B156

The
Evolution
of
the
Book

The
Evolution
of
the
Book

Frederick G. Kilgour

New York Oxford ▓ Oxford University Press 1998

Oxford University Press

Oxford   New York
Athens   Auckland   Bangkok   Bogota   Bombay
Buenos Aires   Calcutta   Cape Town   Dar es Salaam
Delhi   Florence   Hong Kong   Istanbul   Karachi
Kuala Lumpur   Madras   Madrid   Melbourne
Mexico City   Nairobi   Paris   Singapore
Taipei   Tokyo   Toronto   Warsaw

and associated companies in
Berlin   Ibadan

Published by Oxford University Press, Inc.,
198 Madison Avenue, New York, New York 10016

Oxford is a registered trademark of Oxford University Press

Library of Congress Cataloging-in-Publication Data
Kilgour, Frederick G.
The evolution of the book /
by Frederick G. Kligour.
    p. cm.
Includes bibliographical
references and index.
ISBN 0-19-511859-6
1. Books—History.   I. Title.
Z4.K54   1998
002'.09—DC21 97-14430

1   2   3   4   5   6   7   8   9
Printed in the United States of America
on acid-free paper

For
Eleanor

companion
on the
journey

with love,
gratitude,
and
appreciation

Contents

The
Evolution
of
the
Book

Dynamics
1 | of the
Book

IN THE LAST THIRD of the twentieth century, the book in the shape of a long-familiar object composed of inked sheets folded, cut, and bound began to metamorphose into the book as a screen display on an electronic machine; the transformation, in materials, shape, and structure, of the device for carrying written and graphic information was more extreme than any since the original creations on clay and papyrus in the third millennium B.C. Through historical analysis of the societal needs that have invoked the transformations of the book, and the technologies that have shaped them, *The Evolution of the Book* aims to shed light on the present emergence of the electronic book.

This work treats a "book" as a storehouse of human knowledge intended for dissemination in the form of an artifact that is portable—or at least transportable—and that contains arrangements of signs that convey information. The information may comprise stories, myths, songs, and reality; the signs may be representations of human speech or graphic presentations of such things as maps, musical notes, or pictures. With respect to portability, a volume of the elephant folio of Audubon's *Birds of America* and a copy of the Comprehensive Edition of *The Times Atlas of the World* might be looked upon as transportable, and a volume of the Gutenberg Bible as portable, even if a bit difficult to lug about. The electronic-book system, when fully developed, will need to be accessible by a device that will serve as a comfortable vade mecum for an individual user.

Over the last five thousand years there have been four transformations of the "book" in which each manifestation has differed from its predecessors in shape and structure. The successive, sometimes overlapping, forms were the clay tablet

3

inscribed with a stylus (2500 B.C.–A.D. 100), the papyrus roll written on with brush or pen (2000 B.C.–A.D. 700), the codex, originally inscribed with pen (A.D. 100), and the electronic book, currently in the process of innovation. There have also been three major transformations in method and power application in reproducing the codex: machine printing from cast type, powered by human muscle (1455–1814); nonhuman power driving both presses and typecasting machines (1814–1970); and computer-driven photocomposition combined with offset printing (1970–). Extremely long periods of stability characterize the first three shapes of the book; clay tablets and papyrus-roll books existed for twenty-five hundred years, and the codex for nearly two thousand years. An Egyptian of the twentieth century B.C. would immediately have recognized, could he have seen it, a Greek or Roman papyrus-roll book of the time of Christ; similarly, a Greek or Roman living in the second century A.D. who had become familiar with the then new handwritten codex would have no trouble recognizing our machine-printed book of the twentieth century.

The historical pattern of the book, in which long periods of stability in format alternate with periods of radical change, resembles the pattern observed in organic evolution by Niles Eldredge and Stephen Jay Gould in 1972.[1] To paraphrase Eldredge, punctuated equilibria at its simplest entails the recognition of lack of change and the realization that patterns of change in the fossil record, when they do occur, are best explained by extinction and change in geographically isolated species. In short, the theory postulates long-term stability of species (with, at most, minor modifications) in paleontologic time, and punctuating bursts of time in which many species were extinguished. It has been estimated that as many as four and a half million species, or 90 percent of the whole, became extinct at the end of the Paleozoic era; new species evolved from parental species that escaped extinction by virtue of their geographic isolation.[2]

A similar pattern of punctuated equilibria prevails in the evolution of the book. The Sumerians invented writing toward the end of the fourth millennium B.C. and from their ubiquitous clay developed the tablet on which to inscribe it. The Egyptians soon afterward learned of writing from the Mesopotamians and used the papyrus plant, which existed only in Egypt, to develop the papyrus roll on which to write. Although neither the clay tablet nor the papyrus roll changed in form during the next three thousand years, a significant modification related to both book forms did take place in that the numbers of writing symbols were reduced during that period from a couple of thousand pictographs to a dozen or so alphabetic characters, resulting in great increases in the speed of writing. Form aside, the major change throughout the entire history of the book has been in the continuous increase in speed of production: from the days required to handwrite a single copy, to the minutes to machine-print thousands of copies, to the seconds to compose and display text on an electronic screen.

The extinction of clay tablets was ensured by the difficulty of inscribing curvilinear alphabet-like symbols on clay. Papyrus, however, being admirably suited to cursive writing with brush or pen, persisted until the sixth century A.D., together with the writing tablet (made of two or more pieces of wood embedded with wax and held together with threads or thongs), which had been in existence at least since the fourteenth century B.C. The need to find information more rapidly than is possible in a papyrus-roll-form book initiated the development of the Greco-Roman codex in the second century A.D. Although the codex is still with us, the one major change in it having been the replacement of manual writing by machine printing, the introduction of computer-driven photocomposition and the emergence of the electronic book in the last third of the twentieth century provide the next two punctuation points in the book's history of alternating equilibrium and change. Figure 1.1 displays these seven punctuations of equilibria.

For each of the major innovations in the form of the book, five concurrent elements were necessary: (1) societal need for information; (2) technological knowledge and experience; (3) organizational experience and capability; (4) the capability

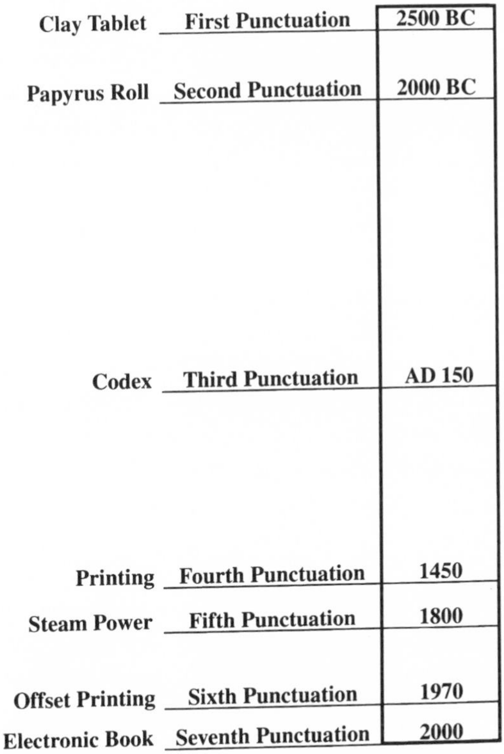

Clay Tablet	First Punctuation	2500 BC
Papyrus Roll	Second Punctuation	2000 BC
Codex	Third Punctuation	AD 150
Printing	Fourth Punctuation	1450
Steam Power	Fifth Punctuation	1800
Offset Printing	Sixth Punctuation	1970
Electronic Book	Seventh Punctuation	2000

Figure 1.1. Seven punctuations of equilibria of the book over forty-five hundred years.

of integrating a new form into existing information systems; and (5) economic viability. The Sumerians, who lived in southern Mesopotamia (now roughly the lower half of Iraq), were the first to create word writing, in 3100 B.C., and the first to produce "textbooks," in 2900 B.C. Their need to record accounts motivated them, about 3500 B.C., to invent an elementary protowriting for marking on spherical or oblong hollow clay balls that contained tokens. During the next four centuries they developed their protowriting system through pictograph and logogram to the full cuneiform system of writing on clay tablets. Production of books in cuneiform script on clay tablets that were either sun dried or kiln baked persisted until the first century A.D.

Pictographic writing was almost certainly introduced into Egypt from Mesopotamia, and the Egyptians first inscribed pictographs—later known as hieroglyphs—on stone about 3100 B.C. A century later, and a century after the Sumerians, Egyptians had converted their picture writing to word writing, and from that time forward hieroglyphs were used only on monuments. For writing on papyrus, mostly done with a rush brush, there evolved a cursive script known as hieratic.

The need both for administrative records, as in Sumer, and for records to support Egyptian religious life shaped the development of the papyrus-roll book. The earliest known papyri date from about 2500 B.C., in the middle period of the Old Kingdom. Their contents encompass descriptions of priestly duties and ceremonies, and temple documents such as income and expenditure accounts. Subsequently the Egyptians produced books containing myths, tales, and magic, and such celebrated works as the Ramesseum Dramatic Papyrus, the earliest illustrated book (c. 1980 B.C.); the Rhind Mathematical Papyrus (c. 1700 B.C.); the Ebers Papyrus, a medical work, and the Edwin Smith Surgical Papyrus (both c. 1600 B.C.); and the Harris Papyrus (c. 1250 B.C.).

The Greeks adopted the papyrus roll for books sometime before the fourth century B.C., the date of the earliest surviving fragments of Greek books. By about the eleventh century B.C. the Greeks had taken over from the Phoenicians an alphabet-like consonantal system of writing, from which they constructed the first complete alphabet by converting four Phoenician consonants to vowels and adding a fifth vowel, thereby writing each sound individually. Although the Greeks continued to employ the papyrus roll for books after the invention of the codex-form book, by the fourth century A.D. only a quarter of Greek literary and scientific texts were on rolls.

The codex-form book of the second century was structurally the same as our present-day book in being composed of leaves bound together between two covers. Its form derived from the wooden writing tablets that had been used for fifteen hundred years to record impermanent commercial and administrative records, notes, school exercises, and the dictated first drafts of books. Codex texts were transferred, at least at first, from papyrus rolls. In 1970 Kurt Weitzmann accurately characterized this introduction: "The most fundamental change in the whole history of the book was that from roll to codex."[3] A quarter century later Weitzmann's evaluation is still accurate, but a quarter century hence it may not be.

Early Christians, like their modern counterparts, were a disputatious lot, given to written and oral debates supported by extensive quotations from texts that were difficult to search on papyrus rolls. For readier access they used the technique of sewing together gatherings of folded sheets of papyrus or parchment and sewing the outermost gatherings to wood, papyrus, or leather covers. In addition to making parts of text more readily available, the codex was more compact and less costly to produce and store than the papyrus roll. The success of the new form is revealed by the fact that 158 of 172 known biblical manuscripts written before A.D. 400 are codices, and only 14 are rolls; of the 118 Christian nonbiblical texts of the same period 83 are codices, and only 35 are rolls.

From 400 to 1300, Byzantium, Islam, and to a lesser extent the Christian West preserved and transmitted to Europe the corpus of Greek writings that fired the Renaissance. Byzantium added new knowledge and literature. Islam led the advance of the book by making innumerable contributions, including the importation of the Chinese method of making paper, until the twelfth century, at which time there began two centuries of decline in Islam and two centuries of advance in the West. By the fourteenth century the West was far in the lead of book production.

From the fifth century until the twelfth the Christian church dominated culture in the West, particularly in its monasteries. Saint Benedict, promulgating his Rule in the first half of the sixth century, prescribed four hours of daily reading, all of which was done orally by selected readers to the rest of the monks. This edict not only impelled copying and preservation of books in monastic libraries but also generated scriptoria in which books were copied. The Carolingian revival of culture in the last half of the eighth century renewed the scholarly activity of interpreting biblical texts and the texts written by the church fathers, generating a consequent increase in copying.

The acceleration, still continuing, of the Western demand for information began in the eleventh century with the appearance of universities, notably a medical school at Salerno and a law school at Bologna. To satisfy the rising number of faculty and student users of books, stationers associated with universities developed a primitive multiple-copy publishing system by lending to clients, for a fee, an exemplar (a university-approved copy) for producing personal copies. Tables of contents and indexes, which began to be added to books of that time, greatly improved retrieval of information from within texts, another boon to scholars. Two other events fueled the increasing demand for books—the invention of eyeglasses, at the end of the thirteenth century, and the development of silent reading, particularly among the elite of the fourteenth century. For four thousand years, "reading" had meant reading aloud and one book could be shared with many listeners, whereas silent readers needed a copy apiece.

In the early fifteenth century, wood-block prints depicting saints, and scenes from the Bible and from legends, began to be produced in Germany and the Netherlands and enjoyed great popularity with the illiterate masses. Later in the fifteenth century captions were added to these prints, and by the 1420s there were book-form sequences composed of block prints, carrying elaborated captions, that outlined the biblical stories and legends. These block books were also extremely popular.

The technologies that Gutenberg successfully brought together to invent printing from cast metal type included metallurgy and the techniques for providing molds, presses, inks, and paper. Gutenberg's typecasting mold, a success in itself, is still used in some shops today. The wooden screw press had been in use in producing papyrus and paper for thousands of years before Gutenberg modified it in the fifteenth century to make it a printing press. Paper technology was well-known by Gutenberg's time, but for printing from type there needed to be developed oil-based inks that would adhere to metal, as the water-based inks previously used by scribes would not.

Gutenberg was an inventive genius, but he did not possess the entrepreneurial skill to crown his immeasurably important creation with commercial success; that was accomplished by Johann Fust, who converted Gutenberg's invention into a business enterprise that could exist on the revenue it brought in. Fust, having financed the development of the process of printing from cast type by lending Gutenberg huge sums of money, none of which was left after Gutenberg finished printing his famous Bible, brought a successful suit for foreclosure, thereby acquiring Gutenberg's shop, equipment, tools, inventory, and supplies. He successfully transformed the moribund printshop into the first major publishing business. The publishing of literally millions of copies of books printed from cast type in the last third of the fifteenth century attests to the volume of society's pent-up demand for book information and the success of the printing press in supplying it.

A century and a half after Gutenberg the need for timely information became sufficiently intense to bring newspapers into being. The oldest known newspaper sheets were printed in the Netherlands in 1605, the first British newspaper appeared in 1621, and the first Paris weekly began publication in 1631; the Swedish court paper started publication fourteen years later and has continued ever since, making it the oldest surviving newspaper. In 1665 the first journals appeared: the *Journal des Sçavans*, published in Paris by the Académie des Sciences, and the *Philosophical Transactions of the Royal Society*, published in London, where it still continues.

Major modifications to the fifteenth-century Gutenberg system of hand composition of type and printing on a wooden press did not come until the nineteenth century. In the first year or two of the nineteenth century, Charles, Third Earl Stanhope, invented the all-metal press. A dozen years later Friedrich Koenig built the first steam-powered press for the *Times*; Koenig's invention, which came to be known as the flatbed cylinder press, would make eleven hundred impressions an hour. In 1846 in the United States Richard Hoe invented the first rotary press, which could print up to two thousand impressions an hour per "feeder." In 1886 Ottmar Mergenthaler produced the first really successful mechanized compositor, the Linotype linecasting machine. All four inventions were direct responses to societal pressure for increased speed in the dissemination of information. The twentieth century has seen remarkable increases in speed of composition and printing. Electronic phototypesetters, a recent development, can produce and compose 36,000,000 characters an hour; the offset press, invented in 1904, can now produce 20,000 sheet impressions an hour. During the last third of the century offset printing, the combination of these two techniques, has superseded letterpress printing from cast metal type.

The transition from the codex to the presently evolving electronic book, the fourth form of the book in history, will not happen overnight. With some preceding forms of the book, as will be seen in the early chapters of this history, the realization of all five elements necessary to effect a transition from an earlier form—namely, users' needs, adequate technology, new organizations, successful integration with existing systems, and cost effectiveness—was a matter of several centuries. Once operational, a system acquires momentum, but its replacement of the previous system is not immediate; to take one example, the roll-form book persisted for four centuries after the successful introduction of the codex. It is doubtful, therefore, that the electronic book, even when widely adopted, will immediately replace the printed book. Its principal initial function will be to fulfill existing societal needs not satisfied by printed books and periodicals.

The ever-increasing informational needs of society, which have driven the evolution of the book, do not admit of clear, simple, detailed analysis, nor have historical analyses been carried out. Indeed, Fritz Machlup's concept of a knowledge industry is but a third of a century old.[4] Nevertheless, the larger picture of knowledge growth is discernible. Since Aristotle men have been aware that the thought processes—meditation, judgment, creation, and invention—require knowledge input if they are to be productive. Learning from sources beyond one's personal experience requires accumulation of knowledge provided by others. The book, and its offspring the periodical, which hold more knowledge than one human memory can retain, have long served as extensions to human memories.

Technological developments in the physical and biological environment have enhanced access to information in books. Improvements in storage of book materials have progressed from the clay-tablet shelves at Ebla of the twenty-second century B.C. to the random-access electronic databases of today. Increases in illumination, from light admitted only through open doors to light admitted through windows, and from illumination provided by oil lamps, candles, and gaslight to that provided by electricity, have meant steadily increasing hours for reading.

Auxiliary marks and displays to facilitate finding information in text have appeared, disappeared, and reappeared throughout the history of the book. Numbering of columns, sheets, and pages is one of the most effective auxiliary markings, yet page numbering did not become common until the printed book. One of the very earliest uses of displays appears in the Edwin Smith Surgical Papyrus, in which the titles and diagnoses of the majority of cases discussed are written in red ink. A capital letter has long designated the start of a sentence, and it has sometimes been embellished with a tick of red ink, as in some copies of the Gutenberg Bible. Over the course of time other conventions have been added to the organization of texts to make them easier to use: headings for chapters and sections; signs, including blank spaces, to signal the beginnings of paragraphs and sentences and the separation of words; and punctuation marks to clarify meaning and separate grammatical structures. Additional helps to the user have been tables of contents and indexes. Computerized screen display of text has already created whole new families of aids, some helpful, some annoying (sparing use of color, for example, is helpful to the reader, but an excess can render a text almost unreadable). Other adjuncts, including audio signals, such as pronunciation of words in electronic dictionaries, impossible to conceive of in printing and hand-produced technologies, will surely follow.

Like biological evolution, technological evolution is predictable only for very short periods of time, largely because the elements required for successful innovation are many and complex. *The Evolution of the Book* cannot foretell informational systems of the twenty-first century except to say that they will be supplying information more effectively than the Gutenberg system.

2 | Incunables on Clay

THE URBAN CIVILIZATION that led to the invention of writing began in south-ern Mesopotamia, in the triangle of land, between the Tigris and Euphrates Rivers and south of present-day Baghdad, that came to be known as Sumer. There men developed an agricultural economy dependent on irrigation, and there, by 3400 B.C., the earliest cities arose. These cities were the nuclei of city-states in which citizens initially made the decisions, but subsequent need for leaders brought about the establishment of kingships, one of the primary duties of which was to protect the poor. The result was an economic stratification from kings to slaves. The need to record and transfer information, a need created largely by the growth of trade, administration, and government in the city-states, gave rise to the invention of writing and the development of the clay tablet.

In 8500 B.C.[1] the food-gathering nomads of James Breasted's Fertile Crescent, who had moved from campsite to campsite as the wild plants and animals that con-stituted their food supply diminished, began to domesticate plants and animals and to build permanent houses, often on former campsites. At first all members of these initial villages were engaged in food production for subsistence, but as they improved their ability to produce crops, raise livestock, and irrigate land, they pro-duced surplus food, freeing some members of the community to develop skills for commerce, industry, social organization, and administration, and to become priests and teachers. Increasing agricultural efficiency continued to free greater numbers for such activities, so that by 3000 B.C. there were a half-dozen Sumerian cities within which almost no one was directly involved in producing food from the land. Although the majority of Sumerian workers remained on farms (a circumstance that has persisted throughout the spread of civilization and still obtains in Iraq, the twentieth-century Mesopotamia, where in 1980, 59 percent of the labor force was in agriculture), much of the new agricultural society had become stratified and specialized into administrators, supervisors, and workers with various skills other than farming, and most of them needed to be reimbursed for their productive activities. Their reimbursement, chiefly in the form of daily redistribution of foodstuffs, necessitated the keeping of extensive records of receipts and disbursals. In a recently published monograph Denise Schmandt-Besserat has shown that a token system that was invented to record the essential accounting information was also the precursor of writing.[2]

Origin and Development of Writing

Of the only three ways to convert spoken language into writing, the first and simplest is to draw a picture to represent a word; for example, a line drawing of a man represents the word "man." Thousands of these pictograms are required to record a significant amount of information. The second method is syllabic, in that one sign, or several signs put together, can represent the sound of a word; syllabic writing requires at most only a few hundred signs. With the third method, alphabetic writing, sounds of words can be assembled from little more than a couple of dozen signs.

Schmandt-Besserat was the first scholar to discover a creditable origin of writing. As she put it, "To recognize that the tokens constituted an accounting system that existed for five thousand years in prehistory and was widely used in the entire Near East was to be my own contribution. I was also able to draw parallels between the shapes of the tokens and those of the first incised signs of writing and establish the continuity between the two recording systems."[3] The tokens to which Schmandt-Besserat referred began to be produced about 8000 B.C. and were perhaps the first artifacts made of hand-molded clay, and also among the first objects to be baked into a ceramic material, which resulted in their preservation. Tokens were in at least sixteen shapes, including cones, spheres, disks, cylinders, tetrahedrons, ovoids, triangles, and rectangles, and most were 1–3 centimeters across.

Later, about 3700 B.C., two techniques for grouping tokens came into existence, namely, running a string through perforations in tokens and tying them together, or enclosing tokens in clay envelopes. Schmandt-Besserat has postulated that these techniques "insured that groups of tokens representing one account were securely held together." The clay envelopes, each measuring 5–7 centimeters in longest dimension and having a cavity 2–4 centimeters wide and clay walls 1.5–2.5 centimeters thick, were hand-molded, closed, and baked, presumably after tokens had been inserted. Their principal drawback was that the number and types of tokens in a closed envelope could not be determined. This shortcoming was soon eliminated by impressing an envelope, before baking, with the number of images of the various types of tokens contained therein. For example, an envelope containing four small spheres and two large spheres would be impressed four times with a small sphere and twice with a large one. Schmandt-Besserat correctly saw that "This mutation of the three-dimensional objects to two-dimensional graphic symbols was the transition between tokens and the first system of writing."[4] This five-thousand-year-long development of the first writing has characteristics analogous to the effects of geographic isolation set forth by Eldredge and Gould in their 1972 paper on punctuated equilibria, which postulates new species coming into being in geographic isolation. Their opening statement concludes: "The history of evolution is not one of stately unfolding, but a story of homeostatic equilibria, disturbed only 'rarely' (i.e., rather often in the fullness of time) by rapid and episodic events of speciation."[5]

Subsequent accounting records, which were maintained on soft clay tablets, were sometimes preserved when buildings that contained them burned down. Bottéro writes that these collections of the earliest clay tablets "clearly constitute accounts of the movement of goods, listing numbers first in detail and then totaled . . . with the single exception of a small number of sign lists evidently prepared especially for the teaching, the training, and the use of scribes." He concludes that "Mesopotamian writing did apparently grow from the needs and necessities of the economy and the administration, and therefore any kind of religious or purely 'intellectual' preoccupation seems to have been excluded from its origins."[6]

Sometime before 3100 B.C. pictograms began to replace impressed signs; these pictograms were the beginnings of Sumerian script, the first written language. The pictographic script, however, presented two problems: first, it was difficult to write curvilinearly with a pointed stylus on wet clay; and, second, there was no standardization of a single pictograph for a given object—at one time there was a cumulation of thirty-four pictograms for "sheep." Both difficulties were resolved by the invention of a triangular stylus that produced regular wedge-shaped impressions, various arrangements of which constructed uniform characters, known as cuneiform, from the Latin *cuneus*, meaning "wedge." The triangular stylus permitted a writing system that employed straight, rather than curvilinear, lines and encouraged the standardization of specific characters for specific words.

After the demise of Sumer, around 2000 B.C., Sumerian as a spoken language slowly dwindled and vanished. However, phoneticization, plus the standardization of signs provided by cuneiform writing, made it possible for the Semitic Akkadians, after they had occupied northern Mesopotamia, to adopt the Sumerian cuneiform script, about 2500 B.C., to represent the word and syllable sounds of their West Semitic language; their neighbors, the Canaanites and Elamites, did likewise for their Semitic dialects. During the second millennium B.C. the Babylonians and Assyrians also took over cuneiform writing, as did other Semitic-speaking peoples, including the Kassites, Hittites, Hurrians, Mitanni, and Urartians. By the middle of the second millennium, Akkadian written in cuneiform had become the lingua franca of the ancient Near East and was being used for most, if not all, diplomatic communication. The so-called Amarna tablets, recovered from that fourteenth-century Egyptian capital, had been written in cuneiform Akkadian by Egyptian royal scribes and their counterparts in other kingdoms.

As mentioned in the previous chapter, the major continuing modification in production of texts for the past five thousand years has been increase in speed. Figure 2.1 reveals three increments in the speed of writing Sumerian. The conversion from the freehand drawing shown in the first and second columns to the cuneiform shown in the fifth column; the simplification of signs after 2500 B.C. and the reduction from 2,000 to 570, of which only 200 to 300 were in constant use. This reduction in the number of signs a writer had to learn and memorize made the work of the scribe go faster.

Cuneiform writing sporadically included signs and displays designed to assist in finding and understanding content information. The beginning and ending of a text were signaled by leaving the right-hand edge of the tablet blank when the front, back, bottom, top, and left-hand edges were all written on. When the text only partially filled the tablet, the ending, and hence the beginning, in the upper-left corner of the front, were obvious. Summaries were sometimes added begin-

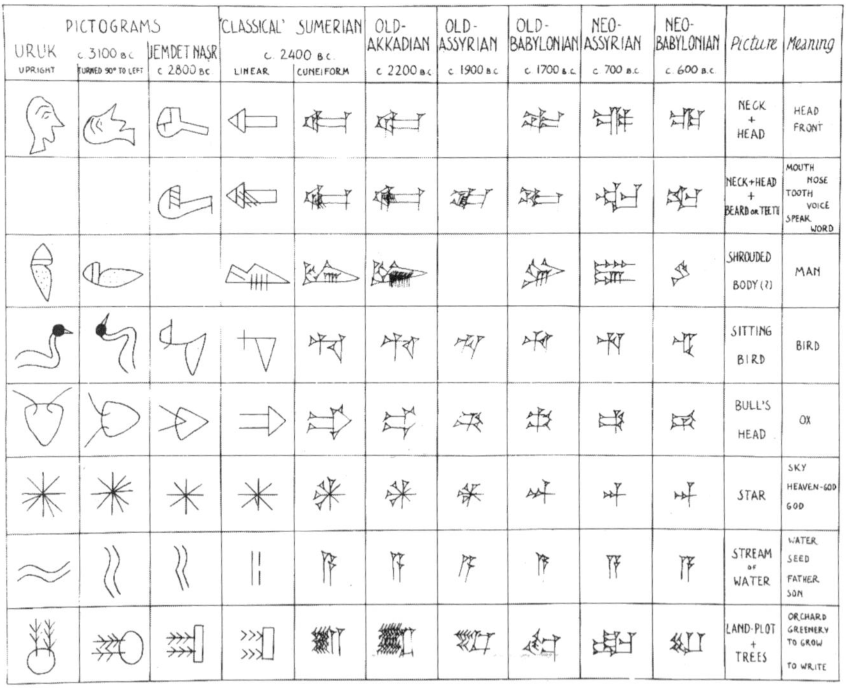

Figure 2.1. Development of cuneiform writing. (Courtesy Dr. Albertine Gaur)

ning in the upper-left corner of the back, and colophons were at times added to later literary texts. These colophons might contain the first line of the text, always treated as the title; the first line of the next tablet when the text was on two or more tablets; sometimes the name of the scribe or owner; and occasionally an attestation to the accuracy and collation of the copy.

Sections, and sometimes sentences, were now and then marked off by lines drawn across the tablet before and after the section, or by blank lines preceding and following. Sometimes the first sign following a marker or blank line was slightly indented. Another auxiliary marking of text was the occasional placing of the figure for the number ten at the beginning of every tenth line.

Four kinds of auxiliary marks were at times used within sentences. A word-separator mark, equivalent to today's blank space, was perhaps the most useful device; when employed it certainly must have been a godsend to the early decipherers of cuneiform text. A name marker often preceded a name—another boon to the readers. Two auxiliary marks that enhanced the specificity of a sign when placed before or after it were a determinative sign and a phonetic complement. Determinatives indicated the class to which an object belonged, such as mammals or birds, men or women, metal or wood, towns or cities, and gods. A phonetic complement specified the correct pronunciation as does the "st" in "1st edition," which signals that the pronunciation should be "first."

Much communication in modern books is nonverbal; machine designs and electronic circuitry are but two of hundreds of examples. Another is maps, which were the first type of nonverbal "writing." The earliest known map, depicting a Sumerian estate, was done in the last quarter of the third millennium. The first urban map, done about 1500 B.C., is of the Mesopotamian city of Nippur. To communicate in words the reality of the information in this map would be impossible. The visual conception and depiction of a map was the first major innovation in the book after the invention of writing.

One immediate result of the invention of writing was training in writing and reading (in the early centuries undoubtedly by the apprenticeship system), the earliest evidence of instruction being lists of words on clay tablets from about 3000 B.C. For the next five hundred years the development of schools, each called a "tablet house" in Sumerian, was slow, as was that of writing itself; nevertheless, pedagogical treatises had come into being by 2500 B.C., and during the second half of the third millennium schools had developed a regularized system of teaching. The chief objective of the schools was the preparation of boys to become "scribes," to use the designation Sumerians gave their administrators; an analogy might be made to the colleges established in colonial America to train young men for the ministry. There were, it might be noted, only a few contemporary mentions of women scribes. Cities, even the earliest ones, needed administrators who could read and write in order to maintain records of income, expenditures, equipment, buildings and their maintenance, taxes, and construction. Scribes, and students in preparation to become scribes, belonged to the elite of Sumerian society; an analysis of the parents of some five hundred scribes revealed that the fathers of students were governors, priests, managers, supervisors, accountants, and archivists.[7]

Clay-Tablet System

The major components of the clay-tablet system, which was mature by 2500 B.C., were manual writing, clay technology, and the organization of collections of tablets, all of which required centuries for development. The clay tablet possessed an advantage in its ease of use, for it would lie firm on a flat surface or could be held in one hand, unlike the later papyrus roll or even some present-day printed books.

Sumer was devoid of wood and stone, and its only mineral was clay, renewed annually, together with silt, by the flooding—sometimes disastrous—of the Euphrates and the Tigris. This alluvial clay was fine grained and required tempering with various materials, including chaff from the threshing floor, before it could be formed in molds. The resultant bricks, which were being produced well before 3500 B.C., have proved remarkably permanent. Seton Lloyd has stated that "The raw material that epitomized Mesopotamian civilization was clay: in the almost exclusively mud-brick architecture and in the number and variety of clay figurines and pottery artifacts, Mesopotamia bears the stamp of clay as does no other civilization; and nowhere in the world but in Mesopotamia and the regions over which its influence was diffused was clay used as the vehicle of writing."[8]

Little is known of the exact procedures the Sumerians used to process clay for writing tablets, but technical analyses of ancient potting methods suggest that their procedures were essentially the same as those of people in the Middle Ages and of primitive peoples today. Thus, one may surmise that the Sumerians repeatedly washed clay with water, allowed it to settle in a vat, then strained it to obtain a fine-grained clay. The tablet formed from it was written on while damp and then dried, usually in the sun but sometimes by being baked in a kiln. These drying and baking processes endowed a tablet with exceptional durability, as witnessed by the existence in museums of an estimated half a million or more tablets and fragments.

The Sumerians contrived with a store of perhaps several thousand tablets what has come to be known as an archive because of the preponderance of administrative records—by some estimates as much as 95 percent—that it contained. For the most part such archives have been unearthed from palaces and temples, but some have even been found in residences. As the accumulation of clay tablets grew into the tens of thousands in the second half of the third millennium B.C., the last major component of the clay-tablet system, organized collections of tablets, came into being.

The best-documented archive, the Royal Archive at Ebla, in northern Syria, contained fifteen thousand tablets and fragments written in the Eblaite language using cuneiform signs. The archive room, measuring only 5.10 by 3.55 meters, was housed in a structure designated as Royal Palace G, which was destroyed by fire about 2250 B.C. The tablets had been stored on three wooden shelves, each 0.8 meters deep, on three sides of the room. The vertical distance between shelves was half a meter. Giovanni Pettinato, the epigrapher at Ebla, "ascertained that the area of the north wall contained texts of a lexical character, while the east sector was reserved for the tablets of a commercial nature. It seems, therefore, that the scribes had ordered the material also, and perhaps chiefly, on a basis of content . . . a fact of considerable importance for library science."[9] Indeed it was, for such shelving of library materials under broad subjects persisted until the last years of the nineteenth century.

Another collection of Mesopotamian tablets, found in a late-third- and early-second-millennium B.C. residential quarter of Ur, has yielded important information about foreign trading; one recorded event is of Mesopotamian goods having been transported to Bahrain, where they were exchanged for copper and ivory. Seven more archives are known in addition to those in Ebla and Ur, five of which were located in temples and two in palaces. Their approximate dates range from c. 2000 B.C., for the collection in the Enlil temple in Nippur, to 612 B.C., when the Ashurbanipal archive of some twenty thousand tablets and fragments, the greatest collection of all, was sacked.

At least fifteen lists of tablets, which contain altogether more than a hundred titles of literary works, have been recovered and analyzed. Although the purposes of the lists have not been determined, it has been suggested that they may be catalogs of collections. No one has been able to detect a principle that guided the organization of the titles within the lists. The most that Samuel Noah Kramer could say about these lists was that they were "prepared by the Old Babylonian men of letters, that is, lists of incipits compiled by them for one reason or another, and arranged in accordance with a varied assortment of scribal procedures."[10]

There is little evidence of the existence of windows in Mesopotamian buildings that would have admitted sufficient light to permit the reading of tablets; where windows did exist they were high in the walls and usually small. Floor plans of palaces and temples reveal that perhaps half the tablet rooms opened through a doorway onto a sunlit area, while the other half opened into a sunlit room. Probably tablets were taken into direct daylight for use.

Cuneiform Texts

The earliest known Sumerian texts are word lists from 2900 B.C. and primers prepared for schools about 2500 B.C. The primers are similar to the small schoolbooks used in teaching modern elementary-school children, but in the middle of the third millennium they encompassed much that was then known. Literary materials included myths, epic tales, lamentations, hymns, incantations, and collections of sayings, proverbs, fables, and essays. Among the several thousand recovered tablets and tablet fragments of these literary documents are a significant number copied by students. An early specimen, a copy of the Enlil myth, is dated about 2400 B.C., an era from which only a few literary texts have been recovered. Among them the epic tale of the hero Gilgamesh is certainly the best known; its popularity persists, for at least sixteen editions have appeared in the twentieth century. The literary genre also included grammars and dictionaries. Most of the known Sumerian literary works, on some five thousand tablets and fragments, are in poetic form and were written between 2100 and 1800 B.C.[11]

Mathematical texts of the early period were arithmetics, of great practical value to students training to become administrators and to officials who would have had to produce and manipulate counts of such things as taxes, supplies, and provisions for trade; reckon payment of wages and time worked, calendar time, land areas, water amounts, and equipment; and keep track of workers, soldiers, and fellow officials. The Sumerian mixed decimal-sexagesimal counting system remains something of a puzzle. George Sarton, the eminent historian of science and himself a mathematician, writing in the mid–twentieth century, observed that "to appreciate their genius it will suffice to recall that the extension of the same ideas to the decimal system was only conceived in 1585 . . . , that its implementation was begun only during the French Revolution, and is not yet completed today."[12] Mesopotamians also invented and developed algebraic operations and could solve simple quadratic equations by the time of Hammurabi (ruled 1792–1750 B.C.), but their mathematics is known only from fewer than a hundred tablets and fragments, no full treatise having yet been discovered.

Scientific texts consisted largely of topics in natural history that were little more than classed lists of mammals, birds, insects, trees, plants, rocks, stones, and minerals. In addition there were lists of villages, cities, city-states, and countries outside Mesopotamia. There were also lists of stars and planets. In the Old Babylonian period, astronomers had distinguished among the stars, moon, and planets and had compiled lengthy tables of positions of Venus including dates of last appearance at sunset and first at sunrise. To make such observations it was, of course, necessary to have a calendar, and well before the end of the third millennium the Mesopotamians had devised a lunar calendar, which required intercalation of an extra month every eight years to keep the lunar and solar cycles synchronized. These texts were not scientific in the modern sense, since they did not seek the regularities that underlie the appearance of nature—it was the Greeks who later invented that basic concept of science—but the Sumerians recorded and contributed many of the observations that the Greeks incorporated into their new science.

Perhaps the earliest medical work is a text of a dozen medical recipes written about 2100 B.C. It says nothing about the ailments that the concoctions were to treat, nor does it contain any mention of incantations, magic, demons, or gods, all of which played a major role in Mesopotamian and other primitive medical systems.

By 2400 B.C. texts of politics, history, and literature had appeared. A political work written by an archivist describes how a new ruler of the city of Lagash had "established the freedom" of its citizenry, a reform achieved by restraining the bureaucratic scribes, who had invented taxes on just about everything that was in sight, and on some things, such as divorce, that were not, and who also made the rounds to collect them. The reform went further, for "men of power" were also restrained from exploiting the poor.[13]

One historical text, which covers two centuries, recounts the troubles that occurred over the establishment of a boundary ditch between the city of Lagash and its northern neighbor, the city of Umma. The original dispute, which arose about 2600 B.C., was settled in favor of Lagash, but soon afterward Umma invaded Lagash and took over the ditch together with some of Lagash's northern territory. Two generations later Lagash attacked and defeated Umma, restored the original boundary ditch, and recovered the territory it had lost. After another generation had passed, Umma invaded Lagash's reclaimed territory, only to be disastrously defeated by Lagash and driven back to its own borders. Soon thereafter the city of Zablam, to the north, conquered Umma and reignited the boundary dispute by withholding water from the boundary ditch and refusing to pay the revenues that Lagash had demanded from Umma. This time a solution was arrived at by compromise rather than by a military clash.[14]

Texts of myths also first appear about 2400 B.C., one of the earliest being an Enlil myth. Enlil, the air god who presided over the Sumerian pantheon of gods for a thousand years beginning about 2500 B.C., was held to have created the concept of universal laws ruling all existence and to have invented the pickax, a basic tool of Sumerian farming, thereby demonstrating an early Sumerian capacity for philosophical thought and practical accomplishment. Another literary form, the lament, appearing at about the same time as the myths, poetically deplored the destruction and looting of temples and other structures in the city of Lagash. It was the beginning of a major category of Sumerian literature that flourished on the seemingly constant internecine strife among the Sumerian city-states.

The earliest known legal text is the Ur-Nammu law code, proclaimed by a Sumerian king sometime after he became the ruler about 2050 B.C. Rules of conduct and rights had long been proclaimed by chiefs and rulers, but the Ur-Nammu code appears to have been the first to set down such rules in writing. The tablet contains an unknown number of laws, of which only five are sufficiently decipherable to be at least partially understood. The next known code is that of King Lipit-Ishtar, dated about 1900 B.C., thirty-seven laws of which have been deciphered in whole or in part. What the total number of laws may have been is not known, but their principle of protecting the economically weak from being overpowered by the strong was clearly stated: "The orphan did not fall a prey to the wealthy; the widow did not fall a prey to the powerful; the man of one shekel did not fall a prey to the man of one mina."[15] (A mina was equal to sixty shekels.) A century and a half later Hammurabi promulgated his celebrated Code, which contained nearly three hundred provisions dealing with such topics as commercial, criminal, and civil law; it is inscribed on an eight-foot-tall slab of stone, however, not on a clay tablet.

The Ashurbanipal Library

The history of clay tablets culminates with the famous library of Ashurbanipal, the last of the powerful kings of Assyria and the most learned, who reigned from 668 to 627 B.C. at Nineveh. The fame of his library rests on its huge size (nearly twenty thousand tablets and fragments are in the British Museum) and on its having been the first to be organized by topic. Ashurbanipal acquired in his youth a thorough knowledge of priestly and scribal learning and knew the Sumerian and Akkadian languages and their scripts. He brought together collections of his predecessors from their neighboring palaces at Ashur, Calah, and Nineveh itself, and added to them a multitude of texts that his scribes searched out and copied from temple collections. Five major groups were (1) lexicographical texts listing Sumerian, Akkadian, and other words; (2) incantations, prayers, wisdom sayings, and fables; (3) omen texts based on all manner of observations and correlations, ranging from heavenly bodies to men's features and events; (4) mathematical and scientific texts; and (5) the ancient epics. Indeed, the Ashurbanipal library is our major source of the Sumerian epics of two thousand years earlier. A decade and a half after Ashurbanipal's death, invading Medes from Persia besieged, captured, and sacked Nineveh. It was probably at that time that fire destroyed the palace containing the library, which soon became forgotten and so remained until British excavators uncovered it in the middle of the nineteenth century.

The discovery revealed that the library contained a wealth of Mesopotamian knowledge that was basic to future transitions of the book. For example, their clay tablets contained information concerning the technical activity of glassmaking, important in the evolution of the book in respect to both the materials used and the resultant products. The latter ultimately included clear glass (ancient glass was colored and ornamental) suitable for eyeglasses, which enabled persons of impaired vision to read. There are some three dozen tablets and fragments concerning glassmaking, all but three of them from the Ashurbanipal archive. They contain descriptions of tools, ingredients, and production, but not precise recipes or instructions. Accurate information about the materials that went into Mesopotamian glass comes from a relatively few glass objects.[16] That lead and antimony were among the ingredients is of interest because of their subsequent inclusion in Gutenberg's type metal. Lead antimonate, which contains both elements, is a yellow pigment that has long been used in glassmaking. Mesopotamian glassmakers also used antimony oxide to partially decolorize glass and to remove bubbles. By 1000 B.C. Mesopotamian glassmakers had discovered that the addition of fairly large amounts of lead reduced shrinkage of glass on cooling, thereby preventing the glass from cracking when it was used as a glaze. Antimony was also available in pure form; a few objects containing pure antimony have been found. Pure lead and pigs of lead were being imported from Cappadocia, in eastern Asia Minor, by 2000 B.C. Pure tin (the third ingredient in type metal) was available by 1500 B.C.

End of the Clay-Tablet System

The clay-tablet book was technologically mature by the middle of the third millennium B.C. and enjoyed a technical stability without change for two and a half millennia. The decline of cuneiform clay tablets began with the introduction of West Semitic alphabet-like syllabaries in the second millennium B.C. Although bulky, they were a vast improvement over the previous cuneiform and hieratic systems with their many hundreds of symbols. By 1100 B.C. the Greeks had taken over the Phoenician alphabet of twenty-two characters in script and modified it by converting four consonants to vowels and adding five new characters, one of them a vowel, to improve its efficiency and accuracy for writing a non-Semitic language. The two dozen or so characters could be learned much more rapidly than six hundred or so signs, and alphabetic writing could be done far more speedily than cuneiform. Furthermore, since it was difficult to render curved lines on moist clay, as was noted earlier with respect to pictographic writing, papyrus, as a far more suitable material on which to draw curvilinear alphabetic writing, began to replace clay by the sixth century B.C. By the second century A.D. the clay tablet was the first form of the book to have become extinct.

At the present time, mention of evolutionary extinction immediately calls to mind mass extinctions such as the one of immense proportions (90 percent of all species was wiped out) during the Permian Period, at the end of the Paleozoic Era, 225 million years ago, and the extinction at the end of the Cretaceous Period, 65 million years ago, that destroyed the dinosaurs. "But there is also 'background extinction,'" as Eldredge has termed it, "in which species drop by the wayside unaccompanied."[17] It is the latter type of extinction that the clay-tablet book experienced, and that we will witness again in subsequent chapters of this book.

Papyrus
3 | Rolls

SOMETIME AROUND 3100 B.C., King Narmer, also known as Menes, united the kingdoms of Upper and Lower Egypt and became the first king of the First Dynasty. It was also at this time that the earliest known Egyptian writing was done; the pictographs on the oft-reproduced slate Palette of Narmer provide one example. Narmer's dynasty and the dynasty that followed, which began about 2900 B.C. and lasted for another two hundred years, comprised the Early Dynastic Period. Thirty more dynasties followed, with the last, the Ptolemaic, ending in 30 B.C.

Egyptian chronology has suffered, and still suffers, from wandering dates generated by various chronological schemes adopted at various times. Flinders Petrie's design of sequence dating, long useful for the study of Egyptian prehistory, was predicated on the assumption that absolute dating was impossible, which was certainly the case in 1901, when Petrie put forth his proposal. In recent decades, however, carbon-14 dating has produced prehistoric dates within usefully narrow limits; although they have replaced Petrie's chronology, there are naturally some older monographs still being reprinted that contain his sequence dates. Further confusion arises as dynastic dates have been, and are still being, changed as knowledge of ancient Egypt expands.

Ancient Egypt, like Mesopotamia, was river dependent, the flow of the Nile for the 750 miles from the first cataract at Aswan north to the Mediterranean Sea providing its nourishment. Measuring south from Aswan to the Nile's sources in Ethiopia and Uganda there are nearly 3,400 miles more of flowing water, making the Nile the longest river in the world. In Ancient Egyptian times the river emptied into the sea through a 150-mile-long delta and had seven mouths; there are now only two. The marshy, flat area of the delta is Lower Egypt; the 600-mile valley to the south, Upper Egypt.

The basis of the Egyptian economy was agriculture, in which most of the labor force was engaged and which still employs two-fifths of modern Egyptian workers. Life on the farm was not easy, at least as it was described with prejudice by a gloating scribe:

> I am told you have abandoned writing and taken to sport, that you have set your face towards work in the fields and turned your back upon letters. Remember you not the condition of the cultivator faced with the registering of the harvest-tax, when the snake has carried off half the corn and the hippopotamus has devoured the rest? The mice abound in the fields. The locusts descend. The cattle devour. The sparrows bring disaster upon the cultivator. The remainder that is on the threshing floor is at an end, it falls to the thieves. The value of the hired cattle is lost. And now the scribe lands on the river bank and is about to register the harvest tax. The janitors carry staves and the Nubians rods of palm, and they say "Hand over the corn" though there is none. The cultivator is beaten all over, he is bound and thrown into the well, soused and dipped head downwards. His wife has been bound in his presence, his children are in fetters. His neighbours abandon them and are fled. So their corn flies away. But the scribe is ahead of everyone. He who works in writing is not taxed, he has no dues to pay. Mark it well.[1]

Mesopotamian influences, as exemplified by artistic motifs, styles, and artifacts, made an apparently sudden appearance in Egypt in the late Predynastic Period in the form of cylinder seals, recessed panels of brick construction for monumental buildings, scalloped battle-axes, and ships. Three cylinder seals of Mesopotamian manufacture have been found in Egypt, one of them in a Predynastic grave; Egyptians took up their use and continued to make them for the next fifteen hundred years. Representations of bizarre creatures, Mesopotamian in concept, also appeared.

Growth of royal administration both before and after the unification of Upper and Lower Egypt yielded an inordinate complexity of bureaucratic activities that required ever more writing of records. Numbers of public works and courts of justice multiplied, movement of products and stone up and down the Nile increased, and censuses of men and animals grew in number. Burgeoning taxation probably required more record keeping than any other administrative function with the possible exception of daily reimbursements. Literally everything was taxed: harvest, herd, land, handiwork, and even the catch of hunter and fisherman. Tax payments were in produce and labor, payments for wages daily and in produce. The immensity of these transaction records sped the development of hieroglyphic writing, particularly the hieratic script, its rapid, cursive derivative.

Two twelfth-century papyri, the Harris and Wilbour, are outstanding examples of administrative record keeping. The most ostentatious of all Egyptian papyri, Papyrus Harris No. 1 (now on permanent exhibit in the British Museum), which had possibly belonged to the great temple Medinet Habu at Thebes, is 133 feet long and 16.5 inches high and contains 117 columns of hieratic script of large proportions. The papyrus records first the donations given by Rameses III (1182–1151 B.C.) to the city of Thebes, then donations, described in detail, that had come from various sources, as well as taxes received and other income. Following these are the benefits that Rameses III bestowed on major deities and temples and on local deities at Heliopolis and Memphis. Another section registers beneficences to local deities in other towns, and the conclusion contains a historical review of events in the distant and recent past. Truly a magnificent book.

The Wilbour Papyrus, written in the reign of Rameses V (1151–1145 B.C.) and now in the Brooklyn Museum, contains another hoard of detailed information about land, taxation, institutions, and people. Measurements of fields for nearly ninety miles south of Crocodilonpolis in the Fayum are given, together with tax assessments in amounts of grain. The taxes were to be paid by institutions owning the land or by the cultivators of the land listed as specific individuals. As the editor of the Wilbour Papyrus has put it, "in one single paragraph, for example, we find side by side, dependent upon the temple of Sobk-Re of Anasha and localized near a place named the Mounds of Roma, plots each of ten arouras occupied by the well-known overseer of the treasury, Khaemtis, by a certain priest, by a temple scribe, another scribe, by three separate soldiers, by a lady, and lastly by a standard bearer."[2] Both the Harris and Wilbour Papyri are splendid examples of the full records maintained in pharaonic Egypt.

Egyptian Writing

The earliest known hieroglyphic writing occurs on stone palettes of the late Predynastic period, of which a dozen have been described in the scholarly literature in whole or in part. These palettes display Mesopotamian influence to such an extent that, as Sir Alan Gardiner has put it, "When the first examples came to light, it was even doubted whether they were of Egyptian workmanship at all, but such doubts were laid to rest by the discovery in 1897 of two more specimens in the temple of Hieracônpolis, one of them the famous Palette of Narmer."[3]

The Tjeḥnu Palette, of the late Predynastic period, contains single hieroglyphs thought to be names of towns; if such is the case, they are probably not pictographs but phonetic signs, being used at a time when phonetic signs had already appeared in Sumer. The verso of the palette portrays seven walled towns and shows a hieroglyph inscribed inside the walls. The Palette of Narmer, from the First Dynasty, a little more than two feet high, is inscribed on the verso with a design that shows two long-necked catlike animals, which have been taken to represent Upper and Lower Egypt, being held apart from attacking one another. These long-necked creatures, as well as other features that depict King Narmer's unification of Egypt, are Mesopotamian in design. Written presentation, however, is absent from the Palette of Narmer. To quote Gardiner again, "It is clear that as yet the learned men of the country had not developed the power of writing complete sentences; the most they could do was to exhibit a complex of pictures which the spectator would then translate into words."[4]

By the end of the Second Dynasty, four hundred years later, the hieroglyphic system was fully developed, at least for inscription or painting on stone. This same period saw hieratic script being derived and abbreviated from hieroglyphs for rapid cursive writing on papyrus. Two thousand years later, about 700 B.C., an even more abbreviated hieratic script, called demotic, came into being. Used at first for official records and later for literary and religious writings, it further increased the speed of writing. Figure 3.1 displays the scripts.

Perhaps the earliest known writing on papyrus is on many fragments of papyri that are dated in the reign of Djedkare Izozi (c. 2409–2383 B.C.), the eighth king of the Fifth Dynasty, but that are concerned with the property and the administration of the burial of Neferirkari Kakai, the third king of the Fifth Dynasty. Among the topics treated were temple ceremonies, temple equipment and its periodic inspection, priestly duties, monthly payments to the head priests and servants of the sun temple, additional types of expenditure, and incomes. Other items included transfer of funds to the king's pyramid estate, presumably to finance his afterlife living expenses, and offerings to his statues and the statue of the queen mother.

With the exception of the Ramesseum Dramatic Papyrus, all the papyri discussed in this chapter, and most others down to the demotic era, contain rubrication, the application of red ink that Egyptian scribes employed to aid users of papyri to find information therein. Georges Posner has identified four apparent rules for writing words in red: to make words stand out; to isolate them as in the modern use of parentheses; to separate them; and to effect differentiation.[5] Also,

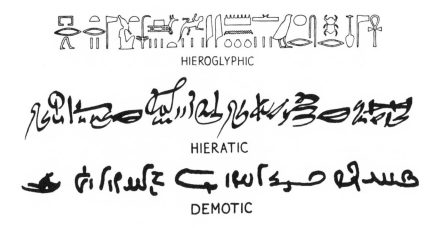

HIEROGLYPHIC

HIERATIC

DEMOTIC

titles and headings, first paragraphs, and first words or first sentences of paragraphs are in red.

The Edwin Smith Surgical Papyrus[6] abounds with rubrication; nearly half the signs are red. The papyrus is 4.68 meters in length and 33 centimeters in height and contains 377 lines of hieratic script in seventeen columns on twelve carefully joined papyrus sheets. Henry Sigerist, a noted medical historian, described it as being the only pre-Greek medical book arranged according to a system, which was *a capite ad calcem* (from head to foot), an arrangement that subsequently became traditional. It contains forty-eight surgical cases but breaks off in midsentence, in the middle of a case involving the spinal column; all of the following cases are missing, and apparently the last half of the work had been missing for a long time before a scribe produced the papyrus, toward the end of the seventeenth century B.C.

The cases in the Edwin Smith Surgical Papyrus comprise twenty-three wounds, fifteen fractures, five dislocations, two sprains, two tumors, and one abscess. The outline for presenting cases is (1) title; (2) examination; (3) diagnosis; (4) treatment; and (5) glosses—sixty-nine in all—explaining words and phrases and enhancing the presentation. To facilitate finding the title of a case, the entire title, or the first part of it, is in red for thirty-five of forty-seven titles (the title of the first case is missing). The general plan of the cases is title in red, examination in black, diagnosis in red, and treatment in black, thereby differentiating among the main sections. Sixty of the sixty-nine glosses begin in red and end in black, six are red, two are black, and one is black, red, black. Each of the twelve black titles is preceded by a case that ends in red, the title being black so that it will stand out; the following examination is also in black, thereby restoring the red-black sequence. Moreover, every title begins with the word "instruction," the first sign of which is a horned head of a member of the Bovidae family, which by itself stands out.[7] In the Ebers Medical Papyrus red ink has mostly been used "for headings and the like," to facilitate retrieval.

In the British Museum's 1985 edition of the Book of the Dead,[8] 156 of 182 headings of spells, or chapters, are in red, to expedite retrieval; the other 26 have either no headings or headings in black. The editors of the British Museum's 1987 edition of the Rhind Mathematical Papyrus (RPM) observed that "Almost every RPM problem has the opening words picked out in red ink, which helps to demarcate the problems one from another."[9] The Book of the Dead occasionally has the first or last paragraph of a spell—or sometimes both—in red, and often the first sentence of a paragraph. The Wilbour Papyrus contains paragraph headings of three lines, the first word of each line being in red. Words interpolated in the Edwin Smith Surgical Papyrus, such as glosses, are sometimes in red.

Manuals of rites frequently used red to isolate certain words; so also did medical texts, wherein the quantity of a drug was often written in red. Red was also used to identify words to be separated within, or from, text, corrections being one example. Also, a vertical or slanting red line might be used to delete an error. Auxiliary marks were in red; a red dot, for instance, signified the end of a long section. A short red horizontal line or lines, or a red dot, might occur at the end of a paragraph. An extreme example of separation is the intercalation in red of a reply to a letter written on the original. In the Rhind Mathematical Papyrus, "Sometimes red is used to set apart certain numbers from the main calculation, as in the case of common multiples necessary for the addition of fractions."[10]

Finally, red was used to differentiate, as in a red total of an addition; the Harris Papyrus and the Petrie Papyri contain examples. Color was also used to differentiate words in a name, with the main part of the name in black and the rest in red. Quantities of wheat and spelt were written in red to set those grains apart from other cereals, and red was also used for numbers of heads of cattle.

Egyptian officials, called "scribes" as in Mesopotamia, increasingly in demand as administrators and recorders as government expanded in the early dynasties, must at first have learned to write by the apprenticeship system, until formal schools were established, apparently during the Middle Kingdom (c. 2040–1786 B.C.). In the schools students practiced writing by copying literary excerpts and lists of words and articles. They also studied arithmetic, a requisite for officials who would be constantly involved in calculating revenues and expenditures. Calculations were amazingly complex, as wages were paid daily in foodstuffs such as bread, beer, beans, dried meat, and salt, coinage being nonexistent. The arithmetic itself was complicated by the fact that it lacked place value for the numbers system. To calculate the number of loaves of bread in 6 sacks each containing 11 loaves, a student had to carry out the multiplication by doubling and continuing to double the multiplicand, starting with 6, until he had a selection of doublings that would add up to 11, as follows:

*1	6
*2	12
4	24
*8	48

Having made the selection (1+2+8=11), he would add the corresponding numbers (6+12+48) to obtain 66.

Egyptians developed graphics more extensively than did Mesopotamians, primarily because papyrus proved far more hospitable than clay to pictorial representation. They also produced line drawings and maps. The oldest Egyptian map, depicting a road through one of Egypt's gold-bearing regions, was drawn about 1300 B.C. and is thus contemporaneous with the Mesopotamian map of fields and canals near Nippur.

Egyptians were responsible for developing "picture books," in which the pictures, with brief explanatory text appended, were the main feature. The *Amduat*, which depicts the netherworld, and the *Book of Gates*, which presents the obstacles to be met with there, are examples of these innovative books. Other examples are the so-called satirical and erotic papyri. The Turin satirical papyrus of the Nine-

teenth or Twentieth Dynasty (1200–945 B.C.) contains depictions of humorous fables in which inferior animals are served by superior creatures that in nature prey
upon the former. Hieratic explanatory text accompanies the pictures. The papyrus
also contains a dozen erotic scenes. These illustrated erotic texts, subsequently
copied by the Greeks, who produced similar texts for centuries, spread into other
cultures.[11]

Papyrus Technology

The technology of the papyrus-roll system comprised five major components: papyrus rolls on which to write, inks for writing, palettes in which to keep the inks
and the rushes with which to apply them, bookselling, and archives in which to or-
ganize the rolls. Papyrus is a coarse paper made, as are all papers, from plant fibers;
the principal difference between its production and that of modern paper is that
preparatory beating of the central pith of the papyrus plant only partially defibers
it, whereas in modern papermaking total defibering is achieved. Pliny has been the
major source of information on production of papyrus paper from the plant, but
some of his description has been suspect. Battiscombe Gunn, following a method
worked out by a Miss E. Perkins, was successful in making an "excellent papyrus
paper." He demonstrated the method to Alfred Lucas, who was also able to produce satisfactory papyrus, as follows:

> The method is to cut a number of sections of the fresh green papyrus stems into
> lengths that can easily be manipulated; strip off the outer rind; separate the inner
> pith into thick slices (not necessarily all of exactly the same thickness) by making a
> cut with a knife at one end and then pulling off the slices; place an absorbent cloth
> on a table and on this arrange a number of slices of the pith parallel to and slightly
> overlapping one another and across them at right angles a further lot, also slightly
> overlapping; cover with a thin absorbent cloth and beat the whole for an hour or two
> with a rounded stone of a size that can be held comfortably in one hand or with a
> wooden mallet and finally place the material in a small press for several hours or
> overnight. The slices become welded together, adhering firmly to one another and
> forming one homogeneous sheet of thin paper suitable for writing upon, the surface
> of which may be improved by burnishing. The colour of the paper produced, al-
> though almost white, was unfortunately marred by being spotted with numerous
> small light-brown coloured specks, which doubtless could be avoided if special pre-
> cautions were taken. Any holes or thin places are easily patched before the sheet is
> pressed and dried by putting a small piece of fresh pith on the defective place and
> beating until it becomes merged into the rest.[12]

Lucas learned from S. Baker of the British Museum that it was necessary to employ
an adhesive to join sheets into a roll, for the juice of the pith was not adequate.

The Egyptian invention of papyrus paper was a major contribution to the evolution of the book. It is likely that the model for the invention of papyrus paper
was the matting of rush fibers interlaced at right angles in mats that were being
produced for several centuries before the First Dynasty. The earliest known pa-

pyrus papers are two unwritten rolls found in a tomb encased in a wooden box dated to the thirtieth century B.C., at the time of the fifth king of the First Dynasty.[13] The earliest existing papyrus-roll books date from about 2000 B.C.; however, there is good evidence that the first writing of one existing book had been in the early twenty-third century. All Egyptian and Greek books were on papyrus rolls for fifteen hundred years, until the more or less regular use of parchment beginning about the sixth century B.C.

The invention of papyrus paper was a major punctuation of equilibria. Not only was Egypt isolated geographically by deserts east and west, but the Nile River Valley was the only location in which the papyrus plant grew. In the latter half of the first millennium A.D., manufacture of papyrus paper drove the plant into near extinction. Parchment and modern writing paper replaced it, the latter having been invented by the Chinese about the time of Christ.[14]

Inks used by Egyptian scribes were mostly black and red inks, the latter for rubrication. Black ink was made from carbon, the source being soot, while red ink was made from red ocher. Ink was prepared in cake form, probably by mixing finely ground carbon or red ocher with gum and water and then drying the mixture into small cakes to be fitted into depressions in a palette. The writing instrument was a brush pen, in use from prehistoric times until the third century B.C., which was dipped into water and rubbed over the cakes.

The Egyptians made their brush pens from a certain kind of rush still prevalent in Egypt by chewing an end into the shape of a fine-fibered brush. Split-reed pens, invented by the Greeks, began to replace brushes in the fourth century B.C. when the Greek alphabet was adopted for writing Egyptian. They were made from reeds about one centimeter in diameter, sharpened at one end and then split in the same manner as the quill pen and the modern fountain pen; like the former, they could be resharpened. Rectangular palettes, with depressions, usually circular, for holding ink cakes, and a recess for holding pens, were made from a great variety of materials, including wood, ivory, alabaster, sandstone, and serpentine. Tutankhamen's tomb contained, in addition to the more usual palettes, a dozen ornate funerary palettes, complete with imitation ink cakes, pens of glass, and gold coverings.

Carol Andrews, in her introduction to the British Museum's 1985 edition of the Book of the Dead, gives a clear picture of ancient Egyptian book production:

> The term *Book of the Dead* was chosen by modern Egyptologists because the texts on funerary papyri are divided into individual spells, or chapters, nearly two hundred in number, although no one papyrus contains all of them. These chapters formed a repertoire from which selection was made. If the prospective owner of a *Book of the Dead* was wealthy and his death not untimely he would commission an expert scribe to write the text for him and it would consist of his own personal choice of chapters. An expert draughtsman scribe would be employed to provide the illustrative vignettes. Others, less fortunate, had to make do with a ready written text in which spaces had been left for the insertion of the name and titles of the buyer. In one instance, in a funerary papyrus of Ptolemaic date (about 200 B.C.) written in the

hieratic script instead of leaving a space for the prospective owner's name the scribe has written on each occasion in demotic, the script in current use for everyday documents, the word *men* meaning "so-and-so." Presumably the papyrus had never been bought.[15]

Compared with clay tablets, Egyptian papyri are relatively rare, as papyrus, like all papers, but unlike clay, can be easily destroyed by various phenomena, including fire, flood, demolition, and even microorganisms. No major archival collections of ancient Egyptian papyri have been unearthed. The largest find consists of the papyri and fragments excavated at El-Lahun by Flinders Petrie.[16] These materials include the temple archive, in which are the usual records, accounts, letters, and similar items, plus texts from residences. Among the latter the most interesting pieces are fragments of a gynecological text and a veterinary text, both of which will be discussed in the following section.

Contemporary literary sources reveal that there was extensive record keeping in government administration and law. Texts of the Fifth Dynasty delineate the activities and responsibilities of the pharaoh's vizier, second only to the pharaoh, who was titled "Superintendent of all works of the King." He was also the supreme judge, applying and interpreting the laws of his king. The departments under him included those of royal writings, sealed writings (registration), archives, and taxation. The centralization of the government suggests that those departments and also the courts must have maintained large files of records, and case records of lawsuit trials have revealed that such files were indeed kept, but none has come to light.

Ancient Egyptian Books

The oldest Egyptian texts were carved in hieroglyphs on the stone walls of the royal burial chambers and vestibules of Fifth and Sixth Dynasty pyramids (2615–2350 B.C.); some survived from prehistoric Egypt. They consist of magical incantations, spells, hymns, and rituals, and all are religious. Their purpose was to glorify and exalt the kings and secure their welfare and well-being in the afterlife.

Just as record keeping had begun to exceed the capacity of human memories about 3000 B.C., so did literary, medical, and mathematical knowledge about 2000 B.C. The oldest known roll-form book is the Prisse Papyrus, dated about 1990 B.C. It contains the maxims of the vizier Ptahhetep, who lived under Izozi in the Fifth Dynasty (2394–2345 B.C.), together with some fragmentary maxims of another vizier. If Ptahhetep did indeed write the Maxims, a contemporary copy, were one ever to turn up, would surely be a strong contender for being the oldest book in the world. The Maxims were popular in later centuries and still are; at least eighteen printings have appeared in the last hundred years, and at the time of this writing the Maxims are still in print.

Other major early literary papyri appeared in the Twelfth Dynasty (1991–1786

B.C.). Sometime after the demise of Ammenemes I in 1962 B.C., his death was recorded—purportedly by himself as in a dream—as a warning to his successor and son, Senswore, to avoid intimacy with his officials and servants (eunuchs involved in a harem conspiracy had murdered Ammenemes). Another tale associated with Ammenemes' death was the *Story of Sinuhe*, which Gardiner has called "the greatest glory of Egyptian literature." He observed that "Both compositions became great favourites in the Egyptian schools, and centuries later were copied and recopied."[17] Many more centuries later the *Story of Sinuhe*, like the Maxims of Ptahhetep, was being printed and reprinted; more than a dozen editions appeared in the twentieth century. The Ramesseum Dramatic Papyrus records a play written to celebrate Sesostris I's ascension to the throne, probably in 1927 B.C. Figure 3.2 is an excerpt of several columns from this papyrus, which is the oldest known illustrated book and the earliest known dramatic composition.

The Book of the Dead, of which there are more papyri in existence than there

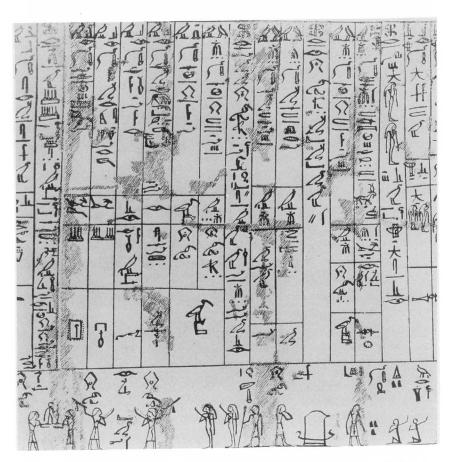

Figure 3.2. The Ramesseum Dramatic Papyrus. (Courtesy Princeton University Press)

are papyri of any other title, is the principal source for major Egyptian religious beliefs, in which the afterlife always played the prime role; the book was the guide for the journey through afterlife and prescribes magic spells for protection. The oldest known copy, written in the early Middle Kingdom period, or about 1950 B.C., contains more than a hundred spells or chapters; a recent edition contains 176.[18] Extant copies, most of them written after 1400 B.C., are housed in Egyptian, European, and American institutions, with the British Museum possessing the largest collection.

Translations of the Book of the Dead have been amazingly popular. A quick analysis made in 1995 of the listings in the union catalog of the Online Computer Library Center (OCLC) revealed 256 editions, printings, and reproductions from 1831 to 1995, (only seven years after J. F. Champollion published his remarkable discovery of how to decipher Egyptian hieroglyphic writing). Among the 256 editions are several translations in French, German, Italian, Polish, and Spanish, and there must be many more in these and other tongues.

The two principal records of Egyptian mathematics are the Golonishev Papyrus, in Moscow, and the Rhind Mathematical Papyrus, in the British Museum, both written about 1650 B.C., with the latter being a copy of an earlier text of about 1825 B.C. Egyptians used a decimal type of system, with a line identifying a unit, and various signs for 10, 100, and 1,000 (like Roman numerals, as in MCCCXXI for 1321), rather than a place-value system. Their arithmetic, an example of which is shown earlier in this chapter, was almost completely additive. Except for the fraction $2/3$, all fractions were unitary, of the form $1/n$. For example, the briefest way they could express $7/8$ was as $1/2 + 1/4 + 1/8$. Mesopotamian mathematics was much further advanced than Egyptian; by the time the Golonishev Papyrus and the Rhind Mathematical Papyrus were written Mesopotamians were solving quadratic equations.

Egyptian medicine, on the other hand, was considerably more advanced than Mesopotamian, and Egyptian physicians were in demand in other lands, as revealed in some of the so-called Amarna letters mentioned in chapter 2. Two medical papyri, the Gynaecologic Papyrus of El-Lahun and the Veterinary Papyrus of El-Lahun, are among the earliest known papyrus-roll books. Both were written about 1900 B.C. and both are fragments. The second is of particular significance, for it establishes the socioeconomic importance of veterinary medicine as of an early date. Henry E. Sigerist pointed out that "loss of a cow or of a bull affected their owner sometimes more than the loss of an infant, which could be replaced without financial sacrifice."[19]

The two most renowned documents in the history of ancient medicine are the Edwin Smith Surgical Papyrus (described earlier in this chapter), in the New York Academy of Medicine, and the Ebers Medical Papyrus, in Leipzig. Both were written about 1600 B.C. and may have been found in the same tomb. The Ebers Medical Papyrus is 65.7 feet in length, or more than four times as long as the Smith. A compilation of several medical treatises, it treats nine areas of medicine in all, one on surgical diseases and eight on internal medicine. Cases are discussed in the same manner as in Smith. In general, primitive and ancient medicine invoked spells, incantations, charms, and other forms of magic, assuming something supernatural to be the cause of disease. However, even for an ancient Egyptian there was nothing supernatural about a head wound caused by a blow from a battle-ax, so it is not surprising that the Smith surgical text is free of magic. And even though magic and internal medicine go hand-in-hand in early medicine, the Ebers calls upon magic in only a dozen cases.

Regression

Egypt's political and economic well-being began a long decline after 1100 B.C. Never again would Egypt be a major power in the world, much less the empire it had been about 1450 B.C., when it had conquered the Western and Eastern Deserts, Nubia to the south, Palestine, and Syria. After 1100 B.C. Upper and Lower Egypt were separate for a century and a half before being reunited. Subsequently, the civil wars that broke out about 730 B.C. so disintegrated political power that the Nubians from the south attacked and conquered Egypt, and in 332 B.C., Alexander the Great (356–323) invaded Egypt and terminated the Thirty-first Dynasty and twenty-eight hundred years of pharaonic rule. Following the death of Alexander one of his trusted commanders, Ptolemy, established the Ptolemaic dynasty, which lasted for the next three centuries.

4 | The Greco-Roman World

S THE GREEKS PRODUCED an outburst of human creativity in the fifth and fourth centuries B.C. such as the world had never before seen, nor was to see again until at least two millennia had passed, which was expressed in all manner of intellectual activity from fine arts to science. In the Greek city-states of that time, a new form of government, a government of many participants, was created and reached its first climax. Western artistic expression, historiography, literature, medicine, philosophy, politics, and science have developed continuously from those centuries. The period produced three intellectual giants: Socrates (c. 470–399 B.C.), Plato (c. 428–347 B.C.), and Aristotle (384–322 B.C.).

The Roman genius for administration and military action enabled Rome to overwhelm the twenty-seven Greek city-states by 146 B.C.; and before the end of the Roman Republic, in 44 B.C., Rome had conquered lands from the Atlantic Ocean to Asia Minor and from North Africa to England and Germany. The Romans, while absorbing Greek art and learning, made their own contributions to both. This author has identified twenty-seven Roman authors as having made creative or original intellectual contributions—twenty-two selected from *The Roman World*,[1] and five from George Sarton's *Introduction to the History of Science*.[2] Of the twenty-seven there were three in the second century B.C. and eleven in the first; eight in the first century A.D. and five in the second. As can be seen from these figures, the first century before Christ was the century of greatest intellectual activity, followed by a steep decline through the first two centuries A.D. to none in the third and subsequent centuries, an extinction not entirely surprising, for the political and economic disintegration of the Western Empire began in the third century.

34

At the beginning of the fourth century A.D., Emperor Constantine moved the capital of the Empire to Byzantium and renamed the city (now Istanbul) Constantinople. By the end of the century the Empire had split into two sections, East and West, each with its own emperor, and in 476 the Western Empire collapsed under repeated military attacks from the north. The Eastern Empire, known by its people as Romana, continued to exist for another thousand years, until 1453, preventing Europe from being invaded from the east and protecting and maintaining Greek and Roman culture and books. Byzantium, as it later came to be called, made two important contributions to the evolution of the book: minuscule writing and multiple-thread binding.

The Greek Alphabet

The oldest writing in an area in what is now Europe is from Crete; it dates from about 2200 B.C. and is in the form of pictographic inscriptions. A script of cursive forms of the pictographs evolved in ensuing centuries into a simplified syllabic writing system comprising some fifty-five signs composed of consonants, some of which were coupled with vowels. Linear A and Linear B used such signs, for the most part inscribed on clay tablets. Linear A, which first appeared about 1700 B.C., is in the Minoan language, and has yet to be completely deciphered. Linear B, in the same script, dates from 1450 B.C. or somewhat later and is the earliest known form of the Greek language; its decipherment was announced in 1952. Not surprisingly the clay tablets of this first Greek writing contain economic and administrative records only, as was the case with Sumerian and Egyptian "firsts." The earliest known Greek literary texts are the Homeric poems of the ninth or eighth century B.C. Greek literary prose does not appear until the fifth century. This chronological sequence—economic and administrative records, then poetry, then prose—was the same as it had been in Mesopotamia roughly two millennia earlier.

The most momentous of Greek accomplishments was the invention of a complete alphabet—complete because it contained vowels: at first five, then six, and finally seven. It was the culmination of the development of writing over two millennia.

The predecessor scripts of the Greek alphabet were in the Proto-Canaanite language (spoken in the area that is now Palestine and Syria) of the seventeenth century B.C. They were followed by various scripts, including Phoenician, in the eleventh century. The West Semitic Proto-Canaanite script was invented about 1700 B.C. by Canaanites who had some knowledge of Egyptian writing. Originally there were twenty-seven consonantal letters in it, which had declined to twenty-two by the thirteenth century.[3] The Phoenician alphabetic script descended directly from Proto-Canaanite in the early eleventh century B.C., and by midcentury its twenty-two letters, written horizontally from right to left, had become stabilized. Although Phoenician never became a lingua franca, it did achieve international status after having been in existence only a century, becoming "a language of prestige." Hebrews and Aramaeans as well as Greeks adopted the Phoenician alphabet and began to write in Phoenician script.[4]

Greek tradition held that a person named Kadmos brought "phoenician letters" to Greece. In support of this tradition the names of Greek letters—alpha, beta, gamma, delta, and so on—have no meaning in Greek, and most of their alphabetic equivalents in Semitic—alef, bet, gimel, and dalet—are Phoenician words. The letter sequence in the Greek alphabet is essentially the same as in Phoenician, and the earliest Greek letter forms (eighth century B.C.) are like those of West Semitic letters. Figure 4.1 relates the Proto-Canaanite alphabet of the twelfth and early eleventh centuries B.C., which is essentially the early Phoenician alphabet, to archaic and classical Greek alphabets (as well as to Latin). The figure also depicts the sequences of letters within each alphabet and lists various local forms of letters.[5]

The majority of scholars have accepted that the Greeks borrowed the Phoenician consonantal alphabet, to which they added vowels, although when the additions were made has been a matter of debate. Writing in 1963, I. J. Gelb stated that it was "still a hotly discussed subject with differences of opinion varying by more than half a millennium," and went on to say that A. Mentz in 1936 had advocated 1400 B.C. while Rhys Carpenter in 1933 went "as far down as about 720 B.C."[6] At that time, when the earliest known Greek inscriptions were eighth century B.C., Gelb recorded that he was "in favour of the ninth century."[7] A decade later Joseph Naveh published a paper in which, on the basis of indirect evidence, he argued for the eleventh century. Classical scholars ignored his proposition and Semitic epigraphists attempted "compromise between the conventional view and the new proposition."[8] However, subsequent publications describing discoveries of the eleventh and twelfth centuries led to general acceptance of the eleventh century by a 1988 symposium attended by archaeologists and linguists, at which one convert stated that "of all the technologies that came from the Near East, the alphabet is the most important."[9]

The Romans derived their alphabet, destined to become the most widely used in the world, from that of the Etruscans, residents of Tuscany, in central Italy. The Etruscan alphabet, which originated about 800 B.C. (the earliest known Etruscan writing is from the eighth century), was based on the original Greek alphabet. Adjustment of the Etruscan alphabet to the Latin language occurred during the seventh century B.C.; the earliest known written Latin is on a brooch from that century. Other inscriptions date from the sixth to the fourth century B.C., but strangely the earliest known Latin on papyrus is from the late first century B.C.

With their new alphabet the Greeks originally wrote from right to left, gradually changing to writing the first line from right to left, the second from left to right, and so on throughout the document. This back-and-forth writing was called boustrophedon, "the way a yoke of oxen turns to plough." It persisted for several centuries, until the fifth century B.C., at which time writing from left to right replaced it.

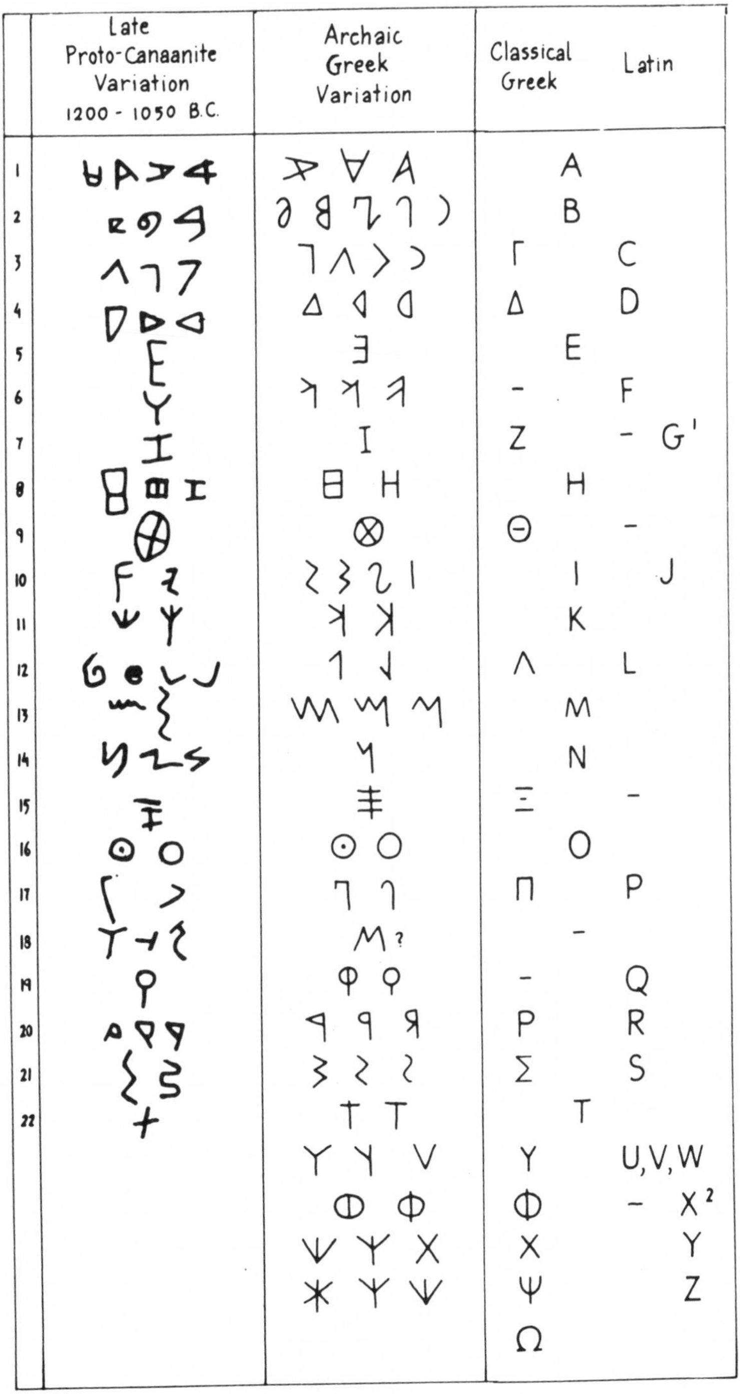

	Late Proto-Canaanite Variation 1200 - 1050 B.C.	Archaic Greek Variation	Classical Greek	Latin
1			A	
2			B	
3			Γ	C
4			Δ	D
5			E	
6			–	F
7			Z	– G'
8			H	
9			Θ	–
10			I	J
11			K	
12			Λ	L
13			M	
14			N	
15			Ξ	–
16			O	
17			Π	P
18			–	
19			–	Q
20			P	R
21			Σ	S
22			T	
			Y	U, V, W
			Φ	– X²
			X	Y
			Ψ	Z
			Ω	

Figure 4.1. Three alphabets. (Courtesy Magnes Press)

For a millennium and a half after the beginning of alphabetic writing in the eleventh century B.C., Greek, and subsequently Latin, were written in full capitals, composed for the most part of straight lines. Writing characters by drawing one, two, three, or even four straight lines is a tedious process; hence, rounded capitals, called uncials, began to replace the original characters in the fifth century A.D. Being much easier to write, they made faster writing possible. An uncial book hand was used exclusively in books until minuscule writing began to replace it about 790, and uncial continued to be used in liturgical texts until the twelfth century.

The earliest known dated example of true minuscule was written in 835, apparently at the Studion monastery at Constantinople. The small, cursive letters of minuscule writing, undoubtedly originating from the cursive commercial and administrative hand that had been in use for centuries, was far more efficient than uncial, in that scribes wrote it more rapidly and in more words per area of parchment. It is widely believed that minuscule came into use in the ninth century because of increased demand for books.

Illustration continued to be increasingly important for communicating complex information difficult or impossible to convey in expository prose. An outstanding example is the *Materia Medica* of Dioscorides, a Greek physician thought to have been born in the second century A.D. in Cilicia, an area in what is now Turkey. His work on medical botany continued to be authoritative until the sixteenth century and is still recognized as a major source of botanical terminology. The Austrian National Library in Vienna is the fortunate possessor of a fifth-century manuscript copy of Dioscorides' work that is handsomely illustrated in color.

Writing Materials

The Greeks made signal contributions in writing materials: parchment, pens, and ink. Of these the two most significant were the manufacture of parchment and the introduction of the sharp-tipped pen to write on papyrus.

A papyrus "as known to Greeks and Romans . . . was a roll of light coloured material, generally about 9 or 10 inches in height, and . . . about an inch or an inch and a half in diameter."[10] The writing on a roll was usually in three-inch columns of lines, parallel to the long dimension, which rarely exceeded thirty-five feet. Owners stored their rolls in baskets, buckets, jars, and cases. Papyrus in roll form continued to be used for literary texts at least until the sixth century A.D., and for records, accounts, and letters until the eleventh. Papyrus-roll books were considerably less durable than the baked clay tablets that preceded them and the parchment books that followed. They required care, as the two following examples reveal. Eric G. Turner reports that "an army doctor writes a letter home giving instructions to shake out his medical books (to prevent the paper sticking and perhaps to get rid of worms)."[11] In 56 B.C. Cicero wrote to his friend Atticus about his library: he requested two slaves "to glue pages together" (evidently his papyrus rolls had come apart) and urgently ended the letter with "remember the library slaves."[12]

Greeks significantly improved writing on papyrus by inventing in the third century B.C. the sharp-tipped pen to replace the rush brush used by Egyptians to paint characters; with the new pen, produced by paring and splitting a hard reed, characters could be drawn. W. John Hackwell has stated that the new pen enabled "a Greek scribe to double the output possible when using the brush technique."[13] Turner was of the opinion that "it is clear that a value is placed on speed, and I should be inclined to think that Plato had in mind a scribe who attained speed by writing some of his capitals 'cursively.'"[14] Turner was referring to a remark made by Plato concerning children learning to write: "We will not insist on a severe standard of speed or beauty in those not naturally inclined thereto." Indeed, the Greeks themselves used the terms "fast writing" and "slow writing."[15]

The Greeks continued to use the carbon black of the Egyptians for ink, as did everyone else until the invention of printing from metal type. They also employed a second kind of black ink that the Egyptians had developed, which was produced by mixing crushed gall with various iron salts. That ink was also used until the invention of printing, but was less satisfactory than carbon-black ink because it was pale brown and did not provide much contrast on the yellowish papyrus.

Parchment, which had been in use since 1600 B.C., began to compete with papyrus as the surface on which to write books in roll form before the time of Christ, but it was not until after the invention of the codex-form book, in the second century A.D. (see the next chapter), that parchment's properties began to be recognized as distinctly superior to those of papyrus. Parchment could be cut in larger sizes than papyrus, was flexible and durable, and received ink on both sides better than papyrus. By the seventh century it had almost eliminated papyrus as a book material, and remained the vehicle of choice until the fifteenth century. The word "parchment" derives from the city name "Pergamum," but why this is so is not clear, particularly as the leading authority on parchment believes that from the sixth century B.C. to the fourth century A.D. there were "no technological developments superior in any way to those used in earlier millennia."[16] It is likely that parchment became known as "stuff from Pergamum" because Pergamum significantly increased the production of it.

The basic difference between parchment and leather is that "parchment is prepared from pelt, i.e., wet, unhaired and limed skin, simply by drying at ordinary temperatures under tension,"[17] most commonly on a wooden frame; leather is always tanned, is not dried under tension, and is usually produced from the hides of larger animals as well as from skins of smaller animals. When parchment is to be used as a writing surface, it must be thoroughly degreased and its surface hardened and smoothed. Vellum, the finest of parchment, being thin and strong, was originally made from calfskin, but today is made from any skin that will produce thinness and strength. Beginning in the sixth century parchment and vellum were for a millennium the book materials of choice.

Leather, and waxen and wooden tablets, played a role in the development of the book. People wrote on leather, as distinct from parchment, before 1600 B.C., perhaps as early as 2000 B.C., and continued to do so at least until the second century A.D. Cuneiform tablets dated 1000–600 B.C. contain recipes for processing leather of a quality to serve as a writing surface.[18] In the fifth century B.C., Herodotus wrote that Ionians were accustomed to call "Papyrus 'skins' because in former times when they had no papyrus they used prepared skins of goats and sheep; and even now in my time foreigners write on such skins."[19] The Dead Sea Scrolls, dated from the second century B.C. to the second century A.D., were on leather.

Presses and Metals

The Greco-Roman era, although a millennium and a half in duration, was surprisingly unproductive of technical invention. Paul-Marie Duval listed only forty-five inventions, plus ten more that originated among the barbarians to the north.[20] K. D. White felt that many of even these claims for invention were "highly speculative, resting either on a literary reference to a supposed inventor . . . or on an alleged first appearance of a device on a bas-relief, painting, or the like."[21] Moreover, some of the inventions, such as the safety pin, and curtains for theaters, were not exactly earthshaking. One of them was, however—the codex book, to be discussed in the next chapter. And another, the screw press, was to be earthshaking fourteen hundred years later.

Hero of Alexandria (fl. A.D. 62) described in his *Mechanics* four types of presses for manufacture of olive oil and wine. The oldest and earliest consisted of a long wooden beam lever, with one end inserted in a wall as the fulcrum and the other having heavy stones hanging from it. Between the center of the beam and the fulcrum was a device pressing down on olives or grapes in a container. In a second type of press a screw replaced the stones; rotation of the screw forced the beam down onto the fruit. The third type was a twin-screw press, and the fourth, the single-screw, direct-pressure press,[22] which was the ancestor of the type of wooden printing press in use from the mid–fifteenth century A.D. to the beginning of the nineteenth.

As the previous two chapters have revealed, the civilizations that preceded the Greco-Roman knew and used tin, lead, and antimony, the components of sixteenth-century type metal. Later, in the Greco-Roman era, advances were made in processing and using these metals. For example, the Romans greatly increased production of tin from "stream tin" (SnO_2), also called tinstone, by constructing, in Spain, aqueducts to wash the stuff, which enabled them to produce literally millions of tons. They also improved the quality: modern analyses have found that they attained a purity of 99.9 percent for both tin and lead.

Sources of lead were nearly exhausted by the seventh century B.C., but fortunately the Greeks discovered rich strata of galena (PbS) at Laurion, not far from Athens. A mine at Laurion, which continued to produce until the first century A.D., was the scene for the development of ore washeries that recycled the large amounts of scarce water needed to clean and grade the ore to ready it for roasting and smelting.[23] New uses that were developed for lead included water pipes as well as sheathing for ships and cisterns. Vitruvius and Pliny, however, called attention to lead as a poison that had a deleterious effect on persons who worked with it and on persons who drank water that had passed through lead pipes.

Antimony was usually obtained by smelting antimony sulfide (Sb_2S_3) with charcoal. Antimony bronzes have been found in preclassical Europe, particularly in Hungary; in the Greco-Roman world antimony was often used in bronze as a substitute for tin. Pliny recorded that "antimony has astringent and cooling properties, but it is chiefly used for the eyes . . . in beauty-washes for women's eyebrows."[24] Pliny goes on to describe its various pharmaceutical applications, including arresting bleeding from "new wounds and old dog bites."

Literacy

For ancient Athenians, reading, which was done aloud, was a social activity. Oral renditions of the *Iliad* and the *Odyssey* continued long after they were written down. Greek drama, like that of today, was written to be heard by large audiences, and Greek oratory, primarily a public exercise, continued in importance for centuries after speeches began to be written following presentation. In noting that Greeks and Romans usually wrote rhythmical prose, intended primarily to be heard, Paul Saenger states: "Since in ancient books verbal concepts were not represented by recognizable images, the Romans developed no clear conception of the word as a unit of meaning. Instead Roman grammarians considered the letter and syllable to be basic to reading. The Roman reader, reading aloud to others or softly to himself, approached the text syllable by syllable in order to recover the words and sentences conveying the meaning of text."[25]

William V. Harris estimated that the level of literacy "for the population of Attica as a whole . . . should probably be set in the range between 5% and 10%."[26] Toward the end of the fifth century B.C. the citizenry of Attica numbered 43,000 out of a total population of 315,000,[27] thus the literacy rate would have been 13.7 percent if all citizens were literate; but since that is most unlikely, Harris's findings seem reasonable. Moreover, there was antipathy to reading; neither Socrates nor Plato was a friend of books. Greeks of the five centuries prior to Alexander the Great's conquests of 336–323 B.C. preferred personal observations and experiences set within the confines of their small city-states. What literary interest they did have was in dramatic plays, recitations of poems, discussions, and lectures. In his *Phaedrus*, Plato has Socrates valuing discussion far above the reading of books, as the following conversation between Socrates and Phaedrus reveals:

> SOCRATES. He who thinks, then, that he has left behind him any art in writing, and he who receives it in the belief that anything in writing will be clear and certain, would be an utterly simple person, and in truth ignorant of the prophecy of Ammon, if he thinks written words are of any use except to remind him who knows the matter about which they are written.
>
> PHAEDRUS. Very true.
>
> SOCRATES. Writing, Phaedrus, has this strange quality, and is very like painting; for the creatures of painting stand like living beings, but if one asks them a question, they preserve a solemn silence. And so it is with written words; you might think they spoke as if they had intelligence, but if you question them, wishing only to know about their sayings, they always say only one and the same thing. And every word, when once it is written, is bandied about, alike among those who understand and those who have no interest in it, and it knows not to whom to speak or not to speak; when ill-treated or unjustly reviled it always needs its father to help it; for it has no power to protect or help itself.
>
> PHAEDRUS. You are quite right about that, too.[28]

Although some Greek boys, and even a few girls, learned to read and write from tutors at home, the great majority learned at schools, which were spread about in towns as well as cities. The earliest known of these date from the beginning of the fifth century B.C. The boys were instructed in gymnastics, music in a variety of forms, poetry, reading, writing, and counting. Learning the "letters" soon became the major objective. Higher education became available with the foundation of Plato's Academy, about 387 B.C., and of Aristotle's Lyceum, in 335. The latter recommended that boys from seven to puberty study gymnastics, music, reading, writing, and enumeration, and from puberty to seventeen, music, mathematics, grammar, literature, and geography. In the Hellenistic age advanced studies became the trivium (grammar, literature, geography) and the quadrivium (arithmetic, geometry, astronomy, and music).

Schools in the Western Empire were based on Greek educational practices with one outstanding exception—many would say improvement: certain schools included girls, at least until puberty. One scholar has described the buildings in which the schools were housed as "makeshift,"[29] and observed that, like the Greeks, the Romans despised their schoolmasters. Reading and writing were still basic in Roman elementary schooling, but at times boys as old as thirteen were still learning their letters. Harris estimated the literacy rate during the High Empire to be well below 20 to 30 percent for males and "perhaps far below 10% for women"; he concluded "that the overall level of literacy is likely to have been below 15%."[30]

Rome's political and economic decline of the third century A.D., induced by the barbarians from the north, included schools, which continued to diminish in number until the final collapse of the Western Empire, in 476. Production of literary and scientific books declined precipitously. Whereas the second century A.D. had produced more than double the number of the first century, the third produced nearly one-third fewer than the second, and the fourth century two-thirds fewer than the third.[31] While this sharp drop cannot be ascribed to a decrease in literacy alone, it surely played a major role.

Publishing, Bookshops, and Libraries

Authors and bookmakers alone do not suffice to make books available to readers and users; they must be supplemented by publishers, booksellers, and libraries. During the Greco-Roman era, publishing and selling went hand in hand and "public" libraries came into being. There is no evidence that there was an established commerce in bookselling in ancient Greece, but Frederic G. Kenyon has brought together enough data to conclude "that at the end of the fifth century and in the early part of the fourth, books existed in Athens in considerable quantity, and were cheap and easily accessible."[32] Aristophanes in his *Frogs* says that each man in the audience has a copy of the play in his hand, and Xenophon refers to "many books" having been in the cargoes of wrecked ships.[33] Much later, scholars at Alexandria were writing to one another requesting that copies of specific books be made for them. One noted, "According to Harpocraton [a colleague] Demetrius the bookseller has got them."[34]

In the peaceful forty-five year reign of Augustus, cultural life flourished to such a degree that an organized book trade and public libraries came into being, both the first of their kind. Bookstore owners were publishers as well as booksellers. Among the best known were Cicero's friend Atticus; the Sosii brothers, referred to by Horace and Ovid; Tryphon, who published works for Martial; and Dorus, mentioned by Seneca. Educated slaves in the shops copied the texts, but authors were often their own publishers in the first instance.

Roman demand for books—whether for information, education, learning, or decoration—brought into being a thriving trade in bookselling as a new kind of commerce. Bookshops were established throughout the Empire, Lyons being one of the best-known provincial centers. In Rome the bookstores, which posted signs listing and pricing both old and new books, were mostly clustered in the business section of the city, offering convenient places for readers and writers to congregate for conversation.

Personal collections of books appear to have existed in Greece before institutional libraries were established; Euripides and Euthydemus, in the fifth century B.C., and Aristotle, in the fourth, possessed significant book collections, for example. By the third century B.C., however, there were already so many books being produced that individuals could not afford to acquire all that they wanted or needed, and an economy for users of books was achieved by institutionalizing book collections to be shared, at first often by a group of scholars. Three institutional libraries of the third century were associated with groups of scholars: the Royal Library of

Alexandria (c. 284 B.C.), the library at the Serapeum (c. 246 B.C.), also at Alexandria, and the Pergamum Library (c. 220 B.C). No building housing the Royal Alexandrine Library has ever been found, but the remains of the Pergamum Library and of the Medical Library at Pergamum (A.D. 132) still exist. The Royal Library was presumably in existence when Zenodotus was appointed the first librarian, about 284 B.C. According to Luciano Canfora, the Serapeum library "seems to have been established as early as the reign of Ptolemy Philadelphus (308–246 B.C.) and was situated in the precincts of the temple of Serapis."[35] The Royal Library served only the scholars at the Museum, a research institute located within the palace precinct, while the Serapeum library appears to have been available to all and sundry. Like the Alexandrine Library, the Pergamum Library was part of an institute and was probably available only to institute scholars.

While there is no archaeological or literary evidence of a library building housing the Royal Library, Canfora supports P. M. Fraser's "idea that the so-called library should be understood in accordance with the first and chief meaning of *bibliothekai*, as consisting of all the bookshelves in the Museum.[36] The oft-quoted statement that the Royal Library comprised 700,000 rolls[37] must be an error, for the structure required to house such a huge collection would surely still provide archaeological evidence, as do the Serapeum and the libraries at Pergamum.

Christian Callmer calculated the capacity of the Pergamum Library as 200,000 rolls "at most," although his arithmetic yielded 212,400. When he computed the wall space available for shelving he used a wall height of three meters (9.8 feet), which is excessively high, a roll diameter of 5 centimeters (1.79 inches), and the actual length of the walls.[38] Before discovering Callmer's article, I calculated the length of wall that would have been required to house 700,000 rolls in the Royal Alexandrine Library, assuming that the average papyrus roll would have been 1.25 inches in diameter and that a layer of 24 rolls could have been laid on a 30-inch shelf. If it is further assumed that the rolls were stacked five layers high and that a wall shelf might have been 1 inch thick, then 1,062 rolls could have been housed in a 30-inch, nine-shelf section. Dividing 700,000 by 1,062 yields 659.13 sections, and multiplying that figure by 2.5 feet gives 1,647.83 feet as the total length of wall shelving on which 700,000 rolls could have been stored. Fourteen alcove-like storage rooms similar to two larger rooms at Pergamum, requiring a stoa 597 feet long, would have been needed to shelve 700,000 rolls. Archaeologists would surely have located a building of this dimension had there been one. Hence it must be concluded that the Royal Library may have been only a tenth or a twentieth the size of the oft-quoted figure and was shelved in the Museum.

Alan Rowe, the archaeologist who excavated the Serapeum, thought it "probable that the [nineteen] chambers in the [excavated] trench were used both for the cult of various deities and for storing some of the books,"[39] a suggestion that Professor Peter Fraser supported.[40] Estimating capacity by the method used for the Royal Library, one chamber would have held 12,740 rolls, a figure somewhat more than one-quarter of the 42,800 scrolls the Serapeum library is supposed to have contained in the first half of the third century B.C.[41] Similar calculations for the Library at Pergamum yield 146,338 rolls shelved in three storage rooms.

Two fourth-century sources give figures for the number of libraries in Rome, none of which survived the Western Empire; one records twenty-eight and the other twenty-nine. As the result of a very thorough search of Latin poetry and prose, Clarence Boyd was able to identify nine by name and to find locations for seven of them. He lists the nine as Bibliotheca in Atrio Libertatis, Bibliotheca Templi Apollinis, Bibliotheca Porticus Octaviae, Bibliotheca Templi Augusti, Bibliotheca Domus Tiberianae, Bibliotheca in Templo Pacis, Bibliotheca in Foro Traiana, Bibliotheca in Capitolio, and Bibliotheca in Templo Aesculapii.

The oldest of these libraries, the Atrium Libertatis, contained both Greek and Latin works and was established sometime soon after 39 B.C. by Asinius Pollio, whom Pliny praised as being the first to make men's talents public property by dedicating a library. Isidorus and Suetonius both refer to the library and to Pollio's role in establishing it.

The emperor Augustus played a role in the establishment of the libraries in the Templum Apollinis and in the Porticus Octaviae. The temple was dedicated in 28 B.C.; the library of the Porticus Octaviae, established in memory of Marcellus, nephew of Emperor Augustus, was erected sometime after the death of Marcellus in 23 B.C. Ovid refers to these two libraries and the Atrium Libertatis as being in operation at the same time. All three contained Greek and Latin works.

The library in the Forum of Trajan, known as the Ulpian Library, is perhaps the best known of Roman libraries. It was constructed during A.D. 112–114, and archaeologists have determined its site. The building provided reading areas, and several Romans recorded that they read there, presumably aloud, with their friends. This library collection contained Greek and Latin books brought together originally by Emperor Trajan and was strong in historical source material: imperial documents, official records, and letters.[42]

Floor plans exist for several provincial buildings that have been positively or tentatively identified as libraries. Professor Lawrence Richardson has proposed that "the building commonly called the *Sacellum Larum Publicorum*" at Pompeii was a library, supporting his proposal with finely reasoned argument.[43] He is of the opinion that it must have been constructed between A.D. 62 and 79. Next chronologically was the beautiful structure reconstructed at Ephesus, founded about 110. Next were the Medical Library at Pergamum and Hadrian's library at Athens; both were built in 132, and the ruins of both can still be viewed. A century later the library at Timgad (modern Thamugadi, in Algeria) was constructed, and one can still see its remains. It was the last of the major Roman library buildings.

The great libraries of the Greco-Roman world had ceased to exist by the middle of the fourth century; Hadrian's library at Athens was destroyed in 267, and the library at Alexandria had met its end by 275. "By the middle of the fourth century, even Rome was virtually devoid of books."[44] It was at this time, January 1, 357, that Themistius (c. 317–c. 388) addressed the emperor Constantius with a plan to preserve the ancient literature then in existence, so that among other things Constantinople would become the literary center of the Empire.[45] According to Jean Irigoin an imperial order of 372 directed the Constantinople city prefect to appoint four scribes skilled in Greek and three in Latin to undertake the transcription and repair of books,[46] so it is likely that an imperial library and a scriptorium had come into being sometime after Themistius had made his plea.

Personal libraries were particularly important because of their large size, and for their role in preserving and transmitting books. Leo the Mathematician (c. 790–c. 869) possessed a library from which it has been possible to identify Porphyry, Aristotle, Plato, and Homer, as well as writers in mathematics and astronomy: Apollonius, Archimedes, Euclid, and Ptolemy. Another ninth-century library owner was Photius (c. 810–c. 893), one of the foremost scholars of Byzantium. He composed an extraordinary work entitled *Bibliotheca*, containing 279 chapters, each reviewing a book. The books reviewed were both Christian and pagan works, the former being slightly in the majority. The dates of original writing extend from the fifth century B.C. to the ninth A.D., with most of the titles dating from late antiquity and only a few from the preceding centuries. Cyril Mango estimated the cash value of the 279 books and doubted "that he would have risked such an investment," adding "that no Byzantine gentleman is known to have possessed as many as 279 books. . . . He probably borrowed them from various quarters."[47]

The best-known private library of the tenth century was that of Arethas (c. 850), archbishop of Caesarea, in Cappadocia (central Turkey). His library probably contained several dozen volumes, of which eight, astoundingly, still exist. Another half-dozen of his texts are probably still extant.[48] Known dates for transcriptions of four of his books are 888, 895, 914, and 932; the book from 914 contains works of three of the eight Christian apologists to be discussed in the next chapter.

Monastic and imperial libraries also contributed to the preservation and distribution of books. The most widely known monastic libraries are those on Mount Athos. Laura, founded in 963 as the first monastery on Athos, had a library and a scriptorium. Iviron followed ten or fifteen years later, and several more came into being in the eleventh century. By 1400 there were forty monasteries on Mount Athos, of which twenty still survive. As revealed in the nineteenth and twentieth centuries, the contents of these libraries were treasures. Convents also produced manuscripts; in 1065 the one at Évegétis had a librarian named Georges who revised manuscripts copied in the convent's scriptorium.

Emperor John II (1088–1143) established the Pantokrator monastery, which produced manuscripts, as did the twelfth-century monastery at Petria. About 1160 Aristippus of Catania brought a copy of the *Almagest* from Emperor Manuel's imperial library in Constantinople to Sicily for translation into Latin—an occurrence that George Sarton called "the greatest astronomical event in Latin Christendom."[49] At the end of the twelfth century, 1201 to be exact, the library of Saint John's monastery on the island of Patmos contained 330 manuscripts, 114 of which are extant.

The western Christians destroyed and looted many of the manuscripts in institutional and private libraries in 1204, but it was still possible over a century later, in 1423, for Giovanni Aurispa (1370–1459), a Sicilian, to bring 238 Greek manuscripts from the east to Venice.

The Greco-Roman Contribution

The Greeks, with some assistance from the Romans, were the prime creators of the Greco-Roman world, the birthplace of Western civilization and culture. The corpus of Greco-Roman writings, in magnitude vastly surpassing what had gone before, was the ancestor from which the literatures of the Western world descended. It embodied Western man's intellectual eruption, which continued to fan out and accelerate, as books became the medium of transport across lands and centuries.

The Loeb Classical Library, whose publisher describes it as "the only series of books which, through original text and English translation, gives access to all that is important in Greek and Latin literature,"[50] comprises 490 volumes. Even though the Loeb Library doesn't absolutely contain "all that is important," the 490 volumes are dramatic evidence of the productivity of Greek and Latin authors. Greek titles, by seventy-one authors, account for 312 of the volumes, and Latin titles, by fifty-five authors, for 178. A search in the online union catalog of the Online Computer Library Center (OCLC) (in mid-1992, when it contained over twenty-six million entries) revealed that eight authors not in Loeb had been published worldwide in the last quarter century to the following extent: Archimedes, 50 editions; Chariton, 5; Euclid, 128; Eratosthenes, 4; Heliodorus of Emesa, 12; Hero, 4; Sappho, 119; and Xenophon of Ephesus, 9. Clearly the creativity of Greek and Latin authors is still with us, transmitted to us by books.

Major Greco-Roman innovations—democracy (limited to be sure and not always prevalent), objective history, the novel, and the basic concepts of natural science, medicine, and engineering—were accompanied by other contributions: improved parchment production, the writing pen, publishing, an organized book trade, and institutional and public libraries, which taken all together made book production more efficient and books more widely available. With respect to bookmaking the two most important Greco-Roman inventions were the complete, simple, easy-to-use alphabet and the codex form of the book, the subject of the next chapter.

5 | The Codex 100–700

THE THIRD MAJOR PUNCTUATION of equilibria in the history of the book was the second-century invention of the codex, the modern form of the book. The clay-tablet book had become extinct in the previous century, having been almost nonexistent for several centuries preceding, and the papyrus roll, still in its two-thousand-year era of stability, was still as awkward to use as it had been in 2000 B.C. The codex, once introduced, came to stay for at least two thousand years. To-day the codex-form book, of which the printed version of *The Evolution of the Book* is one example, occupies most of the space on our shelves, desks, and work-tables. It has been praised as the most efficient technique in existence for storing and retrieving information, and until the 1980s that statement was unequivocally accurate. The need for readily available information, which had been steadily ris-ing, was accelerated by the advent of Christianity. The establishment of congre-gations generated preaching, which in turn required searching out new informa-tion between meetings. Soon the priestly office of reader, a person who read aloud from Scripture, came into being, and readers were so proud of the title that they had it inscribed on their tombstones.

An outstanding example of the necessity for information and its use in the form of books at the time of the invention of the codex is to be found in the defensive and persuasive writing of the second-century Christian apologists, which reveal the use of many sources of information of every conceivable type, from the Bible to pornography (mostly the former). Written and oral attacks on Christians, al-though for the most part rhetorical, were occasionally hysterical. The African theologian Tertullian (c. 160–c. 230) described Christians as being blamed for

48

"every public disaster, every misfortune that happens to the people," and elaborated, "If the Tiber rises to the walls, if the Nile does not rise to the fields, if the sky is rainless, if there is an earthquake, a famine, a plague, immediately the cry arises, 'The Christians to the lion!'"[1] The apologists undertook the gargantuan task of changing this attitude, and although they, too, employed exaggerated rhetoric at times, the major part of their effort was in appeal to man's "love of learning" by organizing and presenting information. Robert Grant has analyzed the writings of eight second-century Greek apologists, and identified their sources.[2] Six of them made specific quotations or referred to a work, and at least 270 of their sources were identifiable; clearly these men both needed information and used books.

Codex technology has proved far more flexible than its second-century inventors could possibly have imagined. Twelve hundred years after its introduction the codex proved to be as hospitable to mechanical printing as it had been to manual writing, and it has been able ever since to respond to society's demands for greater numbers of books, and their offshoots, newspapers and magazines, at an ever-increasing speed of dissemination.

Wooden Tablets

The two precursors of the codex are depicted in a Pompeiian wall painting prior to 79 A.D. (fig. 5.1): in it a woman holds a polyptych—wooden, waxed tablets fastened together into a unit—and a man holds a papyrus-roll book with its title tag. Tablets were the physical model for the present-day book even though only a few, if any, could hold twenty pages of text. The codex forced the roll book into extinction by the seventh century A.D., but the polyptych lived on at least until the seventeenth century.

Wooden tablets, waxed and unwaxed, existed for many millennia. They were made in many shapes, sizes, and forms, and enjoyed many uses: as notebooks, for accounts, marriage vows, birth announcements, contracts, conveyances, and wills, and as the ubiquitous student writing surface. Some wooden tablets, of slices of wood less than an eighth of an inch thick, were written on with ink and served as letters when folded on center and tied closed. In the early second century A.D. folded individual tablets tied together end to end, with the whole folded into an accordion structure, served to record accounts of food supplies at Vindolanda, a Roman fort in north Britain.[3] Homer made an intriguing reference to the use of a tablet for a message from King Proetus to his father-in-law, the king of Lycia, requesting the latter to slay Bellerophon, the bearer of the message: "Many, of fatal import, all graved on a tablet infolded."[4] Homer's "infolded tablet" probably was a thin slice of wood like those found at Vindolanda. Another interesting but relatively recent wooden "book," containing texts thought to be East African chants, consists of a strip of wood 35.2 inches long and 2.2 inches wide folded into sixteen

Figure 5.1. Pompeiian wall painting of woman with tablet and stylus and man with papyrus roll and title tag. (Archaeological Museum, Naples)

sheets encased between two heavy blocks of wood.[5] E. M. Thompson recorded that tablets "inscribed with the names of the dead are found with mummies," and that "In England the custom of using wooden tallies, inscribed as well as notched, in the public accounts lasted down to a recent date."[6]

One example of a temporary record on a waxed tablet is in the British Library. As a courtesy to the author, and after two previous students of Greek had failed, Professor William H. Willis of Duke University succeeded in deciphering the writing in part. It proved to be a listing of agricultural products, such as fodder and flax straw, evidently written hastily and cryptically by an individual named Chairemon. Another temporary record, on the oldest known tablet, a diptych recovered from a fourteenth-century-B.C. shipwreck off the southern coast of modern Turkey, is likely to have been the ship's manifest.[7]

To construct the commonly used waxed tablet a board was hollowed out to a depth of perhaps an eighth of an inch, leaving a narrow frame, and the depression was filled to about one-half with wax, which would be written upon with a hard stylus, often of metal. The woman in figure 5.1 is warming the sharp, inscribing end of the stylus at her lips to facilitate writing on the wax. Presumably the blunt, erasing end of a stylus would rub out writing more easily if it also were warmed. Two or more waxed boards, three-eighths or a quarter of an inch thick and held together with thread, formed a polyptych—two boards forming a diptych, three a triptych, four a quadriptych, and so on. For diptychs, only the inner side of each board was hollowed out; for triptychs and larger, the inner boards were hollowed and filled on both sides. Thompson reported, "On Greek vases of the fifth and fourth centuries B.C., tablets, generally triptychs, are represented, both open in the hands of the goddess Athena or others, and closed and bound with strings, hanging from the wall by slings or handles."[8]

In the fifth century Herodotus tells of the fascinating use of a waxed tablet by Demaratus to secretly inform the Lacedaemonians of the Persian king Xerxes' intended invasion of Greece:

> After it seemed good to Xerxes to lead an host against Greece, Demaratus, being in Susa and learning thereof, desired to send word to the Lacedaemonians. And there was no other way in which he could signify it, because of the danger lest he be discovered, except this which he devised. He took a folding tablet, and scraped off the wax thereof, and thereafter wrote the king's intent upon the wood of the tablet. And when he had done it, he spread the wax over the letters again, that the tablet being carried empty might make no trouble with the guards upon the road. But when at last it came to Lacedaemon, the Lacedaemonians were not able to comprehend the matter, until, as I learn, Cleomenes' daughter, who was the wife of Leonidas, to wit, Borgo, perceived it and advised them to scrape off the wax, and they should find writing upon the wood. And they did so, and found the writing and read it, and thereafter sent tidings to the other Greeks.[9]

Egypt, Herculaneum, Pompeii, and Romania have been fruitful sources of tablets. Twenty-five deeds dated A.D. 131 to 167 have been recovered from the vicinity of modern Verespatak in Romania. In 1875 a box that contained 127 tablets dated A.D. 15, 27, and 52–62 was unearthed at Pompeii. In all, more than 200 tablets have been retrieved in Pompeii and neighboring Herculaneum. Two polyptychs from Herculaneum differed from all the other Herculanean, Pompeiian, and Dacian finds in dimension, form, material, and structure; one is a pentaptych and the other an octoptych, both obviously dated before A.D. 79. Each is made of fine, compact boxwood (whereas most tablets were made of fir), skillfully fashioned and highly polished. Giovanni Pugliese Carratelli has described in detail the octoptych, which is held together by two sets of double threads so anchored in the front and back cover that they do not protrude on the outer surfaces.[10]

An Egyptian diptych of the Greco-Roman period used a similar technique for holding its two boards together.[11] Actually the back board duplicates the technique used in the Herculanean boards. However, all eight holes in the front board are drilled all the way through. The British Library possesses two external boards (Add Ms 33,797 and Add Ms 34,244) belonging to two different polyptychs that are missing; they have drill holes that are the same as those in the Herculanean and Egyptian board types. These four examples represent the model for the codex-form book.

The Technology of the Codex

A high degree of inventive imagination was required to develop the codex-form book from the waxed wooden polyptych and the papyrus-roll book. It would have been possible for any person to observe these two vehicles of writing, side by side, at any time during the fifteen hundred years that preceded the second-century invention (see fig. 5.1), but the transformation from columns written on only one side of a papyrus roll to single sheets of papyrus folded and written on both sides to replace the interior boards of a polyptych reflects the ingenuity and effective imagination of the codex's nameless developers. As Eric G. Turner put it, "The greatest benefactors of mankind are unsung and unknown—the inventor of the wheel, the deviser of the alphabet. Among their number we should place the inventor of the codex. In this form of book the sheets of papyrus or of cut and treated skin are not pasted or stitched together to form a long roll but are superimposed on each other, folded across the middle, and then secured by stitching so that they open into pages. The outside pages can be protected by binding covers and the whole ensemble then forms a durable, sturdy book, easy to store, easy to open and refer to, easy to carry about, and withal capacious since it uses both sides of the writing material."[12]

The quality of the papyrus itself diminished over time. Turner appraised papyrus of the Hellenistic age as "good," but compared it with that of a thousand years earlier as "heavier and thicker. Sheets of the Roman period tend to be clumsier and coarser still; but good . . . till the third century after Christ. Thereafter . . . the quality of ordinary papyrus deteriorates rapidly, and ends up by resembling cardboard."[13] Other shortcomings of papyrus were that it tore easily, became brittle after exposure to damp, disintegrated at a touch following repeated wetting and drying, and required a preservative, usually oil of cedar. In roll form it took two hands to hold it open, and if released by one hand, or both, could spring to the floor like a wild thing, twisting and turning. One Verginius Rufus fractured his hip trying to gather up a roll he had dropped.

The new codex was modeled on the waxen polyptych that preceded it; for example, the protective outer boards of codices have drill holes like those in the polyptych. There was, however, a major problem confronting the inventors of the codex: how to achieve a sturdy, solid block of pages that would also be pliable. The solution arrived at was to fold a papyrus sheet (or stack of sheets) into a single gathering to produce multiple leaves. The majority of the codices produced in the second, third, and fourth centuries were so constructed. At least fourteen early codices are known to have had more than one hundred pages, and two of them had more than two hundred. Other gathering formats varied from two sheets to seven, with four sheets, *quarterni,* from which the English word "quire" derives, eventually becoming the standard.

The single-quire codex lent itself to relatively easy construction. V-shaped slots that would pierce all sheets were cut in the back of the fold (or folds), and a piece of leather cut to enwrap the quire (or quires) was pierced with holes corresponding to the slots in the folds. Then the whole was bound together by threads running from the holes in one side of the leather cover, along the innermost fold from one set of notches to the other, and out through the holes in the second side of the cover. The British Library possesses a cover (PAR 1442) dated in the early eighth century that suggests such a binding.

Successful binding together of multiple gatherings was the key to the invention of the codex. The oldest known complete codex is a 490-page Book of Psalms, in a Coptic dialect, dating from the second half of the fourth century and discovered in an ancient Egyptian cemetery in 1984. It has been described as bound between wooden covers stitched with leather. Texts of other ancient codices are available, but their bindings have been lost or replaced, or else destroyed in the process of preserving the text by mounting the sheets between glass plates. However, enough has been saved of a fourth-century Gnostic manuscript binding to suggest that its nineteen gatherings were held together by two leather thongs, much as two threads held together the Herculanean and Egyptian tablets. This two-thread sewing technique for holding gatherings together was characteristic of the Near East and remained so until this century. Three sixth-century Coptic codices in the Chester Beatty Library in Dublin were sewn in this two-thread manner, which was used in the West at least until the eighth century.

The earliest such European binding is that of the Stonyhurst Gospel of Saint John, dated early in the eighth century (or at least after 698) and now in the British Library. The Cadmug Codex (Cadmug, an Irish monk, was the scribe) is now in the Land library at Fulda[14] and is dated slightly later than the Stonyhurst Gospel. Both books are pocket-size and have similar binding stitching. The sewing together of the gatherings began with the binder cutting four V-shaped slots in two pairs in the backs of the gatherings, and then he used two needles, one for each pair of slots, to sew the gatherings together with flaxen thread. After he attached one of the binding boards to the first gathering, he would then pass one needle in at A and out at B and one in at D and out at C, drawing the threads along the inside fold of the gathering. Next he would insert the needles through slots B and C of the second gathering and draw them out at A and D. Now the needles would go down un-

der the threads from the board to the first gathering and up to the third gathering
for insertion at A and D and along the interior for exit at B and C. This time the
needles brought the threads back down and under the threads passing from B and
C in the first gathering to B and C in the second and on up for insertion at B and C
in the fourth, and so on. This stitch, called chain or kettle, when pulled tight sews
the gatherings together in a solid block.

This two-thread sewing remained in use for manuscripts prepared for churches
in Armenia and Syria until the nineteenth century and was still being used in
Ethiopia as late as the mid–twentieth century. London's Victoria and Albert Museum possesses a large Ethiopic manuscript written in 1947 on vellum, measuring
19.2 inches high and 14.2 inches wide. Four sets of two holes were drilled through
each cover, and four holes were drilled from the back edge of each board to inter-
sect each set of double holes.

Production of Codices

The time and place of the invention of the codex are as unknown as the inventor,
but it may be assumed that the construction and copying of codices took place at
the bookstores described in the preceding chapters. Turner has described the acquisition of books by Egyptian Greeks in the first and second centuries A.D. and
the rates of payment to scribes.[15] The vast majority of codices were found in the
dry, sandy edges of the Fayyûm region of Egypt about 100 miles south of Alexandria and particularly from Oxyrhynchus (el-Bahnasa), another 60 miles further
south. In total some twelve hundred codices and fragments have been recovered
that were produced from the second through the seventh centuries.

Table 5.1 depicts the growth of numbers of codices during the first two centuries
of their existence and at the same time records whether the codices were written on
papyrus or parchment and whether the texts were literary and scientific or Christian.
It also includes dates that span two centuries, such as second/third; editors assign
such dates because of their uncertainty as to the century in which a codex was written. As can be seen in the total column, ten times as many codices were produced in
the third century as in the second. Moreover, more codices are assigned to the span
period, ii/iii, than to the second. Both of these observations suggest that production
of codices did not start until the latter part of the second century.

Another revelation in Table 5.1 is that Christian literature comprised more than
a third of codices produced.

Turner's "unknown, unsung" inventor of the codex may or may not have been
a Christian, but no matter who the inventor or what his religion, the Christians
manifestly seized upon the invention early, exploiting for their own benefit their
recognition of the superiorities of the codex over the roll: the obvious savings of
money in using both sides of the papyrus, the increased speed in production, and
the greater ease in retrieving information from text.

Table 5.1. Codices dated before the fourth century

Century	Papyrus		Parchment		Total	
	G[1]	C[2]	G[1]	C[2]	G[1]	C[2]
ii	6	5	3	0	9	5
ii/iii	14	7	1	0	15	7
iii	81	44	10	5	91	49
iii/iv	26	22	7	3	33	25
	127	78	21	8	148	86

Source: Table 13 on pages 89–94 of *The Typology of the Early Codex* by Eric G. Turner.
[1]Greek, including Latin; [2]Christian (see Turner).

Using several published sources, Colin H. Roberts and T. C. Skeat found "that there are approximately 172 Biblical manuscripts or fragments of manuscripts written before A.D. 400 or not long thereafter (i.e., including items that have been dated fourth–fifth century)"[16]; 98 were from the Old Testament, and 74 from the New. Of the texts 158 were from codices and 14 were from rolls; in other words, during the first three centuries 92 percent of the Bibles produced were codices and 8 percent were papyrus rolls. Examining nonbiblical Christian literature output during the same period, Roberts and Skeat found 118 items, 83 of which were from codices and 35 from rolls. They also collected evidence of the production of popular romances and Acts of the Pagan Martyrs during the first three centuries and found 60 examples, of which only three were codices, a sampling significant enough to conclude that these two types of literature played no role in the development of the codex.

There are more than a dozen third-, fourth-, and fifth-century codex Bibles in existence, all in Greek, all Alexandrine in origin or containing Alexandrine elements, and each ranging from several to many biblical texts. Each has been unbound or rebound several times over. The three most important for documenting the early biblical texts are the Codex Vaticanus and Codex Sinaiticus of the fourth century and the Codex Alexatrinus of the fifth. The first is in the Vatican and the others are in the British Library. Of the three, the Codex Vaticanus is thought to possess the most trustworthy text. The Bodmer Library in Cologny, Switzerland, has three third-century volumes, Bodmer II, XIV, and XV, and two fourth-century volumes, Bodmer VII and VIII. The first three contain most of the Gospels of Luke and John, and the last two, Jude and Peter. The Chester Beatty Library owns three third-century volumes; Chester Beatty I has the four Gospels and Acts, Chester Beatty II the Pauline letters, and Chester Beatty III, Revelation.

Roberts and Skeat have also explored comparative numbers of rolls and codices produced during the first three centuries of the existence of the codex, and they collected and organized dates of production. Table 5.2 is based on the data, which is

Table 5.2. Greek literary and scientific texts

Century	Rolls	Codices	Total	Percent Codices
ii	1133	24	1157	2.0
iii	608	127	735	17.3
iv	66	158	224	70.5
	1807	309	2116	

Source: Table on page 37 of *The Birth of the Codex* by Colin H. Roberts and T. C. Skeat.

in tabular form in their work *Birth of the Codex.* As can be seen in the table, the production of rolls declined and codices increased; apparently the number of codices began to exceed the number of rolls sometime toward the end of the third century or in the early decades of the fourth. Many reasons have been presented for the time it took the production of the codex to surpass that of rolls despite the codex's obvious superiority in usefulness, relatively low cost, and convenience, but certainly a reluctance to accept change was a major obstacle. Nevertheless, codices were much more popular by the fourth century and have remained so ever since.

The writing in most of the early codices was neither the capital nor the uncial discussed in the previous chapter. Turner reported that

> it may be readily admitted that it is not easy to find examples of calligraphy among papyrus codices of the second and third centuries. Their handwriting is in fact of an informal and workaday type, fairly quickly written, serviceable rather than beautiful, of value to a man interested in the content of what he is reading rather than its presentation. . . . These [dozen or so cited codices] give the impression of being "utility" books: margins are small, lines usually long. But the standard by which they are measured and condemned to second-class status is not the contemporary codex of parchment, but the contemporary papyrus roll.[17]

One wonders if uncial writing was used largely in books to be looked at, not read, recalling Seneca's ridicule of Romans who bought books "not for the sake of learning, but to make a show, . . . as decorations for the dining room."[18]

That early codices more often than not were written on papyrus sheets cut from blank rolls had been known by scholars at the beginning of the twentieth century, but it was Turner who discovered that the heights of early papyrus codices conformed to the heights of papyrus rolls.[19] No such uniformity exists among parchment codices, because the skins used to make parchment varied in size and it was economical to use as much of a skin as possible. There were two major reasons for parchment's replacement of papyrus: first, papyrus was harvested into near extinction in Egypt; and second, parchment could be produced locally, from the cattle, sheep, and goats at hand almost everywhere. With the resumption of Greek book production in Byzantium in the ninth century a mature uncial bookhand was written on the parchment, which continued to be used until the advent of paper.

6 | *Islam*
622–1300

ABOUT A.D. 610 an angel appeared to the Prophet Muḥammad (c. 570–632) and proclaimed him "the Messenger of God." From that date on he had frequent revelations, and about 613 he began to preach publicly. His preaching contained implicit criticism of rich merchants, who by 615 had begun to generate the persecution, nonviolent but offensive, that would cause the Hegira—Muḥammad's secret migration in 622 (the first year of the Islamic era) to Medina, some 250 miles north of Mecca. To support themselves Muḥammad and his Muslims followed the usual tribal tactic of raiding caravans to obtain booty. In one raid, in 624 at Badr, three hundred Muslims attacked a wealthy caravan guarded by a force of a thousand Meccans, achieving a victory so total that it is recorded in the Qur'an. In 630 Muḥammad, leading ten thousand Muslims to Mecca, accomplished a nearly bloodless victory and began the conversion of that city into the holiest of Islamic shrines. At the end of the same year he led a month-long raid with thirty thousand men against borderland Syria to obtain booty. It was the first of a series of raids, the grandest ever, that did not end until 718, by which date Islam controlled the areas west of the Aral Sea and the Oxus River that are now Iran, Iraq, Syria, Egypt, Libya, Tunisia, Algeria, Morocco, and Spain.

During four centuries, the eighth through the eleventh, Islam dominated the world in intellectual creativity. By the end of the tenth century Islam had produced nearly ten thousand books. In 988 Ibn al-Nadīm wrote the last chapter of his famous work *al-Fihrist*, which contains brief biographies, often concluding with "among his books there were . . ." followed by a listing of brief titles, such as "Reptiles, Wild Animals, The Disposition of Horses, and Plants." An interval sampling of every tenth page in *al-Fihrist* yielded an estimate of 9,620 titles. This figure falls not far short of the 15,000 titles in Konrad Gesner's *Bibliotheca Universalis*, published five and a half centuries later and a century after the invention of printing from cast type, which attempted to list all existing titles in Latin, Greek, and Hebrew, the learned languages of the West.

Muslims organized knowledge into three main groups: Islamic systematic knowledge, Greek systematic knowledge with Muslim advances, and the literary arts. The topics that al-Nadīm treated in eight of his chapters fall roughly into this organization. Lists of works in the first two categories appear in chapters 1, 2, 5, and 6 and include such topics as the Qur'an, philology, grammar, Muslim sects, and law. Chapters 3 and 4 list history and poetry, in the literary arts. Chapters 7 and 10 contain titles in foreign sciences: philosophy, mathematics, astronomy, medicine, and alchemy. Two other chapters are on topics that al-Nadīm did not hold in high regard: chapter 8, which contains a hodgepodge that begins with "evening stories and fables" and goes on to exorcism, juggling, magic, cosmetic blemishes, omens, military activities, veterinary surgery, falconry, interpretation of dreams, perfumery, cookery, and charms, and Chapter 9, which deals with pagan sects and doctrines.

The Qur'an (the Book), the most famous of all Islamic books, containing the revelations of the Prophet Muḥammad, held sway to a considerable degree over all works written in the Islamic empire; indeed, some Islamic theologians attempted to keep it the one and only book, but failed to achieve their goal. It provided systems of ethics, behavior, law, and economics. Second in importance to the Qur'an was the corpus of traditions of the Prophet that Muslim scholars began to develop after the Prophet's death; these traditions enhance the Qur'anic systems and supplement the Qur'an where it is silent. Many of the tradition texts qualify as belles lettres.

The Arabic language of the Qur'an prevailed throughout the vast Islamic area as the language of religion, scholarship, administration, and the cultured elite. The literary art of Islam, both verse and prose, emphasized beauty of writing, with particular attention to language and linguistic correctness, which generated an extensive study of grammar and philology. The literary arts encompassed all manner of subjects, or at least those of interest to educated men, but literature in the sense of creative, imaginative writing did not flourish in Islam and was held in low esteem.

During the four centuries of Islamic supremacy, Islamic science and medicine far outshone that of the rest of the world and produced at least ten scientific greats, whereas scientists of rank did not appear in the West until the thirteenth century, in such men as Leonardo Fibonacci (c. 1170–c. 1240) and Robert Grosseteste (c. 1175–c. 1253). Two important Islamic scientific discoveries were major contributions to the evolution of the book. First, Abū Musa Jabir ibn Haiyan (fl. 776), one of the two most notable Islamic alchemists, recorded the first use of manganese dioxide, or "glassmakers soap," to produce clear glass, an important invention for the later production of eyeglasses. Second, Ibn al-Haytham (c. 965–c. 1039), known as Alhazen in the West, who was "one of the greatest students of optics of all times,"[1] made experimental discoveries in refraction, binocular vision, spherical aberration, the physiography of the eye, and the focusing of magnifying lenses, and he was the first to produce an accurate account of vision as light traveling from an object to the eye rather than in the opposite direction. Alhazen's findings were also a requisite for the invention of eyeglasses.

Papermaking

The adoption and subsequent introduction to the West of Chinese paper manufacture was Islam's most important contribution to the evolution of the book. Although Muslims also wrote books on papyrus and parchment, they were importing Chinese paper, which had been introduced to the Arab world by the seventh century or perhaps earlier. Chinese prisoners of war built the first Muslim paper mill in Samarkand soon after 751, the date of their capture, and in 794 a mill was built in Baghdad. Subsequently Damascus became a papermaking center, as did Fez in Morocco, probably by the tenth century. Paper gradually replaced papyrus in Islam, and by the middle of the tenth century it had totally displaced papyrus for writing.[2] Another century was to pass before papermaking was introduced into Spain, its first appearance in the West.

Dard Hunter, doyen of the history of papermaking, discussed three important Islamic innovations in paper manufacture: (1) the invention of the modern laid-wires and chain-wires mold; (2) the use of linen rags for pulp; and (3) the trip-hammering of rags to produce pulp. Hunter viewed the mold as "the first real step in papermaking, as it enabled the artisan to form sheets continually upon the same mold," and pointed out that "even the most modern paper-machine employs precisely the same principles."[3] The Muslims used linen rags for papermaking in place of the mulberry bark used by the Chinese but unavailable in Islam. They also replaced hand-beating of pulp with laborsaving trip-hammering. For this procedure a heavy hammer was attached to a long horizontal wooden beam pivoted near the hammer, and a man or boy standing on the end distant from the hammer raised the hammer by his weight; when he removed his weight, most likely by raising himself using an overhead bar, the hammer crashed down on the rags and pulp.[4] In the eleventh century a paper mill was built at Jativa, in Spain, that was probably driven by a waterwheel, thereby eliminating human work from the stamping process.

Writing

Writing was held in high esteem in Islam, for it possessed a particular religious significance; language was considered divinely inspired. Al-Muʿizz ibn Badis (1031–1108), quoted Muḥammad as having said, "Beautiful writing gives to truth more clarity. It demonstrates that when the pens are good, the books smile." Ibn Badis also recorded that Allah said, "Read, by your generous Lord who taught by pen," and added "that the first significant thing that Allah created was the pen."[5] By "read" he of course meant read aloud, and as a Muslim he thought of writing not as self-contained expression but rather as a transcript of oral communication. Writing should be beautiful, he states in the first chapter of his book, and he implies that smaller writing is better, as is writing rapidly.[6] Muslims restrained pictorial art, but did not totally suppress artistic illustration. Scientific and technological illustrations occur in Arabic books, particularly when expository prose fails to communicate information. Figure 6.1 is a star map depicting the constellation that was known as The Crow, together with a table giving the positions of the seven stars in the constellation. The figure is reproduced from a sixteenth-century copy in the Library of Congress of ʿAbd al-Raḥmān al-Sufi's (903–986) *Book of the Fixed Stars*, originally written in the tenth century and characterized by George Sarton as "one of the three masterpieces of Muslim observational astronomy."[7]

Muslims wrote with reed pens and illustrated and adorned with brushes. The constellation in figure 6.1 was done in three colors, red, yellow, and blue, while the table is in two: black for letters, red for numbers. Ibn Badis describes in detail three different types of pens: straight, diagonal, and "the middle one." The straight pen, which could produce writing that was the strongest, smallest, and most permanent, was favored by scribes. The diagonal pen produced writing that was weaker but more beautiful, and the middle one could produce writing that combined strength with beauty. The longer a pen, the faster one could write with it. In the second half of his first chapter Ibn Badis describes the cutting of reeds to produce pens and concludes with a brief description of inkwells.

His next seven chapters contain recipes for inks, starting with black soot inks in chapter 2 and black tannin inks in chapter 3. Chapters 4 through 6 contain recipes for the colored inks—red, pink, yellow, green, blue, violet, and white—that were used for pictorial illustration, and for auxiliary marks and punctuation, capitals, rubrics, designs, and borders of text. Chapter 7 is entitled "On the Writing Art with Gold, Silver, Copper, Tin, and Their Substitutes," and chapter 8 describes writing with secret inks. The last four chapters deal with erasure, glues, polishers, paper manufacture, preparation for writing, and beautifying. The book concludes with a description of adding leather coverings to the binding boards on a codex, but Ibn Badis did not include a description of the structural binding of codices.

Book Production

The Muslims' avid pursuit of learning and knowledge generated a huge demand for books and fostered large private and institutional collections.

In the ninth century, al-Jāḥiz (c. 776–868) pointed out "Were it not for the wisdom garnered in books most of the learning would have been lost. The power of

Figure 6.1. Islamic star map of a constellation named the Crow. (Courtesy Library of Congress)

forgetfulness would have triumphed over the power of memory."[8] Muslims were devoted to books and produced more in their few centuries of ascendancy than did any, or perhaps all, previous civilizations.

Private collectors were the major stimulus for book production, although the royal libraries and later the college libraries created significant demand. Many Muslim humanists, grammarians, lexicographers, philologists, historians, biographers, and theologians possessed exceptionally large libraries that they valued highly. Perhaps the largest private library was that of al-Sahib ibn Abbad (d. 995), humanist prime minister of two Seljuq sultans, who is reported to have declined an invitation to be prime minister of Khurasan, giving as one of his reasons that it would require four hundred camels to transport his books.[9] If one conservatively assumes that a camel could carry two bags each containing fifty two-pound books (camels can actually carry up to six hundred pounds), Ibn Abbad possessed forty thousand volumes. Abu Bakr ibn al-Jarrāh (d. 991) stated: "My books are worth 10,000 dirhems; my concubine, 10,000; my weapons, 10,000; and my riding animals 10,000."[10] Libraries were sometimes acquired by copying an entire collection. The lexicographer Ibn Hani al-Nisāburi (d. 850) owned so many books that he housed them in a separate dwelling.[11] Abu Bakr al-Suli (d. 946), a historian, arranged his books by subject, with each topic having a separate color of binding. Makdisi reports that "He was criticized for depending on his library books, rather than on his memory,"[12] a statement that will surely intrigue modern students of the cognitive sciences. An early thirteenth-century library belonging to Taj ad-Din al-Kindī (d. 1219)—not to be confused with the great Muslim philosopher of the ninth century—contained 440 books on grammar, lexicography, and poetry; 198 on the Qur'an sciences, law, and traditions of the Prophet; and 123 on medicine and other sciences, giving a total of 761.

The authors of most humanistic works dictated their books, often from memory, to copyists or students. When students participated in the publication of a work, the procedures of correction and collation were as follows: "(1) the book was always dictated by the professor to the students, or to a particular student; (2) it was always dictated extemporaneously, the professor not referring to any notes or drafts; (3) the professor heard the dictated text read back to him by a chosen student, word for word; (4) the students were all able to follow the recitation, word for word, in their own copies and to correct their copies whenever the professor corrected, or when the reading was otherwise not in consonance with their texts."[13] Johannes Pedersen writes that "Fantastic stories are often told of the memories of dictating authors: for instance, Abū Bakr ibn al-Anbārī (d. 939) is said to have dictated from memory 45,000 pages of traditions concerning the Prophet and to have been able, according to his own account, to recite thirteen chests of books by heart."[14] More often, however, an author would write his work and dictate from the written version.

By and large, Islamic scholars and authors lived a life of contentment, in that intellectualism was bound up with religion and therefore provided a special sense of satisfaction; but authors must eat, sleep, and work, and they need money for food and shelter. A twelfth-century philosopher-physician provides an estimate of subsistence-level income. Abū l-Fatḥ ʿAbd ar-Raḥman refused a gift of 1,000 dinars from the sultan, "saying that he still had 10 dinars, that he needed only three dinars for annual expenses, and that he lived alone with his cat as companion."[15] Authors were not supposed to write for wages, but they could accept gifts and honoraria, which constituted their income. An author would often dedicate a work to a person of high rank, who would then give the author a gift or honorarium; such honoraria were usually 500 or 1,000 dinars, but there are records of 30,000 and 50,000 dinars. Former students gave what they could—food, or 20 or 50 dinars—but one former student was able to give a teacher nearly 20,000 dinars, thereby making him a rich man.[16]

Calligraphers were skillful writers who produced artistically beautiful copies and rarely, if ever, wrote from dictation. Their writing particularly emphasized elegant form and proportion of letters. Two outstanding calligraphers of the tenth and eleventh centuries, Abū Alī Muḥammad ibn ʿAlī ibn Muqla (d. 940) and Ibn al-Bawwāb (d. 1022), were in great demand for their writing; the former created a beautiful new script and the latter perfected it. They were artists whose work rivals the sixteenth-century Garamond and the eighteenth-century Baskerville type designs.

Whereas calligraphers produced beautiful books, copyists produced the flood. Copying had been a profession in pre-Islamic Arabia, where copyists had been employed for the most part in businesses and administrations, and there is good evidence that the Prophet, himself a businessman, had dictated at least some of the Qurʾan to a copyist. The majority of copyists, who were self-employed and were often also booksellers, became the avenue from authors to book buyers, like the publishers of today. Governmental organization supported most, if not all, of the regularly employed copyists. Al Maʾmun (786–833), caliph from 813 to 833, supported translation as the major activity of his famous House of Wisdom. He employed a staff of scholarly translators and a regular staff of copyists. Sometimes caliphs furnished authors with full-time copyists, as many as four to a single author.

Government officials were often author-copyists. Secretaries, in particular the holders of Offices of Secretary, composed, wrote, and copied original texts, proclamations, and correspondence and also functioned as proofreaders and editors. The texts were concerned with such topics as land taxes, law, financial matters, geography, water regulation, surveying, and biography. The author-copyists also produced legal documents, manuals for secretaries, gazetteers, and road books. Some of these works were important items in a large body of administrative literature; at least one, a book on subterranean irrigation channels, remained authoritative for two centuries.[17]

An Arabic tradition ascribes to the Abyssinians (Ethiopians) the introduction of the codex, or bound book, to the Arabs.[18] Two Arabic manuscripts translated into English by Martin Levey are valuable sources of Arabic bookbinding techniques.[19] Ibn Badis wrote his work in the eleventh century;[20] Abūl ʿAbbas Aḥmed ibn Muḥammad al-Sufyānī wrote his work nearly six centuries later, in 1619.[21] Ibn Badis describes bookbinding in his last and longest chapter. He did not precisely describe the sewing techniques, but said that there were several methods: "Some are used by craftsmen for ease and quickness. It is that the needle penetrates two places. Others work with two needles or three."[22] Presumably this two- or three-needle technique used chain stitching like that employed in the Stonyhurst Gospel of Saint John; the single needle penetrating two places is the technique described in chapter 5. After the quires had been sewn and pressed into a firm block, a spine lining, usually an open-weave linen, was pasted on, as were hinges of strips of paper or leather to attach the book covers. Following the introduction of paper in the eighth century the covers were usually paper pasteboards instead of expensive wooden boards.

Al-Sufyānī described his method of sewing in detail. After collating and aligning the quires, "two lines are drawn on the spine of the quires in the places where you will tie the book. You introduce the needle with the thread in the spine of the quire in the place marked with ink. The thread with which you bind is fine and strong, twisted on either three or four strands. . . . The purpose is to gather the quires of the book by sewing them to each other."[23] Most probably a chain stitch was used. Al-Sufyānī completed the structuring of the book by attaching the pasteboards with paper or leather hinges.

Arabic bindings differed from Byzantine and Western bindings in two distinct characteristics. First, as already described, the boards were pasted or glued to the book with paper or leather hinges rather than being sewn. These hinges often fractured; crudely executed repairs are found more often than not in Islamic codices. Second, they possessed fore-edge flaps made by extending the leather of the back cover and folding it over the fore edge of the book and in under the front page. The entire book was then protected except for the top and bottom edges; some Arabic bindings produced at the end of the eighteenth century still had them. The rapid increase in demand for books that began in the eighth century was undoubtedly the stimulus that brought about faster and cheaper sewing, covers, and attachment of covers. Today this type of binding (mechanized and without the fore-edge flaps) is known as case binding. Like the Muslims, modern publishers use it to provide acceptable protection at low cost.

Bookshops and Libraries

Bookshops and booksellers, of which mention was hardly ever made in Byzantium or the Christian West, abounded in Islam. Tenth-century Baghdad contained a booksellers market said to have comprised a hundred shops of booksellers and stationers.[24] The shops were often meeting places for discussions, and the fourteenth-century traveling scholar Abu ʿAbdallah ibn Battuta "lodged in the college of the Booksellers" when he visited Tunis.[25] Bookselling must have been a thriving activity to have supported a college.

Ibn Khaldūn, the celebrated historiographer, observed that the emergence of the occupation of [copyist-bookseller], which is concerned with transcribing, proofreading, binding, and everything else that has to do with books and office work, had been brought about by the increase in literary pursuits. Copyist-booksellers worked both in and out of stalls, congregating in cities or large towns to such an extent that their clusters of shops became known as "the bookmen's bazaar," "the copyists bazaar," or "the bazaar of books." Ibn Battuta described the Damascus bookmen's bazaar as being near the great Umayyad mosque and comprising stalls "selling paper, pens, ink, and other articles associated with books." The eighth-century author al-Jāḥiz hired booths in which he spent the night reading books to save the purchase cost.[26]

During the eighth and ninth centuries literally hundreds of significant libraries came into being, most of which belonged to private individuals. There were three great caliphate libraries: the ʿAbbāsid in Baghdad, the earliest known; the Fātimid in Cairo; and the Umayyad in Córdoba. There were also innumerable libraries in mosques and colleges.

The ʿAbbāsid caliph al-Maʾmun brought the caliphate library in Baghdad into being in 830 as a major component of his celebrated House of Wisdom, an institution for research, teaching, and translation. Books in the library were in the fields of literary arts; "religious sciences," including Qurʾanic exegesis, tradition, theology, law, philology, and history; and "foreign sciences," embracing alchemy, mechanics, and medicine. Having obtained the permission of the Byzantine emperor, al-Maʾmun sent several copyists to Constantinople, whence they returned with copies of numerous Greek works to be translated.

The Fātimids, whose original caliphate was Yemen, were a belligerent sect professing a theology that was repugnant to most Muslims. Exhibiting threatening political and religious power for more than two centuries, and having gained control of North Africa in 909, they ruled Egypt from 967 to 1171. Immediately after assuming power they built an entirely new Cairo next to the old city, and within thirty years they had constructed a huge palace and a mosque that became, and still is, a center of Islamic culture. The staff of the palace library collected books so vigorously that soon some forty rooms were full of Greek science. The sixth caliph, al-Ḥakim (985–1021, ruled 996–1021) started an academy as an annex to the palace, which he named, as had al-Maʾmun his academy two centuries earlier, House of Wisdom. This academy possessed a huge library of its own, some of which al-Ḥakim had transferred from the palace library. In addition to books there were available, to all and sundry, instruction, paper, pens, and ink. The institute paid fixed wages to its staff and to scholars studying at the institute.

In 1068, following seven years of famine due to the failure of the Nile to flood, Turkish mercenaries temporarily seized power from the Fātimids, ransacking the palace and taking, among other things, books not in inner rooms. They also stole books from the academy as well as from other cities, and used some of the leather bindings as shoe soles. Neither the palace nor the academy library was totally destroyed, and each was extensively built up again. When the Fātimid dynasty ended, with the death of the last caliph in 1171, both libraries were apparently in good shape, but Saladin (1137–1193), who was vizier at the time, abolished the caliphate to become the sole ruler, and began selling off and giving away the books. The Fātimids transferred their base back to Yemen and later to India, taking many volumes with them. As a result, the Fātimid literary heritage resides in Yemen and Indian libraries, as well as, inevitably, in Western European collections.

In 756, members of the Umayyad family found refuge in Córdoba after their eviction from the Damascus caliphate by the ʿAbbāsids in 750. Still claiming the caliphate, they constructed a palace and the Great Mosque, later enlarged and finally completed by al-Ḥakam II (ruled 961–976), a famous patron of learning. He founded twenty-seven schools in Córdoba and provided them with scholarships for the poor. He also carried out an active program of purchasing and copying books for the library, which is thought to have grown to 400,000 volumes.[27] It was the library's zenith; under al-Ḥakam's son, books in the "ancient sciences" were withdrawn and burned to satisfy conservative scholars. In 1011 the minister sold most of the books to obtain money to carry on a war with the Berbers, who plundered the books that remained.[28]

Each Muslim college, beginning with the first, founded by Nizām al-Mulk in 1067, contained a library; it has been estimated that ultimately there were 264 Muslim colleges in seven cities.[29] Major mosques, of which there were a great many, were also centers of learning, maintaining schools and libraries for the benefit of Muslim society as a whole. Mosque libraries, many of which still exist, each comprised one or more private libraries that had been donated.

An astronomer, ʿAli ibn Yaḥyā established in the ninth century near Baghdad a large library, extolled for its size and splendor, that was open to all scholars. Late in the tenth century Sābur ibn Ardashīr founded a large library in Baghdad also for use by scholars, but it was destroyed by the Seljuq Turks a half century later. Further east, in Rayy, south of Tehran, there were a couple of libraries containing thousands of books. Another tenth-century Iranian library was at Shiraz, several hundred miles east of Basra. A contemporary account of the establishment describes it as having two-story buildings set among gardens, lakes, and waterways and containing 360 rooms, one a large vaulted room containing cabinets in which the books were housed. Floors were carpeted and a ventilation system circulated cool air. Another large library was open to all in Basra as part of an academy that was able to grant money to indigent students.[30]

Evaluation

During four centuries, the eighth through the eleventh, Muslim civilization was by far the world center of intellectual activity, producing faith, beauty, justice, and knowledge, accomplishments that were reflected in a production of book titles and copies thereof in amounts never before seen: the total production of books exceeded the total of the Greco-Roman era plus that of Byzantium and the Christian West, discussed in the next chapter. Advanced publishing and bookselling practices were developed, and hundreds of libraries, many still in existence, were established for the dissemination of books. Mechanized manufacture of paper from cloth rags produced a cheap, flexible writing and printing medium that would make possible Gutenberg's invention of printing. Finally, the use of manganese dioxide as the "glassmakers soap" to produce clear glass made possible the invention of eyeglasses, which increased the number of Western readers, creating a demand for more copies that played a significant role in the invention of printing.

As for Arabic manuscripts and books still in existence, Adam Gacek cites with approval an estimate by the authors of *Bibliografia arabskikh rukopisel* of "the overall figure of Arabic manuscripts in the world as 600,000," having rejected another estimate of over 3 million. Gacek estimates that 120,000 have been properly cataloged and that another 180,000 have been listed, and concludes that "some 300,000 or more Arabic manuscripts are still uncatalogued."[31] It should be pointed out, however, that the Muslim aversion to the printing of books led to most books being produced as manuscripts until the last decades of the nineteenth century, although some Muslims had begun to print in the eighteenth.

7 | Western Christendom 600–1400

𝒢 *THE GERMANIC PEOPLES* who brought about the collapse of the Western Roman Empire in the last quarter of the fifth century did not bring an established religion with them, but so complete was the Christianization of the society they had invaded and overpowered that "they had to adopt the religion of those they conquered."[1] In the previous century Christianity had become firmly established in the Empire, with church structures and an organization of parish priests, archbishops, and bishops, headed by the bishop of Rome, with the title of pope. For the continuance of the book it was extremely important that Christianity not only survived but also predominated, for during the following centuries it proved to be the single Western source of development and production of books, through the instrumentality of Christian monasticism, which came into being in the East in the third century and extended into the West not long thereafter.

In the first half of the sixth century, Saint Benedict of Nursia (480–547) composed a rule prescribing the way of life for monks residing in a monastery that became the basis for the conduct of most monastic groups until the twelfth century. In the eighth and ninth centuries, two monks, Paul Warnefrid and Magister Hildebrand, wrote commentaries on the Rule in which they described daily reading and library activities. Monks were required by the Rule to read (aloud or by mumbling) three hours each day in summer and two in winter; in addition, each monk was required to read an entire book during Lent and to carry a small book when traveling.[2] Apparently only a few monks could read text—still a string of letters without word separations—sufficiently well to qualify as readers during meals, the morning assembly, and the evening devotional services. Hildebrand wrote that

Since the Rule orders those to read [orally] who will edyfy their hearers, it is necessary that we subjoin here the instructions of the various holy Fathers who teach how one should read—instructions gathered from the sayings of Augustus and Ambrose, of Bede and Isidore, or even of Victorinus and Servius and other grammarians who teach how to distinguish accurately the obscure meanings and to read according to the accents."[3]

There is no doubt that the major monastic centers of the Merovingian period (sixth and seventh centuries) possessed collections of books, but there is no evidence as to their size. There exist, however, book lists from three eighth-century monasteries that record numbers of books: 20 at Fulda, 34 at Würzburg, and 31 at St. Wandrille. Ninth-century catalogs of libraries at Reichenau and St. Gall list, respectively, "some 415 books" and "264 codices (395 separate works)."[4] The librarian at one of these early monasteries carried out the Rule's provision that "During this time of Lent each one is to receive a book from the library and to read the whole of it straight through. These books are to be distributed at the beginning of Lent."[5] The librarian, assisted by some of the monks, would bring all the books from the library and spread them on a carpet in the cloister. The monks, when each had chosen a book, would sit apart so as not to disturb one another and, presumably, read aloud softly to themselves. At the end of Lent each monk placed his book back on the carpet and was questioned to ascertain if he had read and studied it; if not, it was returned to him. If any book was missing at the end of the reading period the abbot conducted a search until it was found.

Desirably each monastery should have had a collection of books exceeding in number the number of monks who could read. One study has shown that prior to the year 1000 at least one monastery, Corbie, in France, had 350 monks; the fewest was 44, at Inde or Cornelimunster.[6] Hence Corbie could have had 350 volumes, assuming all monks could read. For the most part the books would have been religious in nature, but there certainly would have been some secular works in nearly all, if not all, monastic collections. Along with libraries in Byzantium and Islam, these Western monastic libraries also preserved and transmitted to the modern world the books of the Greco-Roman era.

Book Production in the Monastic Era

The monastic era stretched from the beginning of the sixth century to the end of the twelfth—seven hundred years in which monasteries enjoyed a monopoly in the development and production of books in the West. That era began with an evolutionary period of two centuries during which the conquering Germanic tribes were adapting to a Roman environment and generating a group of entirely new European societies that were neither Roman nor tribal. A second evolutionary period beginning in the twelfth century saw growth in population, production of goods, trade, and wealth, and the advent of a middle class, a learned laity, and the sudden creation of universities.

Magnus Aurelius Cassiodorus (d. 575), a contemporary of Saint Benedict, established a monastery at Vivarium, in southern Italy, in which he encouraged book collecting and introduced monastic book copying. In book I of his *Institutiones*, a work similar to Benedict's Rule, Cassiodorus praises the "tasks" of the scribe, and urges him to read works on orthography to improve the accuracy of his copying. He also describes such scribal appurtenances as a sundial, a water clock for cloudy days, and lamps "that feed their own fire."[7] The scriptorium, as the writing chamber in monasteries came to be called, was sometimes a separate room, which might also contain the book collection. In northern climes the scriptorium was next to the calefactory, or heated room, where monks could warm themselves. Such was the case at St. Gall, in Switzerland, where a ninth-century plan shows a large center table in the interior of the scriptorium with seven writing desks against the walls;[8] the library was in the chamber above the scriptorium.

The scriptoria constituted the principal location of European book production until 1200 and also acted in a primitive publishing and lending capacity. The primary function of a scriptorium was to copy books to be added to its monastery's collection; secondarily it produced copies of its own books to go to other monasteries. A few monasteries made copies for sale.

The copying procedure necessitated searching in other libraries for an existing manuscript if the monastery did not already have a copy. To facilitate finding a title elsewhere, a union catalog of holdings in 185 monastic and cathedral libraries, entitled *Registrum Anglie de libris doctorum et auctorum veterum*, was produced in the early fourteenth century. It contains "roughly 1400" title entries.[9] Nearly a century later Henry of Kirkestede at Bury St. Edmunds completed a bio-bibliographic union catalog from various sources, which included the *Registrum*, entitled *Catalogus scriptorum ecclesiae*; it contained the holdings of 195 English libraries with a total of 674 authors. A number was assigned to each library, and up to nine holding libraries were listed, by number, with each title entry. Richard Rouse has described Kirkestede's purpose in compiling the *Catalogus* as preparing a "list of authoritative and acceptable authors and their works . . . in which ideally the authors and their works would be clearly listed and identified by means of biographical sketches and incipits and explicits, and every work would be located in a library so that it could be found by a monk who desired to read or copy it."[10]

The cost of maintaining scriptoria and libraries was considerable, perhaps the largest part of it being the maintenance of scribes who were not tending fields to produce sustenance. Some monasteries also hired lay scribes, which further increased expense either in cash or in kind. Cost of parchment was high; of inks less so, but significant. The Evesham monastery used "the tithes from Beningworth to pay for parchment and for the maintenance of scribes."[11] This particular use of church tithes was common, as was designation of a specific portion of a monastery's revenue. A not-so-common type of endowment was that at Bury St.

Edmunds, where the scriptorium enjoyed the income of two mills. In France a kind of income tax was imposed on all priests holding benefices from monasteries and sometimes on monastic officials.

Intelligent individuals were required as correctors and proof readers, but presumably a scribe did not have to be able to read the text he was copying any more than a twentieth-century typesetter had to be able to read a Latin text to set it. Moreover, to judge from the following marginalia and colophonic quotations it does not appear that a scribal assignment was greatly desired:

> Writing is excessive drudgery. It crooks your back, it dims your sight, it twists your stomach, and your sides.
> St. Patrick of Armagh, deliver me from writing.
> While I wrote I froze, and what I could not write by the beams of the sun I finished by candlelight.
> Thank God, It will soon be dark.
> As the sick man desireth health even so doth the scribe desire the end of the volume.[12]
> Now I've written the whole thing: for Christ's sake give me a drink.[13]

At the end of a ninth-century manuscript written at Lorsch, the scribe recorded that "Jacob wrote this," and another person added that "A certain portion of this book is not of his own free will but under compulsion, bound by fetters, just as a runaway and fugitive has to be bound."[14] Falconer Madan found that only five of England's monastic houses were "important centres of writing and illumination" and that in the lesser houses "only a small proportion of monks were allowed to take up the work, and often, we may be sure, by accident or design the copying would fall into second-rate hands." Nevertheless, in the seventh and eighth centuries scribes were respected in Ireland, where the penalty for murdering a scribe was the same as that for killing a bishop or an abbot.[15]

Large monasteries had four types of scribes: (1) those who did the common copying work of the house; (2) those trained in calligraphy, who copied fine book manuscripts; (3) the "correctors," who collated and compared a finished book with the exemplar from which it had been copied; and (4) the rubricators and illuminators. Some of the calligraphers and illuminators were laity. The manager of the scriptorium was often the choirmaster; very likely a person who could lead and direct singers could also direct copyists. Only the abbot had the authority to decide that a copy should be made, a scribe could write only with permission from the director, and scribes could not exchange assignments; also, no monk appointed to write could refuse to do so. A thirteenth-century Carthusian statute required unwilling scribes to be punished by depriving them of wine.

In the opinion of Paul Saenger, a foremost student of silent reading, "Word separation was the singular contribution . . . to Western written communication, . . . and a major advance toward silent reading,"[16] The Irish scribes who introduced word separation, in the Book of Durrow (fig. 7.1), which was written about 675, had inherited an ancient oral scholastic tradition that did not include

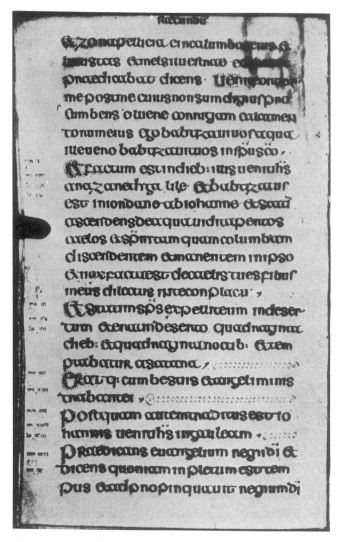

Figure 7.1. Book of Durrow showing word separation.

latinization, Ireland and Scotland never having been part of the Roman Empire. For the Irish monk who did not have Latin as a native or near-native tongue and was not intimately familiar with its varying forms of declension, conjugation, and inflection, reading an unbroken string of Latin words out loud to others was a formidable task. To facilitate oral reading the Irish scribes used space between words to make them more readily visible. Irish missionaries introduced word separation to continental monasteries, but it was not until the eleventh century that the practice was generally accepted on the continent.

Book illumination, in the sense of artistic illustration, was a seventh-century invention, from which the artistic painting tradition developed; "illuminated Books are the most important source for our knowledge of the history of European painting"[17] in the centuries covered by this chapter. One of the earliest illuminated manuscripts is the aforementioned Book of Durrow, which "contains beautiful illuminations" often comprising interlacings of flora and fauna. A quarter century later two other innovative manuscript Bibles were produced. One, known as Codex Amiatinus, was written at Jarrow, on the estuary of the River Tyne near present-day Newcastle, and the other, known as the Lindisfarne Gospels, was written at what is now called Holy Island, off the Scottish coast about fifty miles north of the Tyne. Both are celebrated for text and illumination, the Codex Amiatinus being considered the best early copy of the Vulgate. The Lindisfarne Gospels, written by Eadfrith, bishop of the Lindisfarne monastery from 698 to 721, was bound by Ethiwald, bishop from 724 to 740. Billroth, a monk, "wrought in smith's work the ornaments on its cover."[18]

The Book of Kells, often described as one of the finest books that has ever been produced, was written in an Irish monastery about 800. The work, which has lost some folios at the beginning and end, now possesses 340 leaves. Full-page paintings present scenes from the life of Christ or serve as ornate first pages of the Gospels; one double page does both. All but two of the pages have colorful ornamentation. There are more than twenty-one hundred flamboyant capitals throughout the volume, and the ivy-like decorative page borders entwine all manner of humans, plants, and animals, in forms graceful to grotesque but always lively and interesting.

Manual book illumination continued to thrive for the next seven centuries with many changes in technique, style, and motif. During the first half of the sixteenth it declined to a low ebb but it has never ceased; indeed, it has had a serious revival during the twentieth century.

The Lindisfarne Gospels, 13½ by 9¾ inches with 259 leaves, the Codex Amiatinus, 20 by 13½ inches with 1,030 leaves, and the Book of Kells, 13 by 9½ inches with 340 leaves, were big, heavy books. A recent facsimile edition of the Book of Kells, printed on paper that mimicks parchment, weighs more than twenty pounds. There was no possibility that the ancient chain-stitch binding technique that had been used for the little Stonyhurst Gospel (see chapter 5) could have held such books together. By the late seventh century a new method of binding that produced exceptionally strong books had been developed; it became the traditional method of western bookbinding and continues to be used for expensive new books and the repair of old ones. The artisan used stout cords or thongs of leather in place of threads, looping them through two, or sometimes three, sets of double holes in the upper wooden board and pulling them taut. He then sewed the back of the first quire to each of the lengths of cord. When all of the quires had been attached to the cords and firmly pressed against the upper board, the four lengths of cord were drawn through the four holes in the lower board. At least four of these eighth-century bindings still exist.[19] In the eleventh century a refinement of this technique appeared. A leather band, half an inch wide or less, was slit longitudinally the distance of the width of the back of the book. The two leather strips then had the quires sewn to them, after which the ends of the strips were secured to the boards. These leather-thong bindings were even stronger than the double twine-cord bindings.

Book Production in the Secular Era

Monks continued to copy for their monastic libraries until the beginning of the sixteenth century, but starting in the thirteenth century nonecclesiastic markets for books generated a new kind of organization for copying and providing books in significantly larger numbers than the monastic scriptoria had been able to produce. The new sources of demand for books were spawned by a changing and growing European society. As population increased, villages became towns, cities grew larger. The largest of the cities were Italian: Venice and Genoa each had 100,000 inhabitants, Florence had 90,000, and Palermo and Pisa each had 50,000. North of Italy, Paris led with 80,000 inhabitants, Ghent had 50,000, Bruges and London each had about 35,000, and Cologne had 30,000.[20]

Handcraft manufacturing became organized into capitalistic industries wherein a raw material like wool was "put out" to individual artisans, such as spinners, weavers, and dyers. The resultant increased production of goods engendered an increase in wealth and international trade that required partnering, brokering, warehousing, double-entry bookkeeping, and lending at interest—all new activities. It even introduced a new category of publication—handbooks of commercial practices. The new economy created a middle class between the elite and the poor, a laity many of whose members required education to make their way into the worlds of medicine, law, commerce, the state, and the church.

To provide that education an innovative institution, the European university, arose rapidly, evolving in many cases from urban schools. Schools at Bologna, Paris, and Oxford achieved university status in the last half of the twelfth century, as did schools at Cambridge, Montpellier, Toulouse, Angers, Padua, Naples, Salamanca, and Valladolid in the first third of the thirteenth. In the next two centuries an additional dozen and a half attained university rank. Nearly all of these schools are still in existence. Areas of instruction were medicine, law, theology, and the seven liberal arts: grammar, rhetoric, logic, geometry, arithmetic, music, and astronomy.

The universities generated new users of books—professors who needed books for their studies and teaching, and students who wanted books to supplement and replace lecture notes. To meet this new demand, guilds of stationers, under the control of the universities, came into being in university cities. Their members were professional copyists and stationers. As university bookstores do today, the stationers sold, repurchased, and resold books. They would also provide and sell books copied from "exemplars," master copies that had to be approved by the faculty, who also controlled prices. In one case the stationer could not sell a book to a professor or student for more than four deniers, or more than six to someone outside the university. Quires (*pecia*) of books were "put out," as in the woolen and other trades, to copyists and illustrators and assembled and bound into a book upon return to the stationer. This *pecia* system is an early example, perhaps the first, of nonmechanized mass production with interchangeable parts, since any quire could fit in any copy of a book as long as the quires were composed of sheets of the same quality and dimensions. For a controlled fee a stationer could lend an examplar quire by quire, usually to a student, from which the student could make his own copy. One rough measure of the increased use of books is Marcel Thomas's report that "more than 2,000 copies of Aristotle's works have come down to us from the 13th and 14th centuries";[21] there is no way of knowing how many more have disappeared over the intervening centuries.

Translations from Arabic to Latin in the twelfth century produced "a torrent of new ideas," as one scholar has put it;[22] certainly one of the reasons for the large number of extant Aristotelian manuscripts is that Gerard of Cremona (c. 1114–1187) translated four new Aristotle titles from Arabic in the latter decades of the twelfth century. A century later William of Moerbeke added still more titles to the Aristotelian corpus with his translations from Greek, which only a few Western scholars could read. During these two centuries hundreds of titles previously unknown in the West became available and were rapidly circulated to the universities, dramatically increasing the demand for ever more copying.

Scholasticism completely altered the progression of Western philosophy. Christianity dominated philosophy for a millennium prior to the twelfth century, when "schoolmen" (university teachers) began to reconcile Christian doctrine with the explanation of nature in the newly retrieved works of Aristotle. Scholastic thinking and teaching used a question-and-answer technique that was an effective tool when used by men of superior intellect, the most outstanding of whom was Thomas Aquinas (1225–1274). In his *Summary of Doctrine* he proposed questions, listed objections to them, and then answered every objection, thereby constructing one of the greatest systems in the history of philosophy.

The intellectual complexities of scholastic thinking and findings concerning faith and nature, stimulating to student and teacher alike, resulted in greater student use of books. Instead of taking notes, students began bringing to lectures copies of a book to read silently as the lecturer read it aloud; indeed, a few universities required the practice. What was more important was that a student had a copy to study alone or with others. One author wrote an epitome of one of his larger works so that poor students could purchase it, and some cathedral schools and universities had libraries that lent books to poor students to take to class.

In the fifteenth century the Sorbonne had thirty copies of one manuscript for lending.

A benefit for professors as authors was the evolvement in the thirteenth century of gothic cursive script, which enabled them to write rapidly and to compose their texts in final form for transliteration by copyists for publication. Paul Saenger has pointed out that "The immense productivity of late scholastic writers . . . would have been impossible without the perfection of Gothic cursive script" and added that it "was a unique development in the history of written communication."[23]

Indexes

Subject indexes attached to individual books, eyeglasses that made it possible for those with defective vision to read books, and the development of silent reading, were three major advances that greatly enlarged the use of books and contributed extensive pressure for the development of a system to produce multiple copies of books that would be more effectual than the *pecia* system. A century of invention of various types of indexes and reference tools preceded the advent of the first subject index to a specific book, which occurred in the last years of the thirteenth century. The first subject indexes were "distinctions," collections of "various figurative or symbolic meanings of a noun found in the scriptures" that "are the earliest of all alphabetical tools aside from dictionaries."[24] Richard and Mary Rouse supply an example: "Horse = Preacher. Job 39: 'Hast thou given the horse strength, or encircled his neck with whinning?' Gregory's gloss on this says that the horse means a preacher, to whom God first gives strength to conquer his own vices, and then a whinny—a voice to preach to others."[25] Distinctions were biblical tools designed to assist preachers in writing sermons. The authors of three of the earliest of the extant collections, all of whom died within three years of 1200, provided a good beginning of a useful type of reference book, for distinctions continued to be produced throughout the thirteenth and fourteenth centuries.

By the end of the third decade of the thirteenth century Hugh de Saint-Cher had produced the first word concordance. It was a simple word index of the Bible, with every location of each word listed "by book of the Bible, by the chapter divisions attributed to Stephen Langton, and by one of the seven letters, A–G, to indicate relative position within the chapter."[26] Hugh organized several dozen men, assigning to each man an initial letter to search; for example, the man assigned *M* was to go through the entire Bible, list each word beginning with *M* and give its location. As it was soon perceived that this original reference work would be even more useful if words were cited in context, a second concordance was produced, with each word in lengthy context, but it proved to be unwieldy. By 1386 a third version was produced, with words in contexts of four to seven words, the model for biblical concordances ever since.

The subject index, also an innovation of the thirteenth century, evolved over the same period as did the concordance. Most of the early topical indexes were designed for writing sermons; some were organized, while others were apparently sequential without any arrangement. By midcentury the entries were in alphabetical order, except for a few in some classified arrangement. Until the end of the century these alphabetical reference works indexed a small group of books. Finally John of Freiburg added an alphabetical subject index to his own book, *Summa Confessorum* (1297–1298). As the Rouses have put it, "By the end of the thirteenth century the practical utility of the subject index is taken for granted by the literate West, no longer solely as an aid for preachers, but also in the disciplines of theology, philosophy, and both kinds of law."[27]

Eyeglasses

The invention, in the latter half of the 1280s, of eyeglasses intended primarily for reading probably increased reading by as much as 60 percent. Eyeglasses extended reading capability an average of 15 years beyond the age of 45, a time by which most people would have lost the near vision required to read a printed page. Ninety-five percent of people presently older than 45 use eyeglasses for reading or other close work. George Minois recorded the life expectancy of English males born between 1276 and 1300 as 14.7 years at age 45 and constructed a table of population data from Périgueux, France, that enabled me to calculate the life expectancy at the end of the fourteenth century as 14.45 years at age 45. If one assumes that people began the serious use of books at age 20 and continued to 45, eyeglasses would have increased reading time by 15 years, or 60 percent.

Edward Rosen, author of the most thorough study of the origin of eyeglasses, dated "the invention shortly after 1286" and concluded that although the inventor was unknown "Pisa has a better claim on him than any other locality." Rosen also assembled early references to eyeglasses: two references in the rules of a Venetian guild in 1300 and 1301; the price in Bolognese soldi of "eyeglasses with case" in 1316; a 1322 listing in an inventory of the belongings of a deceased Florentine bishop; and a Tuscan merchant's 1339 complaint listing "one pair of eyeglasses" among goods purchased in Florence and stolen from him. In the 1360s Petrarch wrote that his keen sight "left me when I was over sixty years of age, so that to my annoyance I had to seek the help of eyeglasses," and Guy de Chauliac, surgeon at Montpellier, wrote in his oft-published *Chirurgia Magna*, "if these things do not avail, recourse must be had to spectacles of glass or beryl."[28]

Further evidence of growth in the use of eyeglasses is the establishment of the Venetian guild of eyeglass makers in 1320. Six decades later London imported eyeglasses, mostly from the Low Countries, at the rate of 384 pairs per month over the period from July 1 to September 29, 1384. A century later the rate was 480 per month over the period from November 8, 1480 to July 21, 1481.[29]

The earliest artistic depiction of eyeglasses is in a posthumous portrait of Hugh de Saint-Cher, the aforementioned originator of concordances, painted as a fresco by Tommaso da Modena in 1352 on a wall in a monastery in Treviso. Hugh never wore spectacles, for he died more than twenty years before their invention, but Tommaso apparently thought that a man of Hugh's age would have needed to wear them to read. The painting is sufficiently detailed to enable one to see the structure of the eyeglasses, which are two hand magnifying glasses held together at the ends of the handles by a rivet. The only knowledge of these devices was derived from such paintings until 1953, when "two complete rivetted spectacles as well as fragments of such" were discovered under the planks between the rows of choir stalls in a convent in Weinhausen. Analysis of these eyeglasses revealed many equivalents with eyeglasses in paintings. Horst Appuhn reports that "the general dating of the 14th and 15th centuries is given for the spectacles."[30] Two decades after the Weinhausen find, excavations in a refuse dump at the Trig Lane archaeological site in the City of London uncovered another "Pair of rivetted Spectacles . . . dated by a variety of techniques to 1440 or the years immediately thereafter, [making them] the earliest spectacle frames . . . of known date."[31]

Silent Reading

Silent reading, stimulated by the complex works of scholasticism, prevailed in clerical and professional communities as early as the twelfth century. In the fourteenth century it became popular among the elite—the upper middle class and the nobility, for whom Dante (1265–1321) and Boccaccio (1313–1375) wrote. The nobility in particular turned to silent reading, acquiring books to read as well as reference works such as gazetteers and biographical dictionaries of saints. Books in the vernacular were plentiful, engendering larger and larger royal and upper-class libraries. Most of the populace, however, was illiterate and also unfamiliar with books. As Richard de Bury (d. 1345) put it, "the laity, who look at a book turned upside down just as if it were open in the right way, are utterly unworthy of any communion with books."[32]

Silent reading effected a revolution in the interior design of libraries. Monastic libraries had been cloister libraries. Books were kept in chests or closets within a room, but the oral reading was done in an open cloister, which sometimes had open carrels, or in a monk's own room, for it was imperative that oral reading be done in such a way as not to disturb others. With silent reading a wholly different design was adopted. The floor plan of the new library chamber or hall provided for bookcases around the walls, and tables placed across the narrow dimension of the room, with books for reference chained in the middle of each table. Oxford's new university library of the mid–fourteenth century, an addition to an existing building, measured forty-five by twenty feet. Although Merton College at Oxford constructed a separate library building from 1375 to 1378, it wasn't until the next century that stand-alone library buildings were frequently constructed at church schools, monasteries, and universities. The main purpose of these new libraries was to provide a place for users, not for books.

Silent reading also provoked innovations in punctuation and captions. Paragraph marks came into use to segregate logical units of text, and the comma and period evolved into their modern usage in sentence construction. Modern quotation marks were invented to replace red underlining, a simplification that proved a happy development for printing, which could not produce red underlines easily. Parentheses, an entirely new device, to indicate the oral aside, also appeared at this time. Innovative captions included chapter heads, running headings, and tables of contents listing chapter heads; these three features facilitated access to information within a book, and still do. In 1400 the only significant item of modern format that was lacking was the title page.

Paper

In 1074 one Abū Masaifa established the first European paper mill, at Jativa, in eastern Spain, south of the Jucar River and about twenty miles inland from the Mediterranean Sea. It must have been a good-sized mill, for it had thirty workers. It was located outside the town on a canal and presumably was driven by a water wheel. Sometime before 1148, a Muslim traveler, Idrisi, visited Jativa and described the paper manufactured there as being superior to that found anywhere else in the "universe," and learned that it was being exported to the East and West, as he put it.[33]

In 1238 Valencia fell to Christendom when the forces of James I of Aragon captured it, but the mill continued to be operated by Muslims and Jews. The next European mill was established about 1270 at Fabriano near Rome, to be quickly joined by others in the same vicinity; one is still operational and is a museum. The mill Richard-de-Bas at Ambert d'Auvergne dates from 1326 and was "one of the first mills to see the light of day in France";[34] it too is still operational and is also a museum. Waterwheels drive both mills. The first German mill, at Nuremberg, was established in 1390; the first English mill was established in 1490, more than two centuries after the Fabriano mill. This extraordinarily slow advance across Europe reveals that paper was not in great demand. For single-copy manuscript book production the only advantage paper had over parchment was that it cost less. However, fourteenth-century paper was fragile, had a rough surface, "drank" the water-based ink, and was not hospitable to the pigments of illuminators. Hence early paper was not satisfactory for manuscript book production, though it was occasionally used for that purpose. However, improvements in the drying process led to a paper receptive to inks and pigments that later proved to be an indispensable component of the printing of books.

Throughout the twelve centuries following the invention of the codex the technology of the book remained remarkably stable, but there were three minor modifications in the equilibrium. The first was the invention of cord binding that held together codices of all manner of sizes and shapes; the second was the establishment of the *pecia* system for making copies; the third was the introduction of modern paper as a writing surface, which was to replace parchment and to become the vehicle for Gutenberg's printing. In addition there were seven improvements in the use of books and the presentation of information: eyeglasses to enable reading, silent reading, word separation, subject indexes, tables of contents, artistic illumination, and illustration for comprehension. None of the modifications equaled the invention of the codex in importance, but together they brought the book from antiquity to the modern world except for the invention of printing, which is the subject of the next chapter.

Printing
8 | *1400–1800*

THE LAST QUARTER OF the fourteenth century and the entirety of the fifteenth was a time of remarkable social change. Existing universities expanded in scholarship, size, and number, and several new universities were founded in northern Europe, greatly enlarging the need for information provided by books. Richard Rouse has described the "renewal of northern European spirituality," which brought new vigor to several hundred monasteries of a half-dozen different orders having in common a "practical, individual search for a direct rapport with God through his written word and the interpretation of it. These orders shape the book to serve their needs. What emerges is a book distinctly different from anything the Middle Ages had hitherto seen—a book which in some ways has more in common with the printed book than with the products of the manuscript that preceded it."[1] This innovative religious book wove together four characteristics, none in itself new: (1) access to information within texts via subject indexes, tables of contents, and pages or sheets numbered with arabic numerals; (2) accuracy of text based on codified rules first written out in 1428; (3) clarity of text achieved with a bookhand script named hybrida; and (4) enhancement of bibliographic descriptions in incipits and explicits from "one or two to eight or ten lines."[2] Demand for manuscript books continued to expand into the fifteenth century despite deadly epidemics, but although manuscript production had risen (in France it was 22 percent higher in the fifteenth century than it had been in the thirteenth), manuscript copying could not satisfy the hunger for books.

Printing, best defined as the mechanical production of multiple copies of writing or images, which began in the fifteenth century, twelve hundred years after the introduction of the codex, marks the beginning of the modern book. Printed products from the first half of the century included playing cards reproduced by stencils and engraved wooden blocks, image sheets and books produced from wooden blocks, and books and broadsides produced from cast type. While there was no direct progression from playing card to image print, or from block book to printed book, the printing of images and text from engraved blocks of wood must have encouraged and emboldened the half-dozen men, including Johannes Gutenberg, who sought for a more successful means of reproducing multiple copies of books.

The best evidence that there was a potential market for multiple copies is the number of books printed in the last third of the fifteenth century. In 1935 John Lenhart constructed an estimate "of 20,047,500 copies for the whole of Europe" (though he cautioned that the figure could not "be regarded as mathematically exact").[3] In 1958 Lucien Febvre and Henri-Jean Martin calculated that "about 20 million books were printed before 1500."[4] In 1970 Warren Chappell tallied "some 12,000,000 books,"[5] and in 1981 Richard Rouse estimated "some fifteen to twenty million copies . . . a very large number indeed—perhaps larger than the number of all the manuscripts produced in medieval Europe."[6]

Block Printing

Three single-image prints from wood blocks, impressed with dark brown ink on cut wooden blocks in a system known as xylography, are the earliest dated examples of a process for producing multiple copies: the Brussels Print (1418), the Berlin Print (c. 1420), and the Saint Christopher Print (1423). These and similar prints were all religious in character, portraying devotional scenes in the manner of stained-glass windows in churches, which almost certainly influenced block printing. The prints were inexpensive and could be taken home and put up on a wall for contemplation. Possession of a print of a saint provided protection: Saint Roche protected the owner from plague, Saint Appolina from toothache, Saint Sebastian from injury, and Saint Christopher, the patron saint of travelers, from sudden death (until the latter was decanonized in 1969 one could often see a Saint Christopher medal dangling from the rearview mirror of an automobile).

Block prints of the first half of the fifteenth century are all from south Flanders or south Germany. The Brussels Print is closely similar in design and cutting to the Berlin Print, which contains a poem in Flemish. The Saint Christopher Print was found at Buxheim, some fifty miles southeast of Augsburg in a mountainous region of south Germany. To the various pieces of circumstantial evidence suggesting that the latter print may have been produced in the vicinity of its discovery, a piece of internal evidence can be added. While anyone looking at the print might argue that the terrain depicted in the print seems mountainous only because the artist could not draw perspective (the ragged land masses could equally depict the shores of a river) the waterwheel driving the mill in the lower-left corner of the print is the overshot wheel most often found in mountainous territory.

Block printing, like printing from cast type, is relief printing from an inverted image. The artist could draw the picture directly on the block, inverted right to left, but more likely he drew it on tissue paper and traced it face down on the block; probably text would have been treated in the same manner, to avoid having to write backward. The surface of the block (of a smooth-grained wood, such as pear, cherry, or apple) was usually cut running with the grain, unlike the surface of a wood engraving, which is cut across the grain. The woodcutter used a knife and a gouge, the knife to cut down into the block on both sides of a line and the gouge to hollow out areas between lines. A water-based brownish ink was applied to the block with an inking cushion; a sheet of paper (all single prints were on paper) was then placed on the block and pressure was applied to it by rubbing it with a firm tool, such as a burnisher, or by using a press. All the prints were colored, either freehand or by stencil.

Block books were the assemblage into codex form of sets of image prints that had been popular in manuscript. The Pauper's Bible and the Apocalypse of St. John (one or the other is thought to be the oldest block book) were composed of sets of pictures that had writing added within their borders after the printing. A second type of block book consisted of pictures and text external to the pictures; text might be above or below a picture, or both, or on opposite or consecutive pages. In a third type, text might appear both within and outside the borders of the pictures. Only one known fifteenth-century xylographic book had text with no pictures, the ever-popular *Donatus*, a fourth-century Latin grammar. It also was the only xylographic work printed on parchment, to make it resistant to school-book wear and tear; even so, only fragments of it survive.

The cutting of blocks for block books was the same as for single block prints, except that two pictures were cut side by side to be printed on a single sheet of paper to form two pages by folding. The size of the blocks seems to have been determined by paper size. An examination of the measurements of twenty-five editions of block books revealed that three groups each comprising five editions were printed on paper that varied by only one centimeter in height; in one group of five, for example, three editions were 21 cm. and two 22 cm. The leaves of most fifteenth-century block books were printed on one side only, but the catalog of the Rosenwald Collection in the Library of Congress contains one block book dated "1475?" with "leaves printed on both sides."

The water-based brown ink used for woodcuts was also used for block books until the introduction of the black sticky ink that Gutenberg also employed. Because of the extreme difficulty in keeping a sheet of paper motionless on a block with water-based ink, one experienced wood engraver has held that block-book sheets must have been printed on presses.[7] Some sixteenth-century block books were definitely printed on a press, with black ink and on both sides of the paper.

The printed sheets were bound so that facing pairs of printed and blank pages alternated, with the first and last pages being blank. The blocks for at least one book were cut with letters in alphabetical order, to guide the binder in assembling pages in correct sequence.[8] It is probable that block books were printed singly on demand, as were the manuscript books being produced individually by copyists at the same time; watermarked paper that can be dated gives evidence of individual blocks having been used over a long period of time.

Publication dates of block books are in dispute, with assigned dates varying by half a century. Heinrich Musper maintains, and I agree, that "What is decisive is the wood block itself with the drawing originally cut on it . . . to establish a date or narrow down the period of origin."[9] On the other hand, Allen H. Stevenson holds that "paper [with its watermarks] has proved an unexpectedly competent source of information towards dating."[10] Musper is "convinced that the woodcuts of the *Pauper's Bible* [in the Heidelberg University Library] should on stylistic grounds be placed in the 1420s," whereas Stevenson found that the paper of the "first edition" in the British Library should be dated 1465. Musper has stated that "The original *Apocalypse* could be dated about 1420 because its style corresponds to that of the Brussels woodcut . . . dated 1418."[11] Stevenson, however, dated it 1450–1452. Whatever the date of the earliest block-book may be, it is evident that the woodcutters of the early blocks had already gained extensive experience and acquired superior craftsmanship.

Block books displaying biblical events, thought to have been popular despite the scarcity of surviving copies, were probably produced for priests and other preachers as well as for laypersons. They were of assistance in sermon preparation and helpful in times of human stress. *Ars Moriendi* (Art of Dying), for example, enabled attendants to aid and comfort the moribund by assuring passage of the soul to heaven. *Ars Moriendi* is extant in ten different editions, although known copies are few. Of the Pauper's Bible, also known to have had ten editions, some fifty copies are extant, more than of the Gutenberg Bible. That the total copies of the three dozen known block-book titles number hardly more than a hundred could mean that only a few copies of each edition were printed, but it is much more likely that these picture books were used to extinction.

Xylographic printing preceded typographic printing by at least a quarter century, but it was not a direct technological predecessor. No aspect of xylography is antecedent to typecasting, and it was the casting of type in a mold that was the key to the invention of typography.

Printing from Cast Type

The success of block-book printing in the first two-thirds of the fifteenth century is one demonstration of the burgeoning demand for books. Better evidence is the astonishing number of books printed from cast type in the last thirty years of the fifteenth century, perhaps a larger number than that of all the manuscript books written in the previous nine hundred years.[12]

Five men, working independently, sought to develop a technique for mechanically producing multiple copies of books, but only one, Johannes Gutenberg, came up with a successful invention. The other four were Jean Brito of Bruges,[13] Prokop Waldvogel of Avignon,[14] Panfilo Castaldi of Feltre,[15] and Laurens Koster of Haarlem.[16]

Johannes Gutenberg was born in Mainz sometime during the last decade of the fourteenth century. Although the son of a patrician, he trained in metalworking and was associated with the goldsmiths guild, which led to his exile from Mainz in 1430 during a quarrel between guilds and patricians. He moved to Strasbourg, where he was associated with the goldsmiths guild from 1434 to 1444. Details of his activities in Strasbourg are meager, but he engaged in stone polishing and the manufacture of mirrors, and almost certainly carried out his initial development of printing. In 1442 he borrowed £80 from the Chapter of Saint Thomas in Strasbourg; it was a loan he never paid back. There is no trace of him from 1444 until 1448, when he was back in Mainz, where on October 6 he borrowed 150 gulden. Two years later he borrowed 800 gulden from Johann Fust, a lawyer and a member of a family of wealthy merchant bankers, "to finish the work"; Gutenberg's tools and equipment were security for the loan. In 1452 Gutenberg borrowed another 800 gulden from Fust, to whom he was now in debt for the equivalent of approximately a million 1990 dollars. One provision of this second large loan made Fust a partner of Gutenberg. Curt Bühler has calculated that "The sum which Fust had been willing to risk in this business amounted therefore to at least the equivalent of ten year's wages for a high-living city politician.[17]

Fust would not have risked even the first 800 gulden had Gutenberg not already invented printing from cast type; he was investing in what he foresaw as a profitable business. While still in Strasbourg and sometime before 1439, Gutenberg had engaged a carpenter to build a wooden press, and there is secondary evidence that he may have begun to develop the casting of type. In 1438 he formed a partnership with three other men to manufacture mirrors to sell to pilgrims who would go in the following year to Aachen, where sacred garments of the Virgin and Christ were to be displayed, the belief being that the mirrors would capture magical powers issuing from the garments. It is most likely that the small circular mirrors—mounted in the center of rectangular metal tablets measuring 4¼ to 6¾ inches in height and 2 to 3⅜ inches in width—were made of speculum metal.

A hundred years later Vannocchio Biringuccio described "the ancient method" of producing speculum metal as mixing "three-quarters of copper and one of tin, and in order to make it somewhat lighter in color . . . an eighteenth part of antimony."[18] It is also known that one of the four partners purchased "lead and other materials . . . necessary in this art."[19] Perhaps Gutenberg, the one partner who knew metalworking, substituted lead for copper or tin, both of which were more expensive than lead and more difficult to work. The manufacture of speculum mirrors required experience in making molds and casting metal, skills also required for casting type. The composition of Gutenberg's type metal is unknown, but a spectrographic qualitative analysis of five late-fifteenth- or early-sixteenth-century pieces of type from Lyons revealed that they were made of alloys of tin, lead, and antimony, all metals known since antiquity. One type character was rich in tin, another poor, and three of the five had a small amount of silver.[20] In 1540 Biringuccio described type metal as composed of three parts tin, one-eighth lead, and one-eighth antimony.[21] In 1683 Joseph Moxon reported type metal as being about nine tenths lead and one tenth antimony.[22] Type metal, the kind used for casting type for hand composition as in Gutenberg's day, is a lead-rich composition, approximately 60 to 70 percent lead, 10 to 20 percent tin, and 20 to 30 percent antimony. The main function of the antimony is to harden the type to resist wear. The literature contains frequent statements that antimony causes type metal to expand rather than contract upon solidification, but on this point Bruce Gonser and J. Homer Winkler state: "A common fallacy in accounting for the sharpness of definition of printing characters is to ascribe this excellent reproduction to a slight expansion of the type metal during solidification. . . . In reality . . . all type metals contract slightly."[23] In actuality the antimony in the alloy may inhibit contraction to some extent. An extremely long-lasting variety of a lead-tin-antimony alloy, in continuous use even through the twentieth century, was most probably devised by Gutenberg.

The crucial component of the invention of printing was the mold in which type was cast. As Theodore DeVinne, who was an experienced printer, put it, writing in 1876, "In this type-mould we find the key to the invention of typography. It is not the press, nor the types, but the type-mould that must be accepted as the origin and the symbol of the art. He was the inventor of typography, and the founder of modern printing, who made the first adjustable type-mould."[24] Gutenberg's mold was by far the most sophisticated metallurgical mold of its time and for several subsequent centuries. The function of the mold is to produce types with different raised characters, of uniform height and "body" (the measurement at right angles to the lines of printing), but varying widths, such as "l" and "L". A matrix bearing a reversed and indented letter to be cast is fitted into the mold and the sides of the mold adjusted for width. The typecaster (figure 8.1) then quickly pours molten type metal into the mold. At the same instant as pouring, the caster jerks the mold "to aid the melted metal in making a forcible splash against the matrix . . . the trick of making this throw or cast . . . at the right time and in the right manner, was slowly acquired . . . hand casting was hard work."[25] Relief did not come until 1838, when David Bruce invented a casting machine, but some hand casting continues.

The construction of Gutenberg's wooden-screw printing press was based on the simple screw press that had originally been produced in the first century A.D.

Figure 8.1. Jost Amman's typecaster. (Eigentliche Beschreibung, 1578)

In Gutenberg's time screw presses were used to crush olives, grapes, and other fruits, to compress cloth bales, to smooth and glossen cloths, particularly linen, and to dry freshly molded papers. Presses used for the latter two applications are often cited as precursors of Gutenberg's press. If either one had been, it was likely to have been the paper press, for it had a robust screw much like that in figure 8.2 and much like the one in the first depiction of a printing press in 1499. Both the linen and the paper press had a primitive platen (a flat plate that spreads the pressure of the press across the surface of material being pressed) fitted between the two main vertical press frames, which reveal the need to prevent circular platen motion but hardly suggest a sophisticated device.

The Gutenberg press possessed one important innovation, namely, a hose and platen device that pressed the paper onto the inked type. If the platen had been directly attached to the screw, the twisting action of the screw would have caused

Figure 8.2. A 1507 printing press of Josse Badius.

the platen to smudge the impression. To prevent the platen from rotating with the turn of the screw, Gutenberg suspended a vertical wooden box, called a hose, through a cross-piece attached at each end to the main frame of the press. This hose structure can be seen in figure 8.2, which depicts a Josse Badius press of 1507. Hooks on the bottom corners of the hose and hooks on the platen were held tightly together with several turns of a cord between each set of hooks. The bottom end of the screw, shaped into a conical spindle with a rounded tip, fitted into a cup on the platen and turned independently of the hose as it transmitted the pressure of the screw to the paper. While there is no contemporary or subsequent textual or pictorial evidence that Gutenberg invented the hose and platen technology, the total absence of smudge or slur in the printing of the 42-line

Bible (the so-called Gutenberg Bible) is strong circumstantial evidence of a sophisticated device.

Gutenberg's press had a wooden bench with side rails on which a wooden bed, containing a single page of type locked up in a rectangular metal form (chase), could be moved back and forth. A tympan (frame) was hinged to the bed so it could be lifted up to rest on a support. To protect the margins of the paper to be printed from accidentally receiving ink smudges, another frame, a frisket, was hinged to the end of the tympan to be folded further out. Heavy paper, with a window the size of the type pages, was fitted onto the frisket.

The three men in figure 8.2 are a compositor (on the right), a pressman (pulling the bar), and a second pressman (holding the ink ball). The compositor is apparently about to start setting type in the composing stick that he holds in his right hand. The text he will be setting is in the book mounted on a support to his right. The first pressman, having moved the bed in under the platen, is pulling the bar to make the impression. Next he will rotate the crank in his left hand to move the bed back out from under the platen, unfold first the tympan, then the frisket, and remove the freshly printed sheet. As soon as the first pressman unfolds the tympan, the second pressman moves up to the bench and inks the type for the next impression.

Each sheet to be printed was folded along the center of the longer dimension so that it would contain four printed pages after four printings. To ensure accurate registration (the exact backing up of the type lines on both sides of a single sheet) the pressman pushed the sheet down on the tympan to prick fixed points; when the opposite side of the sheet was to be printed, the pricked holes would be placed over the same points. At first, ten points were used, four each at top and bottom and one in each outer margin; after several quires had been printed, the two middle points, top and bottom, were removed, leaving six. Some years later, when two pages were printed on one sheet of paper, only two points were used, fixed in the center of the sheet, so that the perforations would be hidden when all sheets were bound. When he was ready to print, the pressman would place a sheet of dampened paper on the tympan, fold the frisket over onto the tympan, fold both over onto the inked type, then move the bed into position under the platen and pull the bar to make the impression.

Although the top of the Badius press in figure 8.2 cannot be seen, there almost certainly were stays between the press and the ceiling. An illustration of the earliest known press (1499) shows three braces or stays extended from the head of the press to the ceiling beams to provide stability, and most subsequent illustrations on into the seventeenth century show stays being used. In the late seventeenth century, Joseph Moxon, in what was the original printing manual (1683–1684), described the placement of three stays, two so that "the *Press* will be sufficiently *Braced-up*" and a third to "resist the *Spring* of the *Bar*, if it slip out of the *Pressmans* hand."[26] This consistent use of braces strongly suggests that Gutenberg used them to maintain stability of his presses.

The water-based inks that had been used for four thousand years, including for the printing of block prints and block books, merely forms globules on a metal surface, making them useless for printing from cast type. In 1499 Polydore Virgil thought that Gutenberg had been the inventor of printing ink, but actually the person is unknown. Whether or not he was the inventor, Gutenberg was certainly the first to use it. It is likely that he learned the technique for making it (by grinding a black pigment, such as lampblack, into a boiled-linseed-oil varnish) from Flemish and German painters who were using linseed-oil varnish paints (the familiar "oil" on canvas) in the early fifteenth century.

When did Gutenberg do all the development required to produce cast type, a printing press, and printing ink? The earliest evidence is contained in testimonies given by witnesses in 1439 in an unsuccessful suit brought against Gutenberg for admission to a partnership by a brother of a deceased partner. The evidence of Gutenberg's activities was minimal and circumstantial, to say the least. A "press" was mentioned by five of the witnesses. The second witness to do so was recorded as follows: "Cumrat Sahspach said that Andres Heilman [one of Gutenberg's partners] . . . said to him: Dear Cumrat . . . you made the press and know about the matter; now go there and take the pieces out of the press and separate them, then no one will know what it is."[27] Four other witnesses also mentioned the press, one referring to "four pieces lying in a press" and another to "four pieces lying at the bottom in the press." There has been much speculation about these four pieces being a mold, but they may well have been a device for some other function, such as stabilization of the platen. Three witnesses made statements that referred to "mirror-maker" and "mirrors for the Aachen pilgrimage." Two witnesses spoke of "lead," one of them also stating that Gutenberg "had sent his servant to fetch all the forms; and they were melted down so that he saw it and felt regret for some forms." Finally, "Hanns Dünne the goldsmith said, that about three years ago he earned from Gutenberg approximately [one] hundred *gulden*, solely [for] what pertained to printing [*trucken*]."[28] Aloys Ruppel has pointed out that in 1439 the word *trucken* did not necessarily mean printing in the modern sense. One thing is clear: Gutenberg was not printing books, or anything else, by 1439.

The earliest example of printing from cast type is known as the Fragment of the World Judgement, thought to have been printed by Gutenberg in Mainz in 1445. He had obviously accomplished much since 1439. The fragment is only 3.6 by 5 inches, but it has been possible to calculate that the original (copies of earlier manuscripts and later printings are known) had twenty-eight pages, with twenty-one lines of print on all but one, and was 6.4 by 8.8 inches in size. Gutenberg also printed four editions of the Donatus, a Latin grammar, between 1446 and 1448, and an astronomical calendar in 1447.[29] Hence Johannes Fust had at least a half-dozen printings on which to judge in part the wisdom of making the major investment in 1450.

By 1448 Gutenberg had advanced to the second of the three stages of successful mechanical invention. The first is an intellectual event wherein the invention is conceived and thought through; the second is an area of development in which a prototype is constructed to demonstrate that the new machinery will run; the third is building a machine that will work, in the sense that it will put out a product that is successful in the marketplace. Most of the time the sequence yields a product that is better and cheaper than existing ones for which there is already a well-established market. In Gutenberg's case there was no market mechanism available in which a pent-up demand for books could express itself.

After receiving the first loan of 800 gulden from Fust, Gutenberg launched himself into the third stage of invention without having clear foresight as to the requirements. In the period when he initiated printing of his great 42-line Bible he also printed two single-sheet papal indulgences, some on parchment. The earlier indulgence, the first printed work to bear a date of printing, appeared in 1454, and Gutenberg printed the second in 1455. Aloys Ruppel was of the opinion that work on the Bible went on from 1452 to 1455,[30] and that may well have been the case. Gutenberg was not an experienced book designer, but someone who had presumably had experience with manuscript books laid the Bible out in sixty-six sections, most with ten leaves, to facilitate binding in multiple volumes if desired. All pages have two columns and most of them have forty-two lines of type; the first nine pages, and pages 157 to 164, have forty, and page 10 has forty-one. Every page has spacious margins to allow for illumination. Most copies were on paper, but some were on parchment. As for the pages themselves, "there is something pleasing in their boldness and solidity."[31] The composition, presswork, and inking were well done. Skillful craftsmen produced the great Bible; it was not the product of haste and inexperience.

By 1455 Fust had not received any interest payments or loan repayments. In despair of ever receiving anything, he brought suit against Gutenberg for payment of the loans, as well as the interest, compounded, and the cost of the loans to himself, for he had borrowed the money to lend to Gutenberg and was paying interest on it. The court found in Fust's favor and enjoined Gutenberg to repay the 800 gulden of the first loan, a percentage of the second loan that was to be determined later (the percentage is unknown), and 426 gulden in various kinds of interest. Even if Gutenberg had to repay none of the second loan, he still needed to pay 1,226 gulden—a half-million 1990 dollars or more—which he certainly did not have. Hence Fust received all the tools, equipment, parchment, paper, ink, and books that had been purchased or produced after 1450. Gutenberg retained only the typecasting equipment, the type, and the press or presses that he had possessed before 1450.

From 1455 until his death in 1468 little is definitely known of Gutenberg and still less of his activities. Certainly the type used to print the *Donatuses* and the calendar in 1446–1448 was used to print broadsides and the so-called 36-line Bible, in three volumes with 1,768 pages. Aloys Ruppel was certain that Gutenberg printed this Bible and that he printed it in Mainz,[32] whereas others "presume" that it was printed in Bamberg by Albrecht Pfister and Heinrich Keffer (the latter was one of Gutenberg's witnesses at the proceedings associated with Fust's suit in 1455).[33] However, it is generally agreed that the 36-line Bible was printed in 1457–1458. In 1465, at the time of the so-called Bishops War in Mainz, Gutenberg was again exiled; this time he went to nearby Eltville, west of Mainz. In 1465 the archbishop of Mainz appointed him "Courier," a sinecure that supported him for the last three years of his life. He died in 1468.

Without a doubt, Gutenberg, one of history's greatest inventors and the first of the great ones that we know by name, provided the fourth punctuation in the history of the equilibria of the book by his invention of printing from cast type. His method of book copying had a clear advantage over its predecessors in that it reproduced many copies in a shorter time than had been required to reproduce a single copy manually. The technology he developed, comprising cast type, lead-tin-antimony type metal, wooden press, oil-based inks, and paper vehicle, ushered in a period of stability in book production extending more than five hundred years.

Incredibly, Gutenberg's method of casting type prevailed until 1838—nearly four centuries. His wooden printing press remained the only printing press until 1800—three and a half centuries. And, although he probably never thought of it as such, his method of book manufacture—in which every signature would fit in any copy of a book—signaled the invention of manufacturing with interchangeable parts. The kind of printing equipment Gutenberg had turned over to Fust at the end of 1455 persisted essentially unchanged for the same length of time. His flexible typecasting mold, his crucial invention, experienced no significant improvement for the nearly four centuries that it was the sole source of cast type. The qualitative composition of type metal has remained the same to the present day, almost certainly since Gutenberg and certainly since 1500. In 1800 the wooden press had the same design as the Badius press of 1507 (fig. 8.2) with one seventeenth-century improvement, the substitution of iron for the wooden hose through which the spindle of the screw passed and from which the platen hung.

The most important development following Gutenberg's invention was the establishment in the sixteenth century of independent type foundries, and perhaps the most significant innovation was the introduction of new typefaces. The first departure from gothic was a roman typeface designed by Conrad Sweynheym and Arnold Pannartz in 1465 that was destined to become a standard kind of typeface design throughout the Western world. In 1483, in Venice, Andrea Torresani printed a work in Cyrillic characters, the first book to be printed in a non-Latin alphabet; in 1501 Aldus Manutius, son-in-law of Torresani, issued an edition of Aristotle's *Metaphysics* in a Greek typeface, opening the way to printing in a nonroman alphabet. In the same year, he also printed a Virgil and a Juvenal in a cursive typeface known as italic.

Publishing and the Book Trade

When he took over Gutenberg's assets Johann Fust also acquired Peter Schoeffer, a superb technician who had worked with Gutenberg. Together they created a business, printing and publishing books that would find a market, and they established a distribution network of agents and traveling salesmen. By the time of his death, on a bookselling trip to Paris in the spring of 1466, Fust had already established a bookselling agent in Lubeck. Schoeffer engaged an agent in Paris in 1468, two years before the first book was printed in that city, and in 1470 a traveling salesman selling Schoeffer's books was in Nuremberg. Since it would certainly have cost less to supply a traveling salesman with books than to stock an agency, it is likely that Fust began to retain salesmen as early as 1462, after he and Schoeffer had published four books.

Peter Drach of Speyer, a printer, publisher, and bookseller who had established a large printshop by the 1480s, built a network of agencies and outlets in Strasbourg, Frankfurt, Cologne, Leipzig, Augsburg, Landshut, Prague, Brno, Halberstadt, Stendal, and Basel. Anton Koberger of Nuremberg, a patrician whose family included wealthy bankers, was the largest printer-publisher of the fifteenth century. Koberger, whose business network extended as far south as Lyons, was one of the early printers to contract with other printers to print his books as a technique of maintaining steady work for his own shop, which at times had more than a hundred employees. He exemplified the great printer-publishers who dominated the German market for decades.

Printing spread across Europe with amazing rapidity. More than 110 towns had presses by 1480. Venice became the "capital of printing," with 156 editions published in 1480–1482, followed by Milan (82), Augsburg (67), Nuremberg (53), Florence (48), Cologne (44), Paris (35), and Rome (34). The years 1495–1497 produced 1,821 editions, 447 (24.5 percent) of which came out of Venice; Paris produced 181 and Lyon 95. By the century's end 236 towns had printing presses installed and 35,000 editions of books had been published.[34]

Clearly an effective trade organization for the sale of books had been established by the 1490s. The major expositions for the new trade in books were the great international fairs, particularly those in Lyons and Frankfurt, both of which existed before the invention of printing. Publishers brought books to sell, as well as lists of books yet to appear, and drew up agreements with one another for future sales whereby they gained access to each other's outlets—peddlers, agents, and bookstores. In the sixteenth century the Frankfurt book fair established Frankfurt as the center of publishing in Germany, but in 1597 the imperial censorship commission began to supervise the fair, which led to its slow demise. In the mid–seventeenth century the fair moved to Leipzig, where it flourished until the Second World War, after which it moved back to Frankfurt and became outstandingly successful.

A barter system made possible the widespread distribution of books throughout Europe without transfer of money. Ideally the barter of books for books was negotiated in advance of printing, so that copies could be speedily dispatched, literally as soon as they came off the press, for they often were shipped as sheets. The system was based on trust, confidence, and credit, and its participants realized that if one node of the network suffered financial collapse it could bring down most if not all of the other nodes. Although a primitive system, it built and maintained a book trade.

Title Pages, Pagination, and Illustration

Pagination makes a book easier to use for reference, illustration provides information that complements text, and a title page indicates what the book is about. The first printed title pages were on pamphlets of six sheets containing Pope Pius II's Bull against the Turk, which Fust and Schoeffer published in 1463, some copies of which were printed in Latin and others in German. On their title pages the title stood alone, as did titles on the majority of subsequent fifteenth-century title pages. The first complete title page (title, author, place, publisher, and date) appeared in Venice in 1476, but it wasn't until the 1530s that full title pages appeared regularly. Since the second quarter of the sixteenth century the title page has gone through all manner of variations, from a page completely full of decoration and type to one that is almost blank. Some title pages have been burdened with a table of contents, or with a biography of the author, or crowded "to a point not only of unsightliness but even of illegibility."[35]

Only a few books printed before 1500 possessed numbered pages, although a tenth of fifteenth-century books had numbered folios. By the end of the sixteenth century four-fifths of printed books had arabic-numbered pagination.[36] Ultimately most books were printed with numbered pages, which facilitated indexing and citation.

Book illustration comprises two principal types of graphic representation. The most common is pictorial description, often of high artistic quality, referenced in text; the second type communicates non-verbal information impossible to impart by expository prose, such as the information in maps. Xylographic printing, with elevated lines as in woodblocks, and intaglio printing, with engraved or etched lines below the surface of a plate usually of copper, were the two most often employed techniques for book illustration before 1800.

Albrecht Pfister of Bamberg was the first printer to use woodblocks, incorporating 101 of them in his printing of Ulrich Boner's *Edelstein* (1461), the first book printed with cast type and illustrated; it was also the first dated book to be printed in German.[37] The woodblocks were impressed separately from the type. By 1464 Pfister had produced four or five additional illustrated books using the separate impression technique. The next printer to produce an illustrated book was Günther

Zainer of Augsburg, in 1470. He also used separate impressions, but by 1472 he was able to develop a technique for printing woodcuts and type with a single impression, whereby he continued to print illustrated books for the next half-dozen years. Woodblock printing prevailed in book illustration until the end of the sixteenth century.

Artistic and scientific book illustration began to bloom in the first half of the sixteenth century. Albrecht Dürer led the way with his magnificent Apocalypse printed in Nuremberg in 1498. In 1530 Otto Brunfels and his illustrator, Hans Weiditz, published *Herbarium Vivae Eicones*, in which the plants had been drawn from direct observation, rather than copied from stylized representations as they had been since Dioscorides in the fifth century. (Not everyone has admired this artistic as well as scientific achievement. According to William Ivins, Weiditz's "remarkable woodcuts have been adversely criticized as being portraits of particular plants, showing not only their personal forms and characters but the very accidents of their growth, such as wilted leaves and broken stems, rather than being schematic statements of the distinguishing characteristics of the species and genera.")[38] Leonhart Fuchs produced the second of the magnificent herbals based on nature in 1542.

The next year saw the publication of two of the greatest works in the history of science: Nicolaus Copernicus's *De Revolutionibus Orbium Coelestium*, which established the heliocentricity of the solar system and the astronomy of subsequent centuries; and Andreas Vesalius's *De Humani Corporis Fabrica Libri Septem*, the foundation of modern anatomy. The greater part of each book is based on illustration, with Copernicus explaining geometric figures in his text and Vesalius describing the details of his dynamic anatomical drawings. Vesalius actually invented a new technique for communicating scientific observation in books. As J. B. Saunders and Charles O'Malley have put it,

> the last act [of preparing the book for printing] was the addition to the proof of the elaborate system of cross references between the printed text and the illustrations which made the *Fabrica* unique in the history of the printed book as a medium for the communication of a descriptive science. It was by means of this system that text and picture were woven into an integrated whole. . . . Through many hundreds of cross references Vesalius employed the illustration to eliminate ambiguity and to delimit the verbal statement.[39]

Copperplate engravings replaced woodcuts beginning with the seventeenth century (although intaglio printing had been used as early as 1477, in a copy of Ptolemy's *Cosmographia* printed in Bologna); the finer and closer lines of copperplate engraving permitted more pictorial information to be recorded in a given area. As Ivins put it, "by the end of the century the engraving had taken the place of the woodcut in all but very few of the books made for the educated classes. This . . . was a basic change in modes and techniques made in response to an insistent demand for fuller visual information."[40]

Newspapers and Journals

Newspapers suddenly came into being during the first quarter of the seventeenth century in response to the desire for timely information. Precursors were manuscript newsletters prepared by late-medieval trading companies, such as the Fuggers in Augsburg, that contained commercial and political news. The *Nieuwe Tijdinghen*, thought to have begun publication in Antwerp in 1605, apparently had a commercial newsletter as a progenitor and is often cited as the first newspaper. However, a monthly news publication had appeared in the Swiss town of Rorschach in 1597.[41] By 1610 three German cities and one Swiss city had newspapers; by 1622 the Dutch had two newspapers and the Austrians and British had one apiece. The first Paris newspaper, a weekly, appeared in 1631. Beginning in 1643 the British *Mercurius Civicus* was the first newspaper to use illustrations regularly, but little attention was given to ease of reading until 1787, when John Bell designed an attractive type and a layout with adequate space between lines to improve legibility of his *World*. Two of London's many eighteenth-century newspapers still flourish: *The Times* (1787) and *The Observer* (1785).

Censorship of newspapers was a strong force that worked against the desire and need for news. The Catholic Church had long played the major role in censorship, ever since Pope Gelasius I (d. 496) issued the first list of banned books, in the last decade of the fifth century. A thousand years later, in 1559, the Sacred Congregation of the Roman Inquisition issued the first list that included the word "Index" in its title. The *Index Librorum Prohibitorum*, as it came to be known, was issued and reissued occasionally through the last printing, the twentieth edition, which appeared in 1948; the church suppressed the *Index* in 1966 before further publication.

Various continental emperors and kings enforced the church's decrees, and King Henry VIII of England assumed all censorship powers after his separation from the church. In 1632, a dozen years after the first British newspaper appeared, the infamous Star Chamber decreed that all "newsbooks" be banned, a decree that was removed in 1638. In 1711 a stamp act was passed that increased the price of newspapers, thereby keeping them out of the hands of the lower classes; it was not rescinded until 1854. The American Revolution freed the United States from the Stamp Act of 1765, but in 1798 the United States Congress passed the Sedition Act (one of the four Alien and Sedition Acts), which provided that "if any person shall write, print, utter, or publish . . . writings against the government of the United States . . . then such person being thereof convicted . . . shall be punished by a fine not exceeding $2,000 and by imprisonment not exceeding two years." Twenty-five men were arrested, their newspapers were forced to close down, and ten of the men were convicted. The potential power of newspapers can terrorize governments. All four of the Alien and Sedition Acts were repealed or expired in 1800–1802.

The first periodical journals, five of them, were born in the 1660s. Two had ceased to exist before the decade was out, and a third lived for only a dozen years, but the other two—the *Journal des Sçavans* (Paris, 1665) and the *Philosophical Transactions of the Royal Society* (London, 1665)—are still very much alive. Other countries producing journals in the seventeenth century were Germany, Italy, and the Netherlands. England produced the first magazine designed for women, *Ladies' Mercury*, in 1693. It also produced the first periodical with the word "magazine" in its title, *The Gentleman's Magazine*, established in 1731 and destined to live on until 1907.

The numbers of periodicals grew rapidly throughout the eighteenth century. David Kronick has compiled a table that depicts the growth. There were 4 new titles in 1700–1710, 12 in 1730–1740, 41 in 1760–1770, and 118 in 1790–1800.[42] One observer as early as 1715 "claimed that bookstores were no longer bookstores but journal stores and that bookdealers had become journal-dealers," while another in the 1790s found those years to be "truly the decade of the journal" and felt that "one should seek to limit their number rather than to increase them, since there can also be too many periodicals."[43] One still hears these complaints repeated over and over.

Recapitulation

Gutenberg's concept of the mechanization of copying and his invention of printing from cast type in the mid–fifteenth century are the major innovations of the three centuries covered in this chapter. Lesser innovations, the establishment of publishing as a profession and a book trade network throughout Europe, were followed two centuries later by the birth of newspapers and journals. All books, seventeenth- and eighteenth-century newspapers and periodicals were printed with the same kind of equipment that Gutenberg used. However, the next century was to witness change in almost every aspect of printing technology except the qualitative composition of type metal.

9 | Power Revolution 1800–1840

EXCEPT FOR THE COMPOSITION of type metal and the way type was set, all of printing technology changed dramatically in the first four decades of the nineteenth century, following three and a half centuries of no significant changes—a clear example of the concept of punctuated equilibria. What were some of the reasons that major innovations occurred so rapidly and at this time? New requirements for information sprang from the Industrial Revolution, evangelicalism, and the Napoleonic Wars that spread across Europe. The invention of the semaphore telegraph in France (1793), and its adoption in Britain (1795) provided high-speed transmission of political, military, and commercial intelligence. The invention of electromagnetic telegraphy in the late 1830s and its wide-spread, immediate use in the United States provide striking evidence of the desire for instant information. In England William F. Cooke and Charles Wheatstone, having first demonstrated an electromagnetic telegraph in 1837, established a telegraph line 7.5 miles long in 1839 and by 1843 had extended it to 18.5 miles. In the United States Samuel F. B. Morse formally demonstrated his telegraph line between Baltimore and Washington on May 24, 1844. The demand for information over this line became so great that by December 1846, only thirty-one months later, telegraph lines extended from Philadelphia to Cleveland and Louisville and from New York to Buffalo, Boston, and Portland, Maine. Washington, Baltimore, Philadelphia, and New York were also interconnected. By 1850 lines reached Chicago, St. Louis, Memphis, and New Orleans.[1]

The numbers of newspapers also increased rapidly. "Between 1820 and 1840 at least 2,000 new newspapers and periodicals, many with illustrations, made their appearance in Britain, and in other countries there was similar enterprise."[2] In the United States an extremely rapid growth began in 1783 when the colonies won their independence.[3] The number of newspapers in 1780 was 38, in 1800 260, and by 1820 was up to 582.[4] Population growth during these five decades averaged about 50 percent each decade, whereas the number of newspapers soared at an average rate of 286 percent per decade.

By the end of the eighteenth century the Industrial Revolution had generated a new class of readers in Britain—a small population of "mechanics," who were really civil and mechanical engineers. In 1796 mechanics in Birmingham banded together into the Birmingham Brotherly Society, which, with several later similar groups, proved to be the forerunner of mechanics institutes. Most of these institutes, about seven hundred in number by 1850, had a library as well as a museum, laboratory, and lecture courses. Some had lecture programs, and others had museums, the Glasgow Institute, founded in 1823, being perhaps the first to have all three. "At Glasgow the Gas Light Company provided free light on two evenings a week,"[5] and the London Mechanics Institute, also founded in 1823, had gas illumination by 1825; the installation of gas illumination in these libraries reveals the members' extensive use of books.

Similar institutes appeared in the United States but were not universally successful. Far more effective were "mechanics libraries." The first of these in the United States was the Mechanic Library Society of New Haven, founded in 1793 and still thriving. In 1818 there was a mechanics library in Bristol, Connecticut. In Boston the Mechanics' Apprentices' Library and the Boston Mercantile Library, for young clerks, were both founded in 1820.[6] In 1852 the latter had a circulation of seventy-nine thousand from a collection of only eleven thousand volumes. Books were indeed in high demand by the young employees of Boston's business houses.

Growth in both population and literacy also heightened the desire for books. The population in England and Wales doubled, from approximately nine million in 1801 to eighteen million in 1851. One of the major causes was the decrease in child mortality, which dropped from 74.5 percent for children under the age of five in 1730–1749 to 31.8 percent in 1810–1829.[7] While population was growing, literacy was also gaining ground, if not so dramatically. From 1750 to 1840 in England and Wales the literacy rate of men went from 63 to 68 percent, and that of women from 36 to 52 percent. Similar increases occurred on the continent.[8]

The popular evangelicalism of the British and Foreign Bible Society (1804), the Religious Tract Society (1799), the American Bible Society (1816), and the American Tract Society (1825) generated the printing of huge numbers of Bibles and tracts, which was made possible by the invention by Charles, Third Earl Stanhope, of an effective technique for stereotyping, a process that eliminated the cost of keeping expensive cast type standing in forms for eventual reprinting. Members of the British and Foreign Bible Society "seem to have believed that God . . . provided the invention just in time for the . . . first massive order, in November

1804, for 6,000 Bibles and 5,000 New Testaments in English, 20,000 of the long-awaited Welsh Bibles and 5,000 New Testaments in Welsh, all to be executed in stereotype."[9] The three presses possessing the Royal Privilege for printing the authorized version of the Bible produced nearly 11 million copies of the Bible and the New Testament from 1837 to 1847. This astonishing figure comprised a third of all copies of books printed in England during that period. The British and Foreign Bible Society purchased nearly three-fifths of the 11 million. As Leslie Howsam has put it, "The new technologies of stereotype [1802], machine printing (steam press, 1814) and paper tenacity (Fourdrinier machine, 1807) did not depend on the Bible Society, but the Society's demand accelerated their implementation."[10] In the early years of the Bible societies most of their printing was done from stereotype plates on iron presses.

Iron Hand Presses

According to James Moran, the principal authority on the history of printing presses, the wooden printing press required four major improvements to make it more efficient: "greater stability of structure; ability to print a forme [chase] at one pull; a reduction in manual effort; and an automatic return of the bar after pulling."[11] Moran has shown that Wilhelm Haas (1772) and E. A. J. Anisson-Duperron (1783) produced changes that reduced manual effort, and that Philippe-Denis Pierres (1784) developed a press that would both print an entire chase and return the bar after a pull. While none of these improvements was extensively applied to wooden presses, all of them became standard in iron presses of the early nineteenth century.

A singular innovation of the Industrial Revolution was the development of iron reduction by air blast and coke to produce cast iron, a feat performed by the Abraham Darbys, father, son, and grandson; the last was able by his own improvements to cast the arched iron ribs of the world's first iron bridge (1775), which still stands. In 1784 Henry Cort built a reverberatory furnace that produced wrought iron. Charles, Third Earl Stanhope, designed and caused to have built the first iron printing press sometime before August 1803, when Andrew Wilson referred to it as "the newly invented PRINTING PRESS."[12] The Stanhope press possessed all four improvements that wooden presses had needed: stability, impression of a full chase, far less power required on the lever, and return of the lever by counterweight. However, the cast-iron frame of the first model was liable to crack under tension, so the frame was enlarged beginning in 1806; the cast-iron screw, also subject to fracture, was later replaced by wrought iron. The major innovation in the Stanhope press was a system of multiple short levers that connected the pull lever to the screw, a contrivance that brought the platen down quickly so that manual power was exerted only at the time of impression. Moran has pointed out that these compound levers were the forerunner of the knuckle or toggle joint that replaced the screw in subsequent iron presses.[13]

The advantages of the Stanhope led to its widespread use fairly rapidly. The *Times* almost immediately acquired—in its own phrase—a "battalion" of Stanhopes. In 1811 Stanhopes began to be manufactured in New York. In 1815 a Stanhope went to Germany, where three manufacturers subsequently produced them. Sometime after 1815 a Stanhope was acquired in Paris, and over time there were at least eleven factories manufacturing them in France. Italy possessed two manufacturers, and Sweden one, following an 1828 import of a French Stanhope. Moran records that "in isolated instances, a Stanhope has been used as a production press up to the present day—a tribute to the solidity of its construction."

The Stanhope was a high-quality book press. "Charles Whittingham, the famous 'fine' printer, even went so far as to use the imprint 'The Stanhope Press' on a series of title-pages; and Thomas Bewick, the wood engraver, noted that the typography (in this sense the letterpress printing) of one of his books would be executed in the best style on one of the new *Stanhope* presses."

Four more famous designs of hand-operated iron presses appeared in the early nineteenth-century; all four replaced the screw with different power trains that eliminated possible twisting of the platen, which could cause smudging. In 1813 George Clymer of Philadelphia produced the first, the Columbian, which continued to be produced for a century. The design of the power train of the Columbian was unlike that of the Stanhope or any wooden press in that it had no screw. In its stead Clymer attached the bottom of a square, upright block to the platen and the top of the block to a large lever that was supported by the fulcrum at one end and was attached at the other by a series of short levers to the pull bar. Clymer apparently obtained the idea for the "great lever," the phrase he used in his patent, from Thomas Newcomen, who had used the same phrase to describe the huge lever on the top of his steam pumping engine of 1712. The vertical block was attached to the lever about a third the length of the lever from the fulcrum, giving the lever a mechanical advantage of two, which is significantly higher than that of the screw in a Stanhope press. Moran has quoted several testimonials of the "easier working of the *Columbian*," adding that "as can still be tested, it did require less exertion on the part of the pressman."

In 1820 Richard W. Cope of London introduced the Albion press, which in time became one of the nineteenth century's most popular presses. It had neither screw nor large lever, but a compact and somewhat complex toggle that when straightened depressed the platen. It also had a spring that returned the bar and platen, although after a few years Cope replaced the spring with a counterweight. Cope had produced some two hundred presses by the time of his death, in 1828, but his foreman and successor, John Hopkinson, improved the toggle, discarded the brass links in the mechanism, which had often fractured, and brought fame to the Albion. At the end of his first decade Hopkinson had produced a thousand of the improved presses. By midcentury nearly a dozen manufacturers were producing Albions, and by the century's end they were being built in half a dozen countries abroad.

Samuel Rust of New York patented the Washington, the third highly popular press, in 1821. The Washington was also a toggle press, but the two levers that composed the toggle were of unequal length and joined at the top of the frame; when they were brought toward each other by the pull of the bar, the longer lever depressed the platen to make the impression. Originally the firm of Rust and Turney manufactured the press, but Hoe & Co. acquired the patent in 1835 and enlarged the Washington, building seven different sizes. Subsequently other manufacturers "too numerous to mention" began building Washingtons. In 1940 I, my wife, and several Harvard students used a Washington, under the tutelage of Gehman Taylor, one of Boston's master printers, to compose and print a small book entitled *The Reminiscences of Sarah Kemble Siddons* (1773–1785).

Many American iron presses are known as "acorn presses," because of the resemblance of their cast-iron frames to the profiles of acorns. Presumably the popularity of the acorn design stemmed from the ease of producing the entire frame in one casting. Acorn presses were available well into the twentieth century. Peter Smith of New York, a partner in Hoe & Co., produced and patented in 1821 what was perhaps the first acorn press, which employed a toggle joint similar to one used by John Wells of Hartford, Connecticut, in 1819. By 1840 at least four Boston manufacturers were building acorn presses with toggles. A. O. Stansbury, like Smith a New Yorker, also patented an acorn press in 1821; it employed a so-called torsion toggle to depress the platen. The Cincinnati Type Foundry originally manufactured Stansbury presses and by 1834 was building them in three sizes. After the Stansbury patent expired, Hoe & Co. began making Stansbury presses with torsion toggles composed of three rods that straightened up and pushed down the platen when the bar was pulled.

Iron hand presses have never been entirely superseded for fine book printing. The Albion, which has remained particularly popular, was chosen by Kelmscott in the 1890s and by Ashendene and Doves in the early decades of the twentieth century; indeed, even at the end of the twentieth century, fine-printing hobbyists seem to prefer old Albions.

Large Steam Presses

In the nineteenth century, "the age of the newspaper," as Henri-Jean Martin named it, most of the large steam-driven presses were used to print urban newspapers. Lured to London by the British system of patents, which did not exist on the continent, Friedrich Koenig, a German bookseller-printer, designed the first successful large steam-driven newspaper press, and together with another German, Andreas Bauer, an engineer, he built for the *Times* two double-cylinder presses, each powered by a two-horsepower steam engine, which went into operation on November 29, 1814 (fig. 9.1). Each press cost the *Times* £1,100 but printed eleven hundred sheets an hour, or six times as many as had been required

Figure 9.1. Koenig's steam-driven cylinder press (model, half-size). (Courtesy Science Museum, Science and Society Picture Library, London)

of Parisian pressmen in the mid–seventeenth century. "In no respect did the paper differ [from] previous issues in appearance or quality of impression, but the saving in point of time and of production and cost of labour was considerable"; the principal saving was 250 guineas a year stemming from reduction in number of compositors required "in setting up and working of the duplicate formes" for the battalion of Stanhopes.[14]

The three principal innovations in this machine were the inking system, the "pressing cylinders," which replaced platens, and the steam engine, which replaced human muscles. Without a doubt the most important of the three was the steam engine to drive the press. According to the *Times*'s purchase agreement, "'two Steams Engines of Two Horse Power each to work the said [double] machines' were to cost £250 each," to which was to be added a charge of £100, "to connect by sufficient machinery the said two steams engines with the said two double machines."[15] Details of these two-horsepower engines are lacking, but it is likely that they were high-pressure engines.

Moran has written a concise description of a Koenig cylinder and its action:

The cylinder was . . . divided into three parts, which were covered with cloth and provided with points in the manner of a tympan on a hand press; and iron frames, which continued to bear the name of friskets, were attached to hold the sheets of paper. The surface of the cylinder between the tympans was cut away to allow the forme to pass freely under it on its return. The cylinder made one-third of a revolution for each impression and then stopped. The sequence was as follows: the uppermost frisket seized a sheet of paper and moved it into the next position; the sheet formerly in that position came into contact with the forme and was printed; the third segment moved to the upper position.[16]

The printed sheet in the third segment would be removed and replaced with a fresh sheet. The form, or chase of type in the bed, would then move to the other end of the press, passing under the cutaway section of the cylinder and traveling under the second cylinder to impress the sheet on that cylinder before coming to a stop and reversing its motion to start the next cycle. The *Times*'s editorial for November 29, 1814, correctly evaluated the new press when it said: "Our Journal of this day presents to the public the practical result of the greatest improvement connected with printing, since the discovery of the art itself."

Koenig's second major contribution to printing technology was the first perfecting press, which he patented in 1814; the innovation was that it printed both sides of a sheet on only one pass through the press. Shortly before he and Bauer returned to Germany in 1816, they completed the first of the new perfecting machines for Thomas Bensley, a printer who, with two other printers, had financed Koenig from invention to manufacture. Koenig's new machine was actually two complete presses with only one sheet feeder. Tapes carried the sheet of paper through the machine, first around one cylinder, rotating in one direction for printing one side, and then around the second cylinder, rotating in the opposite direction, for printing the other side; each cylinder had its own bed of type moving back and forth under it. The press could print as many as a thousand sheets, or two thousand impressions, an hour. Bensley first used it in 1817 to print for E. Cox the second English edition of *The Institutions of Physiology*, by Johann Friedrich Blumenbach, that John Elliotson had translated from the third Latin edition.

After the departure of Koenig and Bauer from London the *Times* retained the services of Augustus Applegath to maintain and improve the Koenig machines. In 1828 Applegath designed and installed the first of the big steam-driven newspaper presses; it was approximately thirteen feet high and fourteen feet long. With alterations it was to print the *Times* for the next two decades. The machine, which had four impression cylinders arranged one after the other with the type bed traveling back and forth beneath them, was attended by four "feeders" and four "takers-off" and printed forty-two hundred impressions an hour.

In the history of the book Koenig stands as a colossus, with three immense "firsts" to his credit: he was the first to inject a nonhuman source of power into printing systems, the first to create machines to print both sides of a sheet on one pass, and the first to introduce a practical cylinder printing system. More than any-one other than Gutenberg, Koenig set the printing scene for the next two centuries. Indeed, when he and his engineer returned to Germany in 1816 they established the firm of Koenig and Bauer of Oberzell, which continued to improve and manu-facture presses; in 1990 Koenig machines had the fourth largest share of the world's printing press market.

In the mid-1820s David Napier, a Scottish engineer established in London, be-gan to manufacture perfecting cylinder presses, which were driven at first by hand and then, by 1832, by steam. These presses possessed register superior to that of other machines, due to Napier's "grippers," a device activated from within the cylinder that held sheets firmly onto it; they eliminated the awkward tapes previ-ously used for that purpose. In addition he patented a two-revolution type of cylinder in 1830 that enabled two cylinders to revolve in the same direction; during the second revolution the type bed passed back below the raised cylinders. Napier continued to sell his perfectors for the next three decades.

In their early years cylinder presses were not accepted with enthusiasm by printers, but by midcentury they had transformed printing into an industry and had been sufficiently improved to enable Richard Hoe to build in 1853 a stop-cylinder machine that made three to four thousand impressions per hour. It was dubbed the "little Astonisher" because of the fine work it could print. Two years later a single-cylinder press was so greatly strengthened that it printed excellent il-lustrations. Successful two-color printing was achieved in 1861 and four-color in the 1880s. Improvements and modifications to cylinder presses continued to be de-veloped at least until 1964.

Of the various types of power-driven presses, bed-and-platen presses were long considered to be capable of producing the finest printing, and a few of them continued in operation during the first third of the twentieth century. Essentially machine-power-driven hand presses, they satisfied traditional printers and were used by book printers especially for the high quality of their output. The Riverside Press in Cambridge, Massachusetts, kept one working until 1938, while the Oxford University Press operated one "well into the twentieth century."[17]

Daniel Treadwell of Boston was the first to design a bed-and-platen press and to have it built in the early 1820s. The original, constructed mostly of wood, was horse driven; subsequent models were built of iron and were steam driven until electric motors replaced steam engines. The design mimicked the wooden and early iron presses in that the power source moved the bed to a position under the platen and depressed the platen to make the impression. After the platen was raised the bed retreated to its original position, from which a pressman could remove the printed sheet and replace it with a fresh one.

In 1830 Isaac and Seth Adams built a wooden bed-and-platen press cranked by hand power (soon replaced by iron and steam) with a stationary platen against which the bed was raised after the paper, in a tympan, had been brought into position. When the sheet had been printed, the bed was lowered, and tapes brought the printed sheet to the other end of the press. This design, which did fine work and printed five hundred to a thousand impressions per hour, was popular until the end of the century. At the same time that the Adams brothers were developing their press in the United States, Napier & Son were introducing their Double Platen Printing Machine in England. This press had the advantage of significantly increasing production while running at the same speed as single-platen machines. Each time the bed stopped at the end of its run a platen descended to make an impression; its output ranged from eight hundred to fifteen hundred impressions an hour. Sheets of paper were fed from each end, which led to the machine's being known as a "double feeder." The Napier Double Platen became the most popular book press in England and brought fine reputations to some of its owners. One printing firm of high repute possessed twenty-two of the machines, and in 1930 the Chiswick Press still possessed and used a Napier double-platen machine thought to have been introduced about 1837.

Stereotyping, a process for producing a metal printing plate by infusing a plaster mold of typeset text with lead-rich type metal to produce an exact reproduction of the original type, is particularly useful for printing newspapers, as well as books for which reprinting is anticipated, such as Bibles, textbooks, classics, and other reprints in which there will be no change. Legros and Grant describe its advantages:

> The stereotype made at a single cast is much less costly than the original type in which the matter is composed; it enables the type to be released for fresh work once the proofs have finally passed, and it ensures the absolute identity of one edition with another, so that a carefully corrected work may be reproduced in each successive edition equally perfect in all its detail. It has, moreover, the further advantage that the types need never be subjected to the heavy work of the printing-press, and that they can be returned to the case practically in the same condition as when new. Moreover, a work of great magnitude [such as a Bible] can be produced with a much smaller fount of type, for, as the reading and correcting are followed by the stereotyping process, distribution of the earlier pages can be effected and the type used again for composition. It is in the newspaper office that the introduction of stereotyping has proved to be a step of revolutionary character, for it has permitted the rapid multiplication of an original surface—itself unused in the actual press—and the simultaneous printing of replicas, instead of from the original—on a number of presses.[18]

William Ged of Edinburgh, the inventor of stereotype, produced the first book entirely printed by stereotype in 1739 and reprinted it in 1744, but produced no more. In 1784, Alexander Tilloch and Andrew Foulis, a printer, took out a patent for "making plates for the purpose of printing by or with plates instead of the moveable types commonly used."[19] Apparently Foulis had published at least one book from plates, "a Xenophon of 1783."[20] Charles, Third Earl Stanhope, learned from Tilloch and Foulis the technical information necessary to make plates for printing and perhaps obtained their patent rights. Nearly forty years later, inventors in Russia, England, and the United States developed electrotyping, a process similar to stereotyping. An electrotype is produced by electroplating a thin layer of copper either on a wax mold of type or on a relief graphic and backing the copper layer with a plate of durable metal.

In 1804 the British and Foreign Bible Society (BFBS) came into being, "dedicated to the circulation of the scriptures, in foreign languages as well as in English, to readers who otherwise would have gone without."[21] The BFBS sold Bibles by the thousands on installment payment plans, often with delivery and collection at the door. The society soon became a major publisher, and its entrepreneurial managers were anxious to take advantage of new developments in printing. Their first large order, in 1804, for 26,000 Bibles and 10,000 New Testaments, went to the Cambridge University Press, with the stipulation that the Bibles be printed using the stereotype that the press had just acquired from Andrew Wilson, Stanhope's printer. The Cambridge University Press was one of three presses that enjoyed the restricted privilege of printing the Bible; the other two were the Oxford University Press, which received its first BFBS order in 1809, for 20,000 New Testaments to be printed on stereotype, and the King's Printer, which received its first order in 1812, for 10,000 Bibles and 20,000 New Testaments to be printed on plates supplied by BFBS. During 1804 through 1812 the three presses supplied the BFBS with 1,138,329 books, all stereotyped.

The BFBS furnished the stereotype plates from which the Philadelphia Bible Society published a Bible in 1812, probably the first stereotype book produced in the United States. Four years later the American Bible Society (ABS) was founded in New York and immediately sent to three local printers requests for bids that specified the use of stereotype plates. Before the end of the first year the ABS had received some 10,000 Bibles. During the years 1821 through 1831 ABS printed nearly one and a half million Bibles.[22]

Both societies were proponents of steam-driven printing. The BFBS signed an agreement in 1814 to use a newly patented machine press that failed, but later the BFBS was able to take advantage of steam printing after the King's Printer acquired a Koenig steam cylinder press. In the United States the ABS learned of Daniel Treadwell's successful invention and development of a steam-operated bed-and-platen press, and by 1826 it had installed sixteen Treadwell presses. Both societies were also supporters of papermaking machines and users of the first Fourdrinier machines, to be described later in this chapter.[23]

Mechanized Typecasting

At the start of the nineteenth century all type was still being hand cast, at a rate of some four thousand pieces of type in a ten-hour day. The first improvement appeared in 1807, when A. F. Berte patented a pump to force the molten type metal into the mold to diminish the amount of air in the metal, thereby reducing porosity of the type. In 1811 Archibald Binny of Philadelphia put a spring on the mold that speeded the opening movement, thereby doubling the typecaster's production, according to DeVinne.[24] In 1820 Marc Isambard Brunel invented a technique employing a vacuum to eliminate blowholes in the cast type. In 1822 William Church, a New Yorker living in England, secured a British patent for a hand-operated, multiple-mold casting machine that apparently was an operational failure.

In 1838 David Bruce of New York introduced the first successful typecasting machine to enjoy a long productive life. It was either hand operated or steam driven; the type, like hand-cast type, required finishing in a dressing stick. During the next half century most American and European typecasting machines were adaptations of Bruce's, although patents were granted for machines to mechanically finish the type. In 1883 Frederick Wicks, working for the *Times*, patented a rotary caster having a hundred molds, which in one hour could cast sixty thousand pieces of type that were finished and ready to be set. Such speed meant that used type could be remelted rather than distributed, so that the newspaper was always printed from new type.

Lithography and Photomechanical Processes

Printing from a plane smooth surface was the most novel, unprecedented development in the art of printing in the nineteenth century. The process, which came to be known as lithography, was invented by Aloys Senefelder, a Bavarian, in 1798; a century later, in the form of offset printing, it began to take the place of printing from cast type.

Its invention was prompted by Senefelder's desire to print inexpensively a play he had written. The death of his actor father in 1792 had forced him to drop out of the University at Ingolstadt, but he had fortunately already learned a great deal of chemistry that was to stand him in good stead in his experiments that followed. He began by exploring copper engraving, or intaglio printing, but abandoned it because of the expense of time and money involved in the reuse of plates. After unsuccessfully exchanging zinc for copper, he switched to a piece of limestone, originally acquired for rubbing down various components of his inks, on which to continue his etching trials. Twenty-two years later Senefelder wrote the following, about which A. Hyatt Mayor observed "Lithography is the only major print process whose invention was described by its inventor"[25]:

> I had just succeeded in my little laboratory in polishing a stone plate, which I intended to cover with etching ground, in order to continue my exercises in writing backwards, when my mother entered the room, and desired me to write her a bill for the washer-woman, who was waiting for the linen; I happened not to have even the smallest slip of paper at hand, as my little stock of paper had been entirely exhausted by taking proof impressions from the stones; nor was there even a drop of ink in the

inkstand. As the matter would not admit of delay, and we had nobody in the house to send for a supply of the deficient materials, I resolved to write the list with my ink prepared with wax, soap, and lampblack, on the stone which I had just polished, and from which I would copy it at leisure.[26]

Douglas McMurtrie felt that this "story concerns what may well have been the most important laundry list in all history."[27]

Subsequently it occurred to Senefelder to see what would happen if he covered the stone with dilute nitric acid rather than wiping off the writing. The greasy writing repelled the dilute acid and the writing appeared to be slightly in relief. He was successful in inking the writing and was able to obtain impression with less than half the pressure that he was accustomed to use. However, his dissatisfaction with the smudged impressions produced by his presses forced him to make further investigations into the properties of paper. In one experiment he took a sheet from an old book, soaked it in a dilute solution of gum arabic, lightly sponged the printed side with an oil ink, and pressed a plain sheet of paper on top of it, successfully transferring the text. The sheet having become fragile after several transfers, he substituted a perfectly flat plate of limestone, on which he inscribed images with soap. After pouring dilute gum arabic over the entire surface of the plate, he sponged it with a black oil; where marked with the fatty soap the plate instantly turned black while the rest remained white, and he was able to produce many impressions from it. He recognized that he had invented a simple chemical process in contradistinction to the costly physical processes of printing from an engraved surface or from cast type. In 1799 King Maximilian Joseph granted Senefelder an exclusive privilege, or patent, in Bavaria.[28]

In the following two decades Senefelder proceeded to develop the entire process of lithographic printing in much the same sense that Gutenberg had developed printing from cast type. He continued to improve his inks, and by 1797 he had already built a press for printing from a lithographic stone, in which an inked stone, laid in a bed and with a sheet of paper atop, was moved between two cylinders so that the upper cylinder pressed the paper against the stone to produce the impression. Similar presses are still used for proofing. A decade later he invented an automatic press with mechanical inking and dampening that "could be operated by water and thus work almost without human intervention." It could of course, also be driven by a steam engine. In his own opinion the most important of his later inventions was the substitution of zinc or lead metal plates for limestone.

Throughout the nineteenth century lithography was primarily a graphic art form and as such is still held in high artistic repute. It also excelled in music and map printing. An artist drew the graphic either directly and in reverse on the stone, or on special paper to be transferred to the stone, using pens, pencils, or crayons as tools. The pencils and crayons were composed of tallow, soap, beeswax, and a pigment to render the mixture visible; ink for the pens was a fluid mixture of the same ingredients. In 1836 Godefroy Engelmann introduced his chromolithographic process, the first really successful multicolor lithography, in which the artist drew on a separate stone for each color, using as many as twenty stones for a single illustration. The main problem with Engelmann's process was securing precise registration for each stone during printing. The first lithographic power press became available in 1852, and flatbed presses specially designed for lithography became available in the 1870s. The last quarter of the nineteenth century also saw zinc and aluminum plates replace the stones.

Paper

The mechanization of printing in the form of iron and steam-driven presses led to demands for ever-larger stocks of paper on which to print. Nicholas-Louis Robert, who was associated with a French paper mill, invented the first major departure from traditional hand papermaking in 1798 when he made a hand-cranked machine that produced a continuous roll of paper instead of the customary sheets. The Robert machine did not operate for longer than a few years, but in 1801 John Gamble, a distant English relative of an owner of the mill where Robert worked, brought a model of the machine to England and patented it. Subsequently Gamble became associated with Henry and Sealy Fourdrinier, owners of a London stationery business who were interested in papermaking. Bryan Donkin, a skillful engineer in charge of the Fourdrinier stationery factory, converted the Robert design into a much improved steam-driven machine, which was patented in 1807 (fig. 9.2). The British and Foreign Bible Society was an early user of the machine. Fourdrinier machines were first imported into the United States in the late 1820s and began to be built there in 1829; the first of these became the chief paper supplier to the American Bible Society. The Fourdrinier papermaking machine was a success, and with innumerable refinements still is. Modern machines produce as much as 2,000 feet of paper per minute.

The operation of the Fourdrinier machine essentially mimics traditional paper-

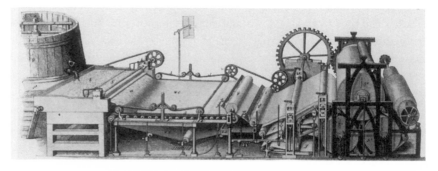

Figure 9.2. An early Fourdrinier papermaking machine. (*Encyclopaedia of Useful Arts*, 1854)

making. It distributes a pulp of 99 percent water and 1 percent fiber into a flat wire screen and removes the water by suction and pressure to produce a roll of dry, compact, continuous sheet of paper. Initially the pulp was made from pulverized rags, in use ever since the first European mill went into operation at Jativa, Spain, in the eleventh century. However, rags became increasingly scarce, to the extent that by the mid–nineteenth century Britain was importing them from many different countries. Esparto grass from North Africa and Spain proved to be the replacement; by 1890 Britain was importing a quarter of a million tons of esparto annually, more than six times the amount of rag import. Esparto was easy to prepare for pulping and its fiber length was uniform, characteristics that produced high-quality paper for printing.

Another major development beginning at midcentury was the manufacture of wood pulp, for which wood chips were—and still are—digested with a chemical in what has been likened to a huge domestic pressure cooker. At first caustic soda was used for the process, and later sulfuric acid, to yield the now familiar sulphite paper. By the century's end chemical bleaching processes had been developed to whiten paper.

Papermaking enjoyed a rapid growth in the last half of the nineteenth century. In Britain production rose from 96,000 tons in 1861 to 648,000 tons in 1900—nearly a seven-fold increase. Speeds of Fourdrinier machines mounted, and their lengths and widths of rolls were enlarged.

Publishing

By the eighteenth century, publishing, which, as Gutenberg had found out, required financial backing in many ways, began to divide from printing and bookselling. Well-to-do patrons often financed book production by printers, while merchant booksellers sometimes invested their own funds in the publishing of a book. William Blackwood (b. 1776) and William Pickering (b. 1796) were both able to amass enough capital in the antiquarian book trade to allow them to become outstanding publishers. Daniel Macmillan (b. 1813) "scratched a living as a clerk in a retail shop in London and Cambridge to accumulate capital and eventually began to publish books."[29] On the other hand, relatively small local printers could sometimes accumulate enough cash from producing primers, catechisms, legal and administrative documents, and the like to finance at least a small book. Moreover, printers in towns and small cities were apt to be aware of the type of books that would be of interest to the populace in contradistinction to the learned books in Latin that had been produced for the elite.

The Oudot family of printers is an example of successful local printer-publishers. In the seventeenth century Nicholas Oudot of Troyes, a small but lively city a hundred miles southeast of Paris, began to print "small-format books . . . with close-set type, using worn type, of the poor quality paper made in the region, covering his volumes with a rough blue paper." These volumes came to be known as the Bibliothèque Bleue. By the early eighteenth century at least three other printers in Troyes had mimicked the Oudots, whose warehouses in 1722 "contained 40,000 small volumes . . . ready for sale for a few derniers each, and 2,576 reams of printed sheets—enough to make up 350,000 octavo-sized books of 48 pages each." By 1789 the inventory of another family's stock was even larger.[30]

In 1780 James Lackington, a London bookseller, broke bookselling custom by refusing to take credit while at the same time selling books with marked-down prices. He bought up books in quantity, lowered the prices, and sold them for cash. In short, he remaindered them, and did so without sustaining losses in the form of lost interest on outstanding bills, most of which "were not paid within six months, many not within twelve months, and some not within two years."[31] Although his enterprise was a commercial success, Lackington earned the wrath and ridicule of his colleagues.

The growth of book publishing in the nineteenth century was dramatic; production of book titles in the last decade was 436 percent greater than that of the first, and the total book production of the nineteenth century exceeded that of the eighteenth by 440 percent, as recorded in the OCLC online catalog. American publishers that were established early in the nineteenth century and that continued into the twentieth included Appleton, Harper, Putnam, and Scribner. Nineteenth-century British publishers were Black and Cassel, Blackwood, Chambers, Constable, Longman, Macmillan, Murray, and Nelson. In France there were Charpentier, Didot, Garnier, Hachette, Havard, Ladvocat, Larousse, and Levy, and in Germany, Brockhaus, Cotta, Mayer, Reclam, and Tauchnitz.

The century started off with continued publication of luxury books. During the early decades in Britain such books as Sir Walter Scott's novels sold for 31 shillings, 6 pence, at a time when laborers were earning 5 to 6 shillings a day. In France, in the period following the Revolution and the Empire, publishers revived the eighteenth-century imperial tradition of books "so sumptuous that one wonders if they were ever really meant to be read."[32] But the multiple economic crises of the second quarter of the century, particularly that of 1847–1848, which destroyed wealth almost everywhere, along with some European political systems, eliminated the market for elitist books and forced publishers to print cheaper books, as cheap as 5 shillings. Even this price was too high for office workers, with the result that lending libraries, such as mechanics and mercantile libraries, began to flourish, as did serialized book publishing. Charles Dickens's *Pickwick Papers* first appeared in monthly installments, beginning in April 1836, at 1 shilling an installment.

Summary

The sudden eruption of new printing technologies in the first four decades of the nineteenth century, following three and a half centuries of quiescence, introduced two centuries of technological advances. Iron presses, steam-engine-driven presses, stereotype, mechanized typecasting, mechanized paper production, and lithography (which would overwhelm printing from type in the last half of the twentieth century) all formed a dynamic platform from which every major development has arisen except for those attributed to the computer in the last third of the twentieth century.

Climax of

10 *Books Printed*

from Cast Type

1840–1940

$\mathcal{G}$ *THE LAST THIRD* of the nineteenth century saw four important inventions in the area of book production, one of which, mechanized typesetting (1890), was as important as the inventions of the first four decades of the century and in a sense completed the revolution described in the preceding chapter. The other three were the rotary press fed by continuous paper coming off a roll (1865), the typewriter (1873), and photomechanical illustrations (1880). Otherwise, with respect to the improvement of printing from cast type, the years from 1840 to the Second World War were occupied mostly with maturing the advances of the early part of the nineteenth century.

The first half of the twentieth century was the apex of relief printing, even though it would still predominate past midcentury. The slow development of offset printing from 1904 on did not seriously challenge relief printing until after the Second World War, when, following the development of efficient techniques for producing offset plates, offset printing rocketed past relief printing and sent it into a steep decline after five hundred years of uncontested predominance.

The last fifteen years before the Second World War saw the establishment of book clubs, providing an important new market for books, and the introduction of a significant new type of book—the paperback. The pioneer Book-of-the-Month Club mailed its first book to its initial 5,750 members in April 1926; at year's end there were ten times as many members and the club had gained the outstanding success that it still enjoys. At the end of the twentieth century there are hundreds of such clubs around the world. The first of the highly successful paperback publishers was Penguin Books in London, which published its first ten books in July

1935. The books sold very well, a second group of Penguins was published three months later, and Penguins are still being published. Pocket Books issued its first ten titles in June 1939; some 10,000 copies were printed for each title. Two decades later every title had sold over 200,000 copies and three had passed the million-and-a-half mark. Pocket Books also opened up a new marketplace for books in the United States, namely, newsstands, drugstores, and five-and-ten-cent stores.

Mechanized Typesetting

There was an amazing growth in the nineteenth century of patented innovation in the field of typographical printing surfaces, of which typecasting and composition are the major components; the growth from 8 patents in the first decade of the century to 1,498 in the last is nothing short of fantastic,[1] but it was not until nearly the end of the century that two eminently successful composing machines appeared, the Linotype and the Monotype. The first of the patented composing machines had been included in William Church's patent of 1822 for a casting machine, but like his casting machine it seems never to have operated. The first composing machine that actually worked was patented by J. H. Young and A. Delcambre in 1840. Their patent described it as having "tubes for containing the type, key-operated pushers for ejecting the type singly to an inclined guide-plate, a composing box for receiving the type from the guide-plate end . . . and a packing-device for pushing the type into the galley." Young had retained Henry Bessemer, later of Bessemer converter fame, as consulting engineer (Bessemer referred to himself as a "mechanician"), and it was Bessemer who devised a machine that worked. In his autobiography Bessemer wrote,

> About 1700 or 1800 letters per hour can be formed into lines and columns by a dexterous compositor, while as many as 6000 types per hour could be set by the composing machine. A young lady in the office of the *Family Herald* undertook the following task at the suggestion of the proprietor of *The Times*, viz: she was to set up not less than 5000 types per hour for ten consecutive hours, on six consecutive days; giving a total of 300,000 letters in a week. This she easily accomplished, and was then presented with a £5 note by Mr. Walter.

Bessemer felt compelled to add, however, "This mode of composing type by playing on keys arranged precisely like the keys of a pianoforte would have formed an excellent occupation for women; but it did not find favour with the lords of creation, who strongly objected to such successful competition by female labour, and so the machine eventually died a natural death."[2] In everyday operation two people were required to operate the Young and Delcambre machine: one at the keys and a "justifier" at the galley.

Although the Young and Delcambre typesetter was used "in a small way" in England and France, it was not until 1853, when W. H. Mitchel of Brooklyn, New York, brought out his typesetter and distributor, that a machine having practical commercial use appeared. At least a dozen other typesetter-distributors were marketed before 1890. Three kinds of these early machines, each coincidentally introduced in 1872, were still in operation at the beginning of the twentieth century.[3]

The Linotype machine, first introduced in 1886 at the *New York Tribune* and improved in 1890, proved to be the greatest of mechanical printing successes by the end of the century, when more than 250 machines were operating in Britain alone. By the time of the First World War, 33,000 were operating worldwide. Ottmar Mergenthaler of Baltimore, inventor of the Linotype, based his design on entirely different principles from those of the Young and Delcambre machine of 1840 and the many machines that followed it. Simply put, the Linotype assembled in a line alphanumeric matrices withdrawn from a magazine, justified the line by inserting wedge-shaped spaces between words, and then cast a type-high slug. After ejecting the slug into a galley, the machine distributed the matrices back into the magazine for reuse. The process required only one operator. The 1890 version possessed a single, interchangeable magazine; later models have had two, three, and four interchangeable magazines and the ability to operate with at least two magazines simultaneously.

The Linotype, in addition to speeding up composition to 8,000 to 10,000 characters per hour per average operator, has many other advantages. Its line-long slugs are easy to handle, and the slug form precludes the disastrous event of an individual type working up above its neighbors during printing; also, since newly cast type is used for every new printing, the printer has at his command a virtually inexhaustible type case. Finally, the Linotype was ideal for newspaper work, where one size of type and one width of line prevail. It was not until 1913 that a substantial competitor of the Linotype appeared, when the first Intertype machine, another line-slug device, was sold to the *Journal of Commerce* in New York. This linecaster possessed only one magazine but was later retrofitted with three. A half century later this Intertype was still in operation.

The last of the important new nineteenth-century machines for composing and casting was the Monotype, which has been extensively used for book setting. Tolbert Lanston, an American, secured patents for the Monotype in 1896 and 1897; it comprises two separate machines, one being a composer and justifier, and the other a caster and setter, each requiring an operator. Depression of a key on the keyboard of the first machine produces perforations in a paper tape that represent the character depicted on the key. A warning bell rings as the end of the line is neared, so that the operator can determine whether to complete the word he is typing, to divide it, or to add another word. When he has added all the type he is going to put into the line, he sets a couple of signals that will notify the second machine of the amount of space to be added between the words to justify the line. The perforated tape then goes to the second machine, which casts each character and each word separator separately and assembles them into a line for printing, usually at the rate of plus or minus 9,000 characters an hour. The popularity of the Monotype stems from its ability to produce good book work, most particularly because it possesses matrices for many of the handsome classical type fonts. The Linotype of 1890 and the Monotype of 1897 completed the mechanization of printing systems that began with Koenig's steam press of 1814.

Cylinder and Rotary Presses

In the course of the nineteenth century Koenig's steam-driven, stop-cylinder press grew to be the first of the two preferred presses for printing books; the second preferred press was the two-revolution cylinder press invented by Robert Miehle in 1884. The most popular of the stop-cylinder presses was the Wharfedale, invented by David Payne and introduced by Dawson, Payne, and Company of Otley, Yorkshire, in 1858 (figure 10.1). (It got its name from the upper, troughlike valley of the River Wharfe where it was manufactured.) At one time there had been seven different factories manufacturing Wharfedales at Otley, and in 1946 there were still two there, as well as others throughout Britain. After the First World War, three Otley firms joined together and subsequently put out the series of Standard High-Speed Wharfedales.

The major shortcoming of the early cylinder presses had been the jarring and vibration generated when the travel of the heavy type bed was arrested and reversed. Payne's solution to this problem was to hang a crank on a rod connecting the rims of two large driving wheels. The "handle" of the crank was connected to the drive mechanism of the type bed, so that the crank would be at dead center when the bed reached the end of travel. The forward motion of the crank slowed

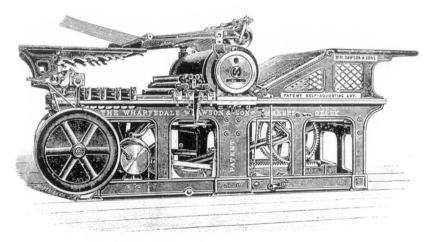

Figure 10.1. A Wharfedale printing press.

as it approached its horizontal dead center, continuously slowing the travel of the type bed as it approached full stop. This arrangement to eliminate the jarring came to be known as "the Otley principle."

The Miehle kind of two-revolution cylinder press was invented in response to the need for a heavy-duty flatbed press to print perfectly registered multiple colors and very fine lines. Miehle's solution was a heavy, sliding pinion gear driving alternately an upper rack and lower rack, each attached to the type bed, to achieve the back-and-forth travel. Miehle borrowed Payne's crank drive to control the bed while the pinion was sliding from one rack to the other and to slow, stop, and reverse the travel. In addition he added two shock absorbers at each end. The Miehle press was manufactured at least until 1970 and was probably the most popular book press during the first two-thirds of the twentieth century (fig. 10.2).

Apparently the first successful rotary press to print a book was developed by Thomas Trench, a papermaker of Ithaca, New York, who is thought to have invented it to print both sides of the roll of paper coming off a Fourdrinier machine. Stereotype plates, presumably containing only a few lines of text each, were fastened to cylinders; the plates made the impression. An 1836 edition of *Robinson Crusoe* published by Mack, Andrus, and Woodruff, owners of the paper mill that employed Trench, may have been the first book printed on a rotary press.[4]

The first of the big rotaries, the Hoe Type Revolving Machine, known as the Quadruple for its four presses, was developed by R. Hoe & Co. in New York in the mid-1840s. In this machine ordinary cast metal type was attached in a relatively simple system to a detached segment of a large, six-and-a-half-foot horizontal cylinder. Unfortunately, if the type was not locked up correctly and securely, the centrifugal force generated when the cylinder started revolving could spray the type around the

Figure 10.2. A Miehle printing press.

print room, an accident that apparently occurred occasionally, but not often enough to take the machine permanently out of operation. It could produce 8,000 sheets an hour printed on one side only; the sheets had to be run through a second time to print the other side. Other shortcomings were that it required a "boy" to feed sheets to each cylinder, and each printed sheet, although taken off mechanically, had to be folded manually to produce the finished newspaper. DeVinne recalled that "The old morning paper pressroom was a Babel of confusion for the work of printing was seriously impeded by feeders and paper-folders, who were often in the way of the pressmen."[5] Hoe installed the first of its Type Revolving Machines at the Philadelphia *Public Ledger* in 1847, and the second, also a four-feeder, at *La Patrie* in Paris in 1848. In 1856 a six-feeder was installed at *Lloyd's Weekly Newspaper* in London, and two years later two immense ten-feeders—which had a nominal production of 20,000 sheets an hour—were set up at the *Times*.

In 1865 William Bullock of Philadelphia installed at the *Philadelphia Inquirer* a major new kind of rotary press. James Moran evaluated this machine "as the first automatic, reel-fed rotary press working from stereotype plates, and printing on both sides of the paper,"[6] three truly magnificent innovations. The paper was fed from a reel, the way it had come from a Fourdrinier machine, and was cut into sheets before it reached the first of two sets of print and impression cylinders; each set printed one side of the sheet. The press could produce 10,000 sheets an hour, but a mechanical device that took the printed sheets off the press and stacked them for folding could handle only 8,000 sheets in the same time. In 1867 Bullock was installing one of his presses at the Philadelphia *Public Ledger* and unfortunately, during the last test, his foot was caught in the drive belt and so badly crushed that he died nine days later.

In 1869 Walter Scott of New York invented an automatic folding machine, which was almost immediately added to a Bullock press to eliminate manual folding. John W. Kellberg produced another major improvement by arranging for the paper to pass continuously through both sets of printing cylinders and be cut into sheets only after both sides had been printed, thereby simplifying the mechanism for moving the paper through the press. The resultant increased speed of paper flow necessitated increasing the speed of the taking-off device, which was also more than doubled. By 1870 improved Bullock presses were running at the hourly rate of 20,000 sheets printed on both sides, and the "Babel of confusion" had been eliminated. Before long, however, improved Hoe presses and a similar press, the Walter, developed at the *Times* in the 1860s, superseded the Bullock.

From Gutenberg onward, paper had been dampened before printing, to produce a good impression, and afterward smoothed and dried in a press. In 1870 Theodore DeVinne began to print the *Century Magazine* using calendered, or coated, paper that he printed dry; the printed lines were sharp and the woodcut impressions greatly improved. Printers of books and magazines everywhere were quick to follow his method.

James Moran has stated that "The technical history of the first fifty years of the twentieth century is . . . one of extension of nineteenth-century methods" and ". . . may now be seen as the final flowering of conventional relief printing and of metal type . . . ," when ". . . the great mass of printing designed to be read, rather than merely looked at, was produced by letterpress and from type. The significant changes [in printing] after 1900 were in the means of setting type and in the size and speed of printing presses."[7] As the century got under way, steam engines and gas engines were still driving the big presses, but they were soon replaced by electric motors, which could be used to drive both large and small presses. The big newspaper rotaries continued to increase in size and speed by the addition of side-by-side presses. An early example was the Hoe Octuple of 1902, which printed from four reels of paper, each four pages wide, and had a theoretical running speed of 96,000 eight-page newspapers an hour. In the latter part of the century these presses were rated at nominal speeds of up to 140,000 newspapers per hour. Improvements that enhanced speed included rapid lockup of stereotyped plates to cylinders (1908), an automatic ink pump (1915), procedures for rapid changing of paper rolls (1896), and splicing of paper while the press was running at full speed (1920s).

Photomechanical Processes

When lithography was introduced into France, about 1812, it aroused considerable interest. Nicéphore Niépce of Chalon-sur-Saone, sixty kilometers south of Dijon, was excited by the new process, but because he had no drawing skill, he set about using chemical methods to try to create permanent depictions of scenes as produced in a camera obscura, first used by the famous Muslim scientist Alhazen (c. 965–c. 1039). In other words, he was inventing photography. He had already achieved considerable success by 1816,[8] and by 1826 had been able to record a view from a window and permanently fix it. The positive image, on a pewter plate, which had required an eight-hour exposure, the oldest known permanent photograph, still exists in the Gernsheim Collection at the University of Texas in Austin. Subsequent to the announcement in 1839 of the daguerreotype, to which Niépce had contributed prior to his death in 1833, and Fox Talbot's announcement of his invention of the negative-positive process, various experimenters worked unsuccessfully on a practical photoprinting process that involved photoengraving in place of photolithography. Indeed the first successful example, the halftone process, did not come until the 1880s.

The invention of photography, announced in 1839, made possible the development of photomechanical printing processes. In Paris in that year Louis Jacques Mandé Daguerre described his production of a direct, unique copy of an image, and in Britain William Henry Fox Talbot reported his discovery of the photographic negative of an image from which any number of exact, repeatable, positive copies could be made. It was Fox Talbot's kind of photography that made possible the photomechanical processes of the last quarter of the century. Both halftone and photogravure produce images from photographic film, but halftone is relief printing, while photogravure is intaglio; both were predominant in printing illustrations throughout most of the twentieth century.

The first of the successful procedures was the line-block technique, developed mostly by Firmin Gillot in the early 1870s. Line blocks, which reproduced line drawings only, in black on white paper, were made by placing a photographic negative of an artist's drawing on a photographically sensitized zinc plate and exposing it to strong light to make a positive image. After exposure the plate was rolled with printers ink, which was attracted to the lines, then washed to remove the ink from the nonimage areas. The plate was then etched with acid to bring the lines into relief, after which it was mounted on a wooden block to raise it to type height for printing.

The ubiquitous halftone, long printed in newspapers worldwide, appeared first in the *Daily Graphic*, New York, in 1880. The principal contribution of the halftone process lay in its ability to reproduce the graduated gray tones of a black-and-white photograph by copying a positive print of a photograph in a special camera equipped with a screen mounted in front of the negative plate or film. Today's screens have between 55 to 200 interstices per inch, which produce an equivalent number of dots on the negative; the dots mimic the grayness of the original photograph by varying from pinpoints in highlight areas to full dots in shadows. The chemical process for producing the printing plate is essentially the same as that for line blocks.

The development of photogravure began in 1878 with Karl Klie. Klie photocopied a positive image onto a copper engraving plate and then photographically printed a crossed-line screen over the image on the plate. Next he etched the plate with a chemical that ate away the spaces between the screen lines to various depths, the deepest of which would provide the areas of heaviest shadow. His printing followed the traditional intaglio process, with thin ink being spread over the plate and the excess being wiped off the surface before the impression was made.

Subsequently, for printing from a rotary press, Klie enhanced his process by copying the image and screen onto carbon tissue—paper coated with a film of sensitized gelatin and carbon powder—and wrapping the tissue around a copper cylinder, which he etched through the tissue. The cylinder was then mounted on a rotary press and covered with a flowing thin ink, which was removed from the surface by a "doctor" or doctor-blade knife, as in flat intaglio printing. In 1895 Klie, joining forces with some calico printers in Lancaster, England, formed the Rembrandt Intaglio Printing Company to use his new process on reel-fed textile printing presses. Rembrandt kept the process under wraps until 1903, when one of its workmen emigrated to the United States along with the secret—not the first time that such an event had occurred.

After improvement in the speed of preparing the cylinder, large-scale printing by rotogravure, as it came to be called, began in the United States when the *New York Times* introduced a regular rotogravure supplement. By the end of 1915 a dozen and a half U.S. newspapers and magazines were using rotogravure, which has since been improved so that it produces long runs of high-quality illustrations having rich colors. Until the last quarter of the twentieth century, it had no significant competition except for the Dultgen halftone intaglio process, which employs a two-step technique for controlling tone by means of two photographic positive copies on film of the illustration to be printed, one a clear copy and the other made through a halftone screen. In the Dultgen process the halftone screen is exposed on carbon tissue, producing dots of various densities, and then the screenless positive is exposed on the same tissue, thereby producing ranges of hardening to the dot images, so that when the tissue has been pressed down firmly on a copper plate and the plate etched, the pits produced are not only of different depths but also of different sizes. Hence this Dultgen method provides a more exact and fastidious quality control of tone than the rotogravure process.

Bookbinding

Until the mid–eighteenth century, publishers sold books in sheets to be bound by booksellers or by the purchaser, but by the mid–nineteenth century publishers were commonly binding their books, which stimulated the mechanization of binding. The first major step in this direction was the introduction of case binding in the 1820s. Originally case-bound books continued to have their signatures sewn by hand, but the case, comprising boards, covers, and spine, was produced on a machine. The case was attached to the hand-sewn quires by a vertical adhesive tape. The next decade saw the advent of a press that decorated the entire cover in one operation.

In 1879 David M. Smyth patented his "book-sewer" machine, which in the same year was awarded the American Institute Gold Medal. The first machine went into operation sometime in 1880 at the Riverside Press in Cambridge, Massachusetts; a half dozen years later Riverside owned seven Smyth sewers. In that same year, 1886, Smyth Manufacturing brought out its Improved No. 3 machine. Frank Comparato states that "According to company history, more No. 3 Smyth book-sewing machines have been sold than any other in the world."[9] The success of the Smyth sewers led to other innovative introductions, and as one British author has viewed the development "The last few years of the nineteenth century saw an invasion from America of many fast-running machines for the binding trade, with automatic feeds and all especially designed for intensive mass-production."[10]

The last major development in bookbinding before 1940 came with the paperback book revolution in the last half of the 1930s. The new process was called "perfect binding"—something of a misnomer, as the unsewn pages tend to come loose with use. The procedure involves folding printed sheets into quires, assembling the quires in perfect order and guillotining the folds off their backs, and then dipping the quires into an adhesive and pushing them onto the spine of the cover. Some 18,000 books can be bound per hour. Tests of the number of readings that these bindings will support have yielded findings ranging from six to twenty-eight.

Newspapers and Magazines

The first truly daily newspaper, the London *Daily Courant*, began publication in 1702. As Martin described it, "the governing classes took fright when they saw newspaper reading beginning to make headway among the people,"[11] with the result that in 1712 Parliament passed the Stamp Act, which taxed every copy of a newspaper or pamphlet. This act, with its successive increases in the tax, retarded growth of British newspapers until its repeal in 1854. John Feather has characterized the effect of the repeal as "the economic equivalent of steam-printing. It was now possible to produce a daily paper which sold for a penny or even a halfpenny."[12]

The nineteenth- and twentieth-century history of newspapers depicts a struggle among competing forces: technological development to increase availability of news, taxation to restrict that information to the elite, and outright political control except in the United States, where freedom of the press was guaranteed by the First Amendment of the U.S. Constitution. As a result the United States "developed an aggressively independent press, less trammelled by libel laws and governmental secrecy than anywhere else in the world,"[13] and it is not surprising that some of the most significant inventions and developments in newspaper production throughout the nineteenth century occurred in the United States. First there was David Bruce's invention of the typecasting machine in 1838; after later development in Britain, which increased its output to 60,000 characters an hour, the typecasting machine made it unnecessary for newspaper printers to distribute type after use, as it was cheaper to melt the used type and cast it anew. Next came Richard Hoe's installation of the first rotary press in 1847; a decade later, a Hoe rotary built for the *Times* of London was producing 20,000 impressions an hour as compared with the 1,100 impressions an hour produced by its Koenig machines of 1814. The third major American invention was the Linotype composing machine, first built by Ottmar Mergenthaler in 1886; William Turner Berry evaluated it as having "opened a new era in the history of printing, especially newspaper-printing."[14] Finally, Henry Alexander Wise Wood of New York patented the Autoplate in 1903, which automatically cast semicylindrical stereotype plates for use in high-speed rotary newspaper presses. Legros and Grant, in praising the Autoplate, pointed out that the London *Evening News* "on the occasion of receiving intelligence of the foundering of the *Titanic*, cast 1150 plates for one edition," which "would have been quite impossible by the methods of stereotyping in use but a few years ago."[15]

In the eighteenth century magazines began to fill the information gap between books and newspapers. Three of the earliest—Defoe's *Review*, Steele's *Tatler*, and Addison and Steele's *Spectator*—became immensely influential among the upper and middle classes. In the second quarter of the nineteenth century "cheap" magazines began to be published for the lower classes. In 1832 the Society for the Diffusion of Useful Knowledge started its weekly *Penny Magazine*. Its circulation rose to 200,000, but it was discontinued in 1846 when circulation fell to 40,000. A more successful example was *Chamber's Journal*, published from 1844 to 1956; its circulation was up to 90,000 in its second year. The first of the picture magazines was the *Illustrated London News*, which started publication in 1842 and still continues. It soon began to print scenes of current events, as newspapers had been doing since shortly after the turn of the century.

The same technologies used to mass-produce newspapers also fostered the development of popular magazines, so called to distinguish them from the "quality" magazines, such as *Century*, *Harper's Magazine*, and the *Atlantic Monthly*. One author said of the new culture: "A structural equivalence between Eastern, feminine, past, dull, and sickly on the one hand and virility, masculinity, Western, timely and lively on the other was explicit . . . in the editorial features."[16] While newspapers remained mostly local in character, popular magazines were being addressed to the educated, literate middle class nationwide. By 1890 many of them had moved to the Midwest, often locating at the junctions of the east-west and north-south railway lines that had already spanned the continent for two decades.

The high-speed presses employed by the leading magazines made it possible to lower the price of an issue to ten cents, resulting in large, nationwide circulation that attracted advertisers, so that magazines rapidly came to rely on advertising income rather than sales revenue—a brand-new development for publishers. There was a 148 percent rise in the total circulation of six leading general-interest magazines in the first dozen years of the twentieth century (even though four of the six succumbed in the 1920s). The total circulation for the six in 1912 was slightly more than 4.5 million, with an average of 765,000; only one exceeded 1 million: the *Saturday Evening Post*, at 1,855,000. In 1940 there were fifty-two American magazines with a circulation of 1 million or more.[17]

Since the time of Gutenberg, publishers had been plagued with distribution problems, first for books, then newspapers, and finally magazines. By the first half of the nineteenth century a few publishers had reasonably effective distribution systems, but most publishers relied on independent agencies, or on the wholesalers who began to come into being at midcentury, to provide distribution. "The largest wholesaler was A. S. Tuttle, who moved New York newspapers on his own railroad cars to dealers outside the city by 1854. When his company expanded into the American News Company [1864], it owned or controlled over 20,000 newspaper agencies across the United States."[18] Growing rapidly, it branched out into whole-saling books "and eventually hundreds of other items," and it created a new mar-ket—selling periodicals to passengers in railroad cars. It "practically monopolized the distribution of periodicals when the low-priced magazine appeared in the nineties." By 1955 it "serviced some 95,000 dealers . . . imported and exported, wholesaled, and retailed newspapers, magazines, and books" and was "the largest wholesaler of books in the world."[19]

Typewriters

The first American patent for a typewriter, issued to William Austin Burt of De-troit in 1829, had characters mounted on a semicircular band of metal. Four years later Xavier Progin of Marseilles produced a typewriter that operated with type-bars, as do most modern manual typewriters. As was the case with type-composing machines in the nineteenth century, the next half century was spent in develop-ment, for it was not until 1873 that the first commercially successful typewriter was marketed. Nevertheless, typewriters of various designs attracted much attention in the world's fairs of the 1850s and 1860s. These midcentury typewriters had various styles of metal vehicles bearing type characters—bands, wheels, or sleeves. All of the designs produced accurate line registration, but all were slow, because of the time required to move a character into position before striking the impression.

Finally, in 1867, Christopher L. Sholes, usually thought of as the inventor of the "modern" typewriter, made a typebar model that worked rapidly because the operations of moving a character into position and striking the impression were combined into one movement. Remaining alignment problems were resolved by fine tuning, and the problem of two adjacent or near-adjacent bars clashing to-gether during rapid typing was solved by changing from an alphabetical arrange-ment of the keys to an arrangement in which bars having often used characters were widely separated. The result was the "qwerty" keyboard, still with us, on which the international "azerty" keyboard is based. The Remington Company put the Sholes typewriter on the market in 1873.

Samuel Clemens—Mark Twain—was undoubtedly the first author to purchase a typewriter. In early December 1874 he acquired a Remington Type Writer and on December 9 typed a letter to his elder brother, Orion, and a second to his close friend and publisher William Dean Howells, editor of the *Atlantic Monthly*. In the first he recounted the typewriter's benefits: "The machine has several virtues. I be-lieve that it will print faster than I can write. One may lean back in his chair and work it. It piles an awful stack of words on one page. It dont muss things or scatter ink blots around. Of course it saves paper."[20] On December 11, Howells replied to the letter he had received with "When you get tired of the machine, lend it to me," to which Clemens responded, on December 15, "I guess I shall have to afflict you with the machine before long: it is most too tearing on the mind." On November 5,

1875, nearly a year later, Howells wrote that he had received the "type-writer," adding, "Of course it doesn't work: if I can persuade some of the letters to get up against the ribbon they wont get down again without digital assistance. . . . It's fascinating . . . and it wastes my time like an old friend."[21] It was not a surprising ending to an early trial of a machine that produced only capital letters, wrote nonvisibly (i.e., on the bottom of the cylindrical platen), and was crippled by innumerable bugs.

By the end of the century two important improvements in typewriters had been introduced. In 1878 the Remington 2 came onto the market with a shift-key mechanism that had uppercase and lowercase type characters on the same typebar, and in 1895 Underwood introduced its No. 1 with visible typing. With these improvements the nineteenth-century typewriter was, as one historian has described it, "the most complex mechanism produced by American industry."[22] Successful portable typewriters began appearing in 1909 and their popularity increased throughout the century. The first successful electric typewriters began to appear in the 1920s. They possessed many advantages over manual typewriters, including less operator fatigue, resulting largely from lighter touch, and better legibility, greater speed, and more uniform copy. Sales greatly increased after the First World War, to the extent that by 1940 publishers expected to receive typed versions of manuscripts.

Essentially all typewriters until 1960, both manual and electric, were typebar mechanisms with one font only. In 1960 IBM introduced its Selectric typewriter, which had an interchangeable, spherical typeface carrier that enabled a choice of fonts. Another improvement was that the type ball moved across the paper from left to right, so that the platen carrying the paper no longer had to move from right to left and be returned manually by the typist. The last of the IBM introductions, the Magnetic Tape/Selectric, came in 1964; some look upon this machine as the first of the modern word processors.

Book Publishing

During the period from 1840 to 1940 publishing grew into an industry that generated a huge increase in numbers of titles published and copies produced. At the century's end a few titles sold over a million copies each, an event that would have been unheard-of at the beginning of the period. It was a sudden addiction to novel reading that produced these rocketing sales. Another surge in book sales had occurred in the 1870s with what is sometimes called a paperback revolution, but this was hardly a skirmish compared with the eruptions of Penguin and Pocket Book paperbacks just before the Second World War.

Works of fiction became amazingly popular in the last half of the eighteenth century, in large part because they could be borrowed from circulating libraries, which, in the sense that they were available to all, were the forerunners of public or municipal libraries. They imposed a small lending fee of pence or pennies that the "masses" above the poverty level were able to pay. And pay they did, mostly for novels. As in 1712 the elite took fright, but this time taxation did not appear to be the weapon for depriving the "masses" of something to read. Instead vitriolic attacks were mounted against the circulating library and—in the words of one magazine—"that common herd of Novels (the wretched offspring of circulating libraries) which are despised for their insignificance."[23] Novels comprised from one-fifth to one-half of the stock of circulating libraries well into the nineteenth century. Mudie's Circulating Libraries, the best known in midcentury Britain, had at its peak of activity more than twenty-five thousand subscribers in London alone, and purchased as many as three-quarters of an edition of a novel. Some publishers would not risk publishing a novel without Mudie's approval.

Low prices and mass production of books are two major success stories of the first half of the twentieth century. In 1919 Emanuel Haldeman-Julius brought the Little Blue Books into existence in, of all places, Girard, Kansas. The first two titles were *The Rubaiyat of Omar Khayyam* and Oscar Wilde's *Ballad of Reading Gaol*. The little books, 3½ by 5 inches, had blue covers, saddle-wire bindings, and sixty-four pages on average. They first sold for 25 cents, but the huge number of copies sold brought the price down to 10 cents and then to 5. During the next three decades some 300 million copies were sold. At the start their competitor was the Little Leather Library, which published short classics, beginning with a collection of Shakespeare's plays. Pocket-sized books, they were bound in imitation limp leather and priced at 10 cents a copy. Sales declined in the mid-1920s, and the owners initiated a new project, the Book-of-the-Month Club (BOMC). The first book, *Lolly Willows*, went to some 4,750 members in April 1926. Membership was ten times that number at year's end; at the century's end the BOMC had hundreds of thousands of members, had distributed hundreds of millions of books, and had been joined by at least another hundred specialized clubs. They answered a real demand for books, particularly by readers distant from bookstores and libraries.

The main advance in book publishing in the first half of the century was the introduction of mass-produced paperback books in Britain and the United States to be sold at extraordinarily cheap prices—6 pence (12 U.S. cents) in Britain and a quarter in the United States. Paperbacks had long been published on the European continent, but not at such low prices or in editions of tens of thousands. In 1946, the British Penguin publisher announced the simultaneous issue on one day of a million copies of books by one author, a set of George Bernard Shaw's plays.

Sir Allen Lane, the founding publisher and editor of Penguin Books, issued the company's first ten titles in July 1935. As he put it three years later, "we worked on the principle that the first thing art has to do is to entertain; that if a book is boring no amount of literary excellence can atone for the failure to perform that elementary function."[24] His first ten titles were novels: *Ariel*, by André Maurois; *A Farewell to Arms*, by Ernest Hemingway; *Poet's Pub*, by Eric Linklater; *Madame*

Claire, by Susan Ertz; *The Unpleasantness at the Bellona Club*, by Dorothy L. Sayers; *The Mysterious Affair at Styles*, by Agatha Christie; *Twenty-Five*, by Beverly Nichols; *William*, by E. H. Young; *Gone to Earth*, by Mary Webb; and *Carnival*, by Compton Mackenzie. Sir Allen printed 20,000 copies of each title; he had calculated his break-even point as being 17,500.

Not unsurprisingly the book trade responded with the same kind of negativism with which it had greeted James Lackington in 1780 when he began to sell remaindered books at low prices (see chapter 9). Readers immediately liked Penguins to such an extent, however, that Sir Allen had difficulty keeping up with the demand for the original ten titles. Nevertheless, he was able to issue in October 1935 a second set of ten titles, which also sold well. Emboldened by the success with fiction, he initiated in 1937 a new series, Pelican Books, that "was all very serious stuff, much of it heavy going." His reaction to the immediate and overwhelming success of the Pelicans was "Who would have imagined that, even at 6d, there was a thirsty public anxious to buy thousands of copies of books on science, sociology, economics, archaeology, astronomy, and other equally serious subjects."[25] Another series, Penguin Specials, was also begun in 1937; it dealt with politics and other contemporary topics.

In 1956, two decades after the appearance of the first ten titles, Penguin Books sold 10 million copies worldwide. At that time 1,000 titles of Sir Allen's books were in print, out of the total of nearly 2,400 that had appeared. Of that total, 1,200 were Penguins, 400 were Pelicans, and 170 were Penguin Specials; the rest were in all manner of topics. At the century's end bookstores are still displaying shelves full of Penguins.

In 1938, in the United States, Robert F. de Graf approached the publisher Simon and Schuster with the idea for a paperback series called Pocket Books, which led to the incorporation of a company in which de Graf and the firm each invested $15,000, with de Graf holding 51 percent of the stock. Lincoln Schuster, Leon Shimkin, and Richard Simon, as well as de Graf, played very active roles in the early years of the new company (whose logo, a bespectacled kangaroo reading a book held in her forepaws, with a second book in her pouch, was named Gertrude, after the mother-in-law of the artist who drew her).[26]

In the summer of 1938, de Graf, having designed a book he described as pleasing to the eye and agreeable to the touch, printed a thousand copies of *The Good Earth*, by Pearl Buck, and made a market test by sending them to a thousand readers to obtain their reaction. He also sent a questionnaire to forty-nine thousand readers to see how they would respond to being able to purchase good books at a quarter apiece. The findings of the market survey being favorable, the four men set about selecting ten works of literary merit for their first publications. On June 19, 1939, they published a full-page advertisement in the *New York Times* announcing the Pocket Book publishing venture and the first ten titles published that day. Several New York publishers telephoned de Graf on the morning of June 19, voicing the same kind of negativism that London publishers had expressed to Sir Allen Lane in 1935; they urged de Graf to drop the new enterprise before it was too late. But as was clear before the day was out, Pocket Books was, literally, an instant success. Table 10.1 lists the ten titles and the number of copies of each that were sold over the next several years. The total sale—nearly nine million copies—was a huge success. By the end of the year Pocket Books had published thirty-four titles and had sold 1,508,000 copies, an average of 44,000 thousand copies in an average time of three months.

The Cambridge University Press was the first of the university presses, having been authorized on July 20, 1534, in the royal charter that established the university. However, it was not until May 3, 1583, that Cambridge appointed its first university printer, Thomas Thomas, who printed his initial seven books in 1584; ever since, the press has issued at least one book a year. Incited by Cambridge, Oxford appointed its first printer in 1584, and the Oxford University Press published its first book the next year. It was nearly three centuries later, in 1887, that the first university press came into being in the United States, when the Johns Hopkins Press, founded a decade earlier, published its first book. Presses at the University of Chicago, Columbia University, and the University of California started in the first half of the 1890s. By 1900 there were fourteen university presses, but by 1910 only eight existed (including one outstanding newcomer, the Princeton University Press). By 1919, however, there were thirty-eight university presses and by 1965, sixty-seven.

Publishing associated with universities came into existence before the invention

Table 10.1. Sales of first 10 pocket books, 1939–1957

Copies	Titles
289,000	*Bambi*, Felix Salten
431,000	*The Bridge of San Luis Rey*, Thornton Wilder
210,000	*Enough Rope*, Dorothy Parker
2,101,000	*Five Great Tragedies*, William Shakespeare
1,759,000	*Lost Horizon*, James Hilton
653,000	*The Murder of Roger Ackroyd*, Agatha Christie
1,546,000	*Topper*, Thorne Smith
420,000	*Wake Up and Live*, Dorothea Brande
210,000	*The Way of All Flesh*, Samuel Butler
1,176,000	*Wuthering Heights*, Emily Bronte
8,795,000	

Source: Frank L. Schick, *The Paperback Book in America* (1959), pp. 128–29.

of printing, as was discussed in chapter 7. At first, however, such publishing was mostly rewriting of texts for instructional purposes, and even after Gutenberg, presses that became associated with universities were largely concerned with reprinting. It was not until the first half of the nineteenth century, when European universities began to emphasize research as well as teaching, that university presses took on the mission of publishing scholarly works containing new knowledge. It is still their mission, and many of their publications would never see the light of day were only the commercial publishing industry available to print them.

The Age of Libraries

The most important development in the nineteenth-century literary world was the invention of an entirely new kind of library—the municipal library, whose collection was freely available to all the citizens of a community. This event occurred simultaneously at midcentury in the United States and Britain and a decade later in France.[27] Prior to the 1850s the phrase "public library" meant a library that was a private library available to a few but not to all; after 1850 it came to mean a library financially supported by taxation whose book collection was available free of charge. In general it was the increasing desire for information, particularly information for self-improvement, that brought the public library into being, just as it had brought the mechanics and mercantile libraries into being earlier in the century. There can be no doubt that the economic crisis of 1847–1848, following so soon after that of 1837–1842, triggered the legislative action in Massachusetts (1848 and 1851), in New Hampshire (1849), and in Great Britain (1850) that authorized the use of tax money to support public libraries. The same kind of need that caused the establishment of public libraries propelled the soaring use of them during the Great Depression of the 1930s.

The public library in Manchester, England, opened in 1852, and that in Boston, Massachusetts, in 1854. Four years later, when it possessed 100,000 volumes, the Boston Library moved into its own building. Two decades later it had nearly 300,000 volumes and was circulating more than a million volumes a year—more than three books per inhabitant per year.[28] At the century's end it had more than a million volumes. This growth of a million volumes in a half century exemplifies the remarkable new market for books that came into being in just the last half of the century. The vast majority of the library users who borrowed those million volumes yearly were unable themselves to purchase the books they used.

Academic libraries had a growth history similar to that of the new public libraries. Until shortly after the enactment of the Copyright Law of 1870, which provided the Library of Congress with large numbers of free new books, Harvard possessed the largest library in the United States. From 1849 to 1876 Harvard added books at an average rate of 5,926 volumes per year; from 1876 to 1900, the average rate was 34,000 volumes a year—nearly six times as great as in the previous quarter century.[29] This accelerated growth was due to the introduction of German research techniques into American institutions in the 1870s and the simultaneous shift in instruction from a single textbook to assignments in multiple works. Indeed, it was the Harvard College Library that, in the 1890s, first introduced the reserved-book procedure that made multiple copies of multiple books available to many students.

Britain and the United States were in the forefront of developing municipal and academic librarianship and furthering its professionalism and education. The American Library Association was founded in 1876, and Great Britain's Library Association was founded in the following year. Melvil Dewey established the world's first university library school at Columbia University in New York City in 1887. He transferred the school to Albany two years later because the Columbia trustees would not permit him to teach women students; seventeen of his first class of twenty had been women.

Denmark, Norway, and Sweden developed public libraries on a par with those in Britain and the United States. Notably, Denmark, with its dense population, has been able since the Second World War to bring library service—directly from a library, or by book truck, or by mail—in reach of every citizen, a major and unique achievement. France and Germany achieved networks of municipal libraries; however, German libraries suffered two disasters. First, the Nazi government after 1933 exercised control and censorship of public libraries: acquisition of foreign books by Jews was prohibited, and "communist" authors' books were removed and often burned. Subsequently a half-dozen years of air raids destroyed and severely damaged many German libraries. In Italy and Spain library service had not advanced as far as it had in northern Europe by 1940; at that time only 3 percent of Spanish municipalities had public library service.

Although it is likely that some library users could have purchased some of the books they borrowed from libraries, very few, if any, could have purchased all. By and large, public libraries stimulated a demand for books and increased their sales.

Summary

From 1840 to 1940 remarkable increases in speed and quantity of print production were achieved by major technical advances: the mechanization of typesetting, bookbinding and writing (in the form of typewriters), the photomechanical fabrication of illustration, and the introduction of cylinder and rotary presses.

The new typesetting machines, the Linotype (1890), a boon to newspapers, and the Monotype (1897), which largely benefited book printing, were the most important inventions of the hundred years covered by this chapter. Two cylinder presses, the Wharfedale (1858) and the Miehle (1884), became the predominant book presses by the time of the Second World War, and William Bullock's power-driven rotary press (1865), with its innovative rollfed and perfecting design, was another outstanding invention, particularly for printing newspapers. The introduction of David Smyth's power-driven booksewing machine (1880) enabled binding to keep abreast of the increased speed of book printing. Finally, Fox Talbot's invention of negative-positive photography (1839) not only made possible the development of photomechanical processes of illustration, but also was a major component in the development of photocomposition, which enabled the rapid development of modern offset printing.

11 | Computer-Driven Book Production

THE HALF CENTURY following the Second World War was a revolutionary era, for it encompassed the sixth and seventh punctuations of equilibria in the history of the book: the development and introduction of photocomposition, which made offset printing so economical that it replaced cast type; and the introduction of electronic books, to be discussed in the next chapter. Gutenberg's seminal concept—that the act of physical writing by humans could be mechanized, and that the mechanism could be used to make multiple copies of a book at a low cost—remains basic to modern printing technology, although the technologies Gutenberg had available more than five centuries ago were different in every regard from those of the late twentieth century. As has already been said, when new technologies furnish new solutions to problems, they rarely do so by mimicking earlier technology.

For the new technologies of printing during the last decades of the twentieth century the enabling force has been computerization. It was entirely responsible for the replacement of cast type in the production of offset printing, largely responsible for elimination of presses and inks in electrostatic printing, and totally responsible for the absence of presses, inks, and paper in electronic books. In addition, the ubiquitous personal computer, which has all the advantages of a typewriter, plus flexibility in composing, correcting, and formatting, has enabled authors to transmit text directly to publishers.

Early Offset Printing

Offset printing, a lithographic process, was the most important printing innovation to attain maturity in the twentieth century. The first of the planographic techniques used to print from a flat, smooth surface began as lithography, which was invented in the last decade of the eighteenth century and was used throughout the nineteenth almost entirely to print illustrations. The original stone printing surface began to be replaced by zinc metal plates about 1860, and by 1904 aluminum plates were also in use.

Offset printing has two major characteristics that sharply differentiate it from printing with cast type. One is that the material is printed from a perfectly smooth and very thin continuous sheet of metal plate, treated to increase its porosity and receptivity to water and overlaid with a thin layer of photosensitive material. Originally, for book printing, a negative film copy from a photocompositor was placed on a plate and exposed to an intense light that passed through the clear letters on the film, chemically hardening the image on the plate and making it receptive to greasy ink and repellent to water. The most recent type of photocompositor projects a low-power laser beam in the form of digitized characters directly onto a presensitized plate to produce the same result. In both cases, the plate is mounted on a plate cylinder and dampened with water; the greasy ink that is subsequently applied to the plate is absorbed by the characters and repelled by the dampened area.

The second characteristic that differentiates offset printing from relief printing is that the inked plate does not print directly onto paper, as in traditional relief printing from cast type. Instead, the plate, wrapped around a plate cylinder, prints an inverted image onto a rubber-blanketed cylinder, which in turn prints onto the paper passing next to it and pushed against it by a rubber impression cylinder (fig. 11.1). On blanket-to-blanket machines the impression cylinder is replaced by a second blanket cylinder onto which a second plate cylinder prints; the second blanket cylinder prints on the opposite side of the paper while pushing it against the first blanket cylinder (fig. 11.2). Offset sheet presses can produce up to 10,000 impressions an hour; roll-fed offset presses up to 20,000.

The first successful offset press was constructed in Britain in 1877 or soon thereafter and was based on two patents granted to Robert Barclay in 1875. It was designed for multicolor printing on tin from lithographic stone. The press closely resembled the flatbed cylinder press except that the traveling bed contained a stone bearing the image to be printed, rather than a chase of cast type, and the press had two cylinders instead of one: an offset cylinder, on which the image was printed as the bed passed under it, and an impression cylinder, mounted above the offset cylinder. The offset cylinder was blanketed with a rubber-coated canvas that made printing possible on the irregular surfaces of the sheets of tin that were passed between the two cylinders. Such offset presses were built for individual firms for tin printing until 1892, when George Mann and Co. of Leeds introduced its Improved Climax, which remained in production into the twentieth century and earned a bronze medal at a London exhibition in 1904. The Improved Climax sold for £300, with "£8 extra if adapted for paper-printing." It would be of considerable interest

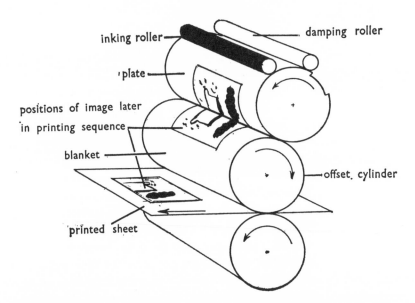

inking roller

damping roller

plate

positions of image later in printing sequence

blanket

offset cylinder

printed sheet

Figure 11.1. Diagrammatic representation of the three cylinders of an offset printing press.

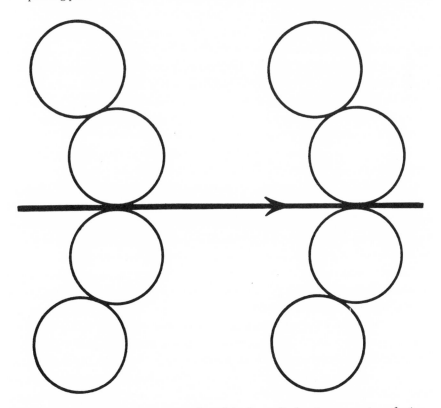

Figure 11.2. Diagrammatic representation of the four cylinders in a two-unit perfecting blanket-to-blanket offset printing press.

to know the extent, if any, to which the Improved Climax was used to print on paper. In 1903 George Mann & Co. patented a rotary offset tin printer, with a design, still in use, that won a "special silver medal" at its public introduction at the same exhibition.[1]

Ira W. Rubel, in the United States, Arthur Evans in Britain, and Caspar Hermann, in Germany, share the glory for having developed Senefelder's lithographic press into an offset press that has become the major printer of books. Stephen H. Horgan described Rubel's rediscovery of offset printing: "Ira W. Rubel, a [New] Jersey lithographer, missed an impression one day and it was printed on a rubber blanket. On the next impression the sheet was printed on both sides of the paper, from the stone as usual and offset from the rubber blanket on the back of the sheet. He found the offset impression was better on rough stock than could be had from the smooth stone, and so offset printing came into use and photolithography was revived."[2] Rubel had been using a litho press of essentially the same design as a stop-cylinder press, such as the Wharfedale (fig. 10.1); its main difference was a device for raising or lowering the bed on which the stone rested to bring the surface of the stone into correct printing position.

Rubel designed a new type of offset press with three cylinders of the same diameter arranged as shown in the stylized representation in figure 11.1 and arranged with the Potter Press Printing Company of New York to build the machine. Potter sold a machine in England in 1906 and eventually sold the machines all over the world. Rubel died in 1907 without having patented his design, so that other companies were free to manufacture them. In 1909 in Britain, Waite & Saville Ltd., one of the first manufacturers to mimic Rubel's design, began to build an offset press based on the Potter, or American, system of three equal cylinders.

In 1906, George Mann & Co. of Leeds introduced and patented a highly successful offset press designed by Arthur Evans. It embodied a two-revolution system, in which the paper-carrying impression cylinder made two revolutions for each turn of the blanket and plate cylinders. The latter cylinder bore two copies of the same plate, and the former cylinder two blankets from which impressions were made twice on the paper on the impression cylinder. The Mann Company sold more than two thousand of these presses in the next quarter century.

Caspar Hermann, a native of Königsberg, Germany, went to the United States in 1889 at the same age, eighteen years, as Ottmar Mergenthaler had done. As he worked in print shops in Richmond, Washington, and Baltimore, he began to develop an idea for an indirect or offset printing machine. His application for a patent was rejected in 1903, but he did succeed in rebuilding a small letterpress machine to convert it to an offset press. In 1905 he contracted with the Harris Automatic Press Co. to convert to an offset printing design one of the Harris automatic rotary book presses. In 1906 Harris sold its first offset press to the Republic Bank Note Company in Pittsburgh. Returning to Germany in 1907, Hermann began a successful collaboration with European printing press manufacturers. His initial accomplishment, in the year of his return, was the design of the "Trumpf," the first offset press produced in Germany. The manufacturer was G. G. Röder in Leipzig. In 1908 he patented the practical perfecting offset press for printing on both sides of the paper simultaneously. Hermann worked with the Frankenthaler Press Co., Albert & Cie, A G VOMAG, and George Mann & Co. in Leeds. In 1912 the VOMAG firm was the first to manufacture roll-fed offset presses; these machines could print up to 7,500 impressions an hour.[3]

An automatic sheet-paper feeder for presses had been invented in 1897 to replace the "feeder boys." It was an unpopular device, but when the "boys" went off to the First World War or to better paying wartime jobs, automatic feeders took their places. Otherwise there were no significant innovations during the war, but following the war German manufacturers renewed innovative activity by developing offset presses small and large. By the mid 1920s, large web-fed perfecting offset presses were printing German newspapers, and at least one such press had been exported to Australia. In 1929, at a major printing exhibition in London, nineteen exhibitors displayed offset machinery; of all the offset related exhibitors most were from Germany and other parts of Continental Europe. At that time the leading American printing journal was publishing nearly two thousand pages a year, of which three-fifths were devoted to advertising, but only two firms advertised offset presses, on average only once every three months.

The most important innovation in the 1930s was the introduction of a press design, widely used today, that came to be known as the "unit principle," in which each unit is a complete offset press minus a feeder and folder and has three cylinders of the same size, the so-called American or Potter system. Such units are arranged in tandem with two units providing for two-color printing; two unit presses can be converted to perfecting by activating an apparatus to tumble sheets between the two units. In 1933 the Webendorfer-Wills Co. introduced a web-fed, multicolor press that could operate with two to five units.

Subsequently the blanket-to-blanket unit principle perfecting press evolved, in which the impression cylinder was replaced by a second printing cylinder with a plate cylinder mounted below it. Both printing cylinders also act as impression cylinders. Originally blanket-to-blanket machines were either sheet or web fed, with the former having a double-size transfer cylinder mounted between the two units. As the end of the century approaches, blanket-to-blanket machines are web fed, with the paper passing directly from one unit to the next.

Early in the 1930s, American printers, faced with the loss of business induced by the Great Depression, began to trend toward offset printing as a way of reducing costs. Those with a wide variety of commercial jobs found that they could achieve "enormous saving in composition costs" by "merely photographing the copy as was," as one printer put it. Elimination of the expense of etching and blocking of illustrations, as described in the previous chapter, was another incentive. An area of advantage where offset was in a class by itself was in the printing of large color work beyond the physical limits of photoengraving plates. In general, copy for publications, including books, could be set on mechanized composition machines, proofed, transferred to thin zinc plates, and mounted on a cylinder ready to print, without the costly tasks of overlay patching with paper or underlay cutting away that had been necessary to obtain good impression from type and blocks. Offset printing sometimes consumed only a quarter of the time required by letterpress printing. The cost benefits of offset increased demand for offset presses and brought new manufacturers into prominence.

Photocomposition

During the two decades between the wars, several men patented and constructed photocomposition machines, but none was a success. It was not until three years after the Second World War that the first successful photocomposition machine was introduced. Then invention and development of photocomposition devices advanced through four decades, with output speeds going from keyboarding speed to close to 36 million characters an hour. Designs moved from mimics of the highly mechanical slug-casting and type-casting machines, namely the Intertype of 1913 and the Monotype of 1897, to designs having almost no mechanical motion. The first of the photocompositors was the Intertype Fotosetter, introduced in 1950, and the second was the British Monotype's Monophoto of 1954. The first high-speed device was the Photon machine, developed by two French engineers, which had a nominal projection speed of 70,000 characters an hour. "The first book printed by photocomposition using the Photon system" appeared in 1953.[4] The Photon's high speed was achieved by flashing a high-intensity beam of light through photographic matrices on the rim of a spinning disk. These early machines produced positive images of characters on sheet film that were later transferred to offset plates.

The popular Linotron, first installed in 1968, represented the next major design advance. Although the new design still used physical photographic characters, a computer converted them to digitized form as they were called for. The digitized image was projected by an electron beam and focused by a magnetic field onto a cathode-ray tube (CRT); a lens focused the CRT image onto film. The most recent development uses computer memories to store digitized characters, which are projected directly onto a sensitized offset plate, usually called a "direct-digital plate," by a low-power laser beam. Two widely used photocompositors of this design were first installed in 1983 and 1984. Their nominal speed is 36,000,000 characters an hour, which approaches the speeds of power-driven presses, leading some to speculate that computerized photocomposition machines may eventually replace printing presses altogether.

Modern Offset Printing

Beginning with the development of successful photocomposition machines immediately following the Second World War, and through the advent of computer-driven photocomposition in the 1970s, offset printing evolved so rapidly that it had become the preferred method of book printing by 1980. As Moran wrote in 1978, "The pace of change so quickened that it is easy to understand how the period 1900–1950 has now entered into technical history."[5] At the same time a reengineering of sheetfed presses had begun that continued throughout the 1980s. A major change was made by the introduction of the four-cylinder blanket-to-blanket design (fig. 11.2), which enabled offset presses to print simultaneously on both sides of the paper and in effect doubled their output. From 1970 to 1980 the proportion of commercial printing done by offset increased from 52 to 63 percent.[6]

Some realization of the suddenness of the shift from relief printing with cast type to offset printing with plates can be gained from the experience of the distinguished typographer Joseph Blumenthal in 1971, when he liquidated his Spiral Press, which he had started forty-five years earlier. Intending to sell his three presses, he telephoned dealers in secondhand machinery, only to be told that there was no market for letterpress equipment and that he should call a junk man and pay him to take the presses away. Fortunately he was able to give two of them to two other fine printers, and the third to a group of undergraduates at Yale University.[7]

Prior to the Second World War most offset printers prepared their own plates, but after the war a new industry for producing presensitized plates began to emerge, and before the century's end it had developed and marketed improvements to traditional plate technology and produced two major innovations: (1) plates for waterless offset printing; and (2) direct-digital plates onto which digitized characters are projected by a laser beam.[8] Manufacturers also provided both negative-working and positive-working plates. The first are exposed with negative film, producing a positive image on the plate that hardens the light-sensitive coating, while the coating in nonimage areas is chemically dissolved away. The chemistry of positive-working plates works in the opposite manner; the unexposed image areas are hardened and the exposed areas are dissolved and washed away.

Offset plates are analogous to cast type; plates replace type in the offset printing system. In Rubel's day, at the beginning of the twentieth century, lithographic plates were primarily aluminum and zinc; at the end of the century other metals, such as copper, chromium, and stainless steel, were added as the base or support metal of the plate. In addition, a plastic support base has come into use, particularly for job presses; images on the plastic plates are produced electrostatically in xerographic machines. Bimetal or trimetal plates are customarily used to support durable image surfaces. For runs of a million or more impressions, the surface metal, which is often copper because of its ability to accept ink, is either laminated or electroplated to the base metal beneath it.

Waterless negative-working plates have been available since 1978 and waterless positive-working plates since 1985. Japanese printers have widely accepted them and they seem to be gaining acceptance outside of Japan. Water being known to engineers as notoriously "tricky stuff," one might think that getting rid of it might be a sufficient benefit in itself, but the process has not been enthusiastically received in the United States. A waterless plate has five layers: from the bottom up, a layer of aluminum, a primer, a photographic layer, a silicone rubber layer, and a protective transparent film. The plate, either positive or negative, is exposed to ultraviolet light in a vacuum frame. With the more commonly used negative-working plate, ultraviolet light passing through the text characters weakens the bond between the silicone rubber and photopolymer layers in the image areas, allowing the protective film to be peeled off. The plate is desensitized with a solution that strengthens the bond between the rubber and polymer layers in the nonimage areas, and finally the rubber is brushed off the exposed characters, leaving them slightly recessed to retain ink.

Until the advent of offset lithography it had not been possible to print a lithographic illustration along with type. Only relief illustration, such as woodcuts, relief etchings, and halftones could be printed with cast type, to which lithographic and intaglio surfaces are not hospitable. Prints produced by a relief process had to be sewed into a book as a gathering of one or more folded sheets, or be tipped in separately by the bookbinder, which involved attaching the back edge of a print to the appropriate page with a quarter inch of glue. Offset printing enables photographic images to be projected onto sensitized plates along with text to produce black-and-white illustrations appropriately placed.

Before the development in the 1990s of computerized control of color and registration, preliminary copies were produced on proof presses, some on small, hand-inked presses, others on large presses designed to mimic the operation of the presses that would produce the final copy. Even with the latter it was almost impossible to duplicate the tints of the proof colors and to maintain them consistently during the print run. With computerized control the slogan is "What you see on the proof is what you will get from the press." Where formerly the press operator had to have additional operators to maintain color and registration for the entire production run, he could now sit at a remote console at the delivery end of the press and from that point adjust the ink keys that had been automatically set before the run, adjust the lateral and circumferential plate registration, and manipulate a variety of other variables to produce accurate images.

The first commercially successful, albeit not widely popular, color photographic process was marketed by the Lumiére brothers in 1907. The Kodak Kodachrome transparency of 1935 was the first color film to enjoy great success, and many designers still prefer it for four-color offset printing. The printing process involves making a separate printing plate, often on an electric color analyzer, for each color—magenta (red), yellow, cyan (blue), and black—to be run on four separate printing cylinders. Great design skill is required to assure accurate overlap registration, as the four cylinders operate at high speeds and employ inks that have no chance to dry completely as the paper speeds from one cylinder to the next.

Flexographic and Electrostatic Printing

C. A. Holweg of Alsace-Lorraine obtained a British patent in 1908 for analine printing, a new kind of relief printing directly from a flexible surface. Holweg described his invention as "a method of printing paper bags on a rotary printing press equipped with elastic blocks and using analine colours dissolved in alcohol."[9] As analine printing developed during the next forty years the "elastic blocks" became flexible rubber stereo plates wrapped around the printing cylinder, which could print all manner of packaging paper; paper for nonpackinging applications, such as forms, securities, and stationery; and nonpapers, such as cellophane, plastic curtains, and upholstery materials. These versatile presses were high-speed, perfecting, and web fed.

Analine printing offered so many advantages—low machine costs, speed of printing (particularly multicolor printing), rapid ink drying, and long runs—that it induced new developments for mass produced printing on paper and was renamed flexography by the printing industry in 1952. The most important development after midcentury was the replacement in many flexographic machines of rubber plates by metal wraparound plates, seven-thousandths of an inch thick, which are coated with a fifteen-thousandths of an inch of photopolymer. These plates are processed in the same manner as that described for waterless plates. In the mid-1990s flexographic presses printing from photopolymer plates predominate in letterpress printing, and are used mostly for mass-produced paperback books and newspapers.

Chester F. Carlson invented electrostatic printing when he made the first electrostatic, or xerographic, copy in 1938. He obtained the first patent in 1940. A score of companies rejected his request to develop the invention for the marketplace before the Battelle Memorial Institute agreed to the development. There was even resistance at Battelle, where, it is rumored, one of the engineers had asked, "What's wrong with carbon paper?" Nevertheless, Battelle was successful in fabricating a copier. The Haloid Company, later the Xerox Corporation, acquired the commercial rights to Carlson's invention in 1947, but it was not until the late 1950s that the first Xerox Copier reached the market. It was an unqualified success, and Carlson, who had gone to work when he was fourteen to support his invalid parents, became a millionaire before his death in 1968.

Electrostatic copying, or xerography, has been in widespread use since its introduction. Its principal advantage is its simplicity, for it transfers image to paper without physical contact, press, or ink. Adaptable to providing either single or multiple copies, one-sided or two-sided, it is particularly useful for reproducing a single copy of a book from a microfilm copy. Microfilming, the first process available to reproduce a single copy economically, was introduced in libraries in the 1930s to preserve books and newspapers printed on self-destructing papers and to reduce the amount of space required by the original. In the last decades of the century, following the appearance of electrostatic printing, the two processes have been combined to reproduce books and other documents on demand. This microfilm-electrostatic technique was probably the first successful on-demand printing.

Further advances were introduced when the Eastman Kodak Company and Xerox introduced electrostatic book-printing systems in 1990. Both produce printed books in small numbers economically, albeit employing somewhat different techniques to do so, and both can print merged files from various sources. One of the earliest users of the Kodak 1392 Printer, "the world's first mixed-data stream printer," was R. R. Donnelly & Sons, who employed it to produce two or three dozen copies of the first customized textbooks to be published by the Mc-Graw-Hill Book Company.[10] The 1392 printer, a component of the Kodak Lion-Heart system announced in 1990, made it possible to retrieve requested texts, or sections of text, from various databases, combine them with a course syllabus and other course documents, and electronically interfile the indexes for each section to produce a single index. In 1987 McGraw-Hill began to build a database of their digitized texts, and in 1989 announced the first publishing system for producing textbooks customized for specific courses of instruction.

A second book-production system, the Xerox DocuTech Production Publisher, comprises a digital document scanner, a 6135 DocuPrint printer[11] (DocuTech), and an automatic binding operation that produces a finished book or booklet. Xerox first announced DocuTech in 1990 and subsequently improved and enhanced it. The DocuTech accepts both hardcopy and digital books, pamphlets, and newsletters. The 6135 DocuPrint makes sheet copies, and online finishing converts the printed sheets into copies of books or brochures. The system has the capability to reduce the entrepreneurial publishing risk associated with many new books by initially printing copies in hundreds rather than thousands. The DocuTech can electronically scan original hardcopy to produce bit-mapped masters with a resolution of six hundred dots per inch, and the scanner can accept sheets, either singly or bound, as well as halftone illustrations and photographs. Once materials have been converted to digital masters they can be edited or electronically cut and pasted to combine pages of text and graphics retrieved from separate sources. Since the DocuTech puts out a hundred copies or fewer economically, it can solve many out-of-print problems for publishers.

Electrostatic printing, in addition to enabling the production of increasingly greater numbers of impressions per hour, also provides the capability to print ever fewer copies economically, a capability that has served me well, for I obtained on request two books, each in an edition of one copy only, to use in the preparation of *The Evolution of the Book*. It provides a further benefit to both publishers and users by opening up a market for small numbers of customized books, such as customized textbooks for a specific number of students in an academic course of instruction, a market that can be expanded to include other types of books and users and customized books compiled from more than one publishing source. Publishers can also reap an economic benefit in being able to make a conservative initial print order that can later be supplemented by additional orders of a few dozen copies, thereby saving on warehousing costs and reducing the wastefulness of shredding books that are no longer saleable.

Word Processing

In 2025 those information specialists who look back at the twentieth century to discern the origin of the mighty databases that provide them with all sorts of information will see computerized word processing systems as a significant component of that original source. Computerized word processors composed of programmed minicomputers driving several hardwired terminals, at first exclusively used by organizations, were widely available by the mid-1970s; their cost was in the vicinity of $15,000. Twenty years later word processor programs for personal computers were available for $400, and by the early 1990s more than a million copies of one of the most popular word processor programs for desktop and laptop computers had been sold.

In the 1990s electronics firms were manufacturing machines ranging from a portable "typewriter" weighing 4.5 pounds to a word processor weighing 11.5 pounds and advertised as "virtually a complete publishing system"; each is a computer with a program built into its circuitry and does not need software. The former provides a spelling checker/corrector, over three hundred characters in as many as twenty-one languages, and a printer "so quiet you could type in the library." The word processor possesses a batch of capabilities for manuscript preparation—a program for composing, editing, and formatting text, a spelling checker/corrector/thesaurus, several type fonts, a display screen, a disk drive, and a jet printer that prints up to 160 characters per second—to say nothing of other functions for other purposes. It is so totally different from the machine with which Mark Twain struggled that comparison is impossible.

Word processors and word processing software for personal computers have speeded manuscript preparation from author to publisher to printer. The publishers of one scholarly journal announced in its January 1995 issue that "Authors are strongly encouraged to deliver the final, accepted version of their manuscripts on diskette," but added that "manuscripts prepared on any microcomputer word processor are acceptable." It was but one of many such announcements, intended to spare the publisher the expense of digitizing paper copy. In submitting the final text of a manuscript on diskette the author has much more responsibility than formerly for every aspect of the printed version while enjoying more authority over it, for he or she not only "writes" the manuscript but also does the basic composition or typesetting. The publisher prepares the manuscript for the photocompositor by doing the final editing and inserting computer instructions for subsequent composition. The resultant machine-readable version of the manuscript then goes to a computer-driven photocomposition machine to produce the films from which offset plates are made, and the plates are mounted on an offset press for printing. Except for editing proof, the process is entirely mechanized. Either the printer or the publisher retains the offset plates for possible future reprinting. The publisher also keeps the final manuscript in a database for future electrostatic printing, electronic publishing, or some other application.

These computerized systems give publishers an advantage not previously available, by replacing what had been blocks of printed words, having almost no capability for variable use, with databases that make possible a variety of products, including electronic books, books on compact discs with read-only memories (CD-ROMs), customized textbooks in editions of only a few dozen copies, and on-demand books and text.

Book Publishing

In the last four decades of the twentieth century, publishing underwent transformations far greater than any since its establishment two centuries earlier. While some publishing houses grew by merger and acquisition, others were acquired as subsidiaries by huge conglomerates involved in activities other than publishing, an unprecedented change. Book sales and numbers of new titles rose continuously, mass marketing was introduced, book clubs expanded, and superstores emerged. Specialty publishers arose to supply particular categories of books, from romance novels to scientific and technical publications, and desktop publishing opened a novel avenue of communication between authors and readers.

The story of the Houghton, Mifflin Company of Boston exemplifies the development of the modern publishing house. In 1864 H. O. Houghton & Co., owner and operator of the Riverside Press, was practically forced into the publishing business by the cancellation of long-term printing contracts. Melancthon Hurd came forward with $50,000 of his own money and another $20,000 from his father; he became a partner, and the firm was renamed Hurd and Houghton. In 1878, when the company merged with James R. Osgood Co., Hurd departed. Houghton, Osgood & Co. was in turn dissolved two years later, at which juncture George H. Mifflin, who had been with the firm for a dozen years, came forward with money and became a partner. As Houghton Mifflin, the house prospered, weathering the national financial panics of 1893 and 1907 that drove other publishing houses into receivership. The first two-thirds of the twentieth century progressed smoothly for the firm, and as a result of growing revenue it went public in 1967. This event attracted the attention of conglomerates. A decade later Western Pacific Industries purchased enough Houghton Mifflin stock to push its holdings above 10 percent and generate an uproar from loyalists, who feared that Western Pacific would force Houghton Mifflin out of trade-books (adult fiction and nonfiction, juvenile books, and paperbacks) and into publishing textbooks only. To avoid another Boston Tea Party, Houghton Mifflin bought back its stock from Western Pacific, which received somewhat more than an estimated one-third return on its investment. At the same time, 1977–1980, Houghton Mifflin was indulging in buyouts of a half-dozen smaller houses, which became its subsidiaries. In a couple of decades it had become, like many others, a new type of publishing house.

These new houses contributed to the unprecedented increase in the production of new trade titles, which soared in the last four decades of the twentieth century, as shown in figure 11.3. After rising from 11,022 titles in 1950 to 15,012 in 1960, numbers of new titles began a rapid escalation, passing a 300 percent increase over the 1960 number before the end of the century. One factor that played a major role in this remarkable increase, which surpassed the increase during all of the century's earlier years, was the significant rise in demand for information that originated in the Second World War. In addition, offset printing empowered by computerized photocomposition enabled faster and less costly book production. (Nevertheless, the prices of books rose as the number of titles rose. From the average price of $8.29 in 1963–1965, the cost of books rose to an average price of $45.07 in 1988–1990, an increase of 546 percent.)[12]

The fundamental basis of the remarkable growth of book production, however,

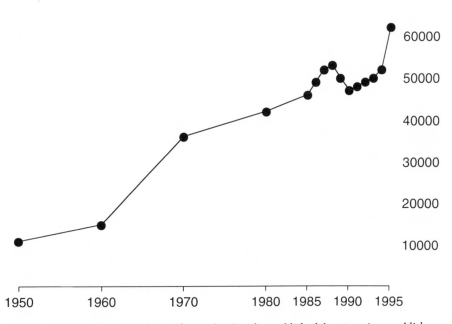

Figure 11.3. Growth in numbers of new book titles published by American publishers, 1950–1995. Source: *Bowkers Annual.*

was the astounding increase in the U.S. gross national product (GNP). In 1945, at the end of the war, the GNP was at $200 billion, and it increased by $100 billion for each of the next three five-year periods, reaching $500 billion in 1960. By 1965 it was at $700 billion and by 1970 had passed $1 trillion; in ten years it had doubled its entire previous growth and continued to maintain a high rate of growth. From 1960 to 1987 the publication of new titles increased at an average annual rate of 13.7 percent of the 1960 total. It is interesting to observe that the economic recession of the late 1980s and early 1990s, when the percentage increase in U.S. gross domestic product (GDP) declined in 1988 through 1991 and then went up in 1992 and 1993, mirrored the fall and rise of book production. After a meager increase of 2.4 percent from 1987 to 1988 the publication of new titles plummeted annually at 19.1 percent for 1989 and 1990. During the next four years it climbed back to the 1988 level.

During the Second World War publishers had gained experience in reprinting and distributing large numbers of books to the armed services, and after the war they began to develop mass-marketing techniques for paperbacks, as Penguin and Pocket Books had done before the war. Payments for paperback reprint rights rocketed skyward beginning with $35,000 for *The Naked and the Dead* in 1949. Four years later *From Here to Eternity* brought $100,000; in 1971, *The Drifters* brought $1 million. These mass-marketed reprints were distributed through such outlets as drugstores, supermarkets, newsstands, and book clubs, and later by mail order. A new type of reprint began to appear in 1953 under the imprint of Anchor Books, a subsidiary of Doubleday. Anchor's "quality" reprints were distributed through bookstores, where they did not have competition from the mass-market publications. There can be no doubt that mass marketing drove the conversion of publishing into an industry.

The explosion could not have occurred if book publishers had not had available the long-existing distribution system for magazines. For example, when Pocket Books started operation in 1939 it engaged the American News Company to distribute its books. Not long after that it began to operate its own distribution system, engaging local distributors, and it soon had contracts with some six hundred local independents.[13] Other paperback publishers followed the Pocket Books example or contracted with one of the half-dozen large distributing companies.

The number of mass-market titles published each year continued to increase slowly compared with trade titles until the 1980s. Just why this flattening—or the two-year, 29 percent decline following 1992—should have occurred is not clear, but it is likely that multiple factors played a role. For example, demand for reprints may have become satiated, or the distribution channels burdened, or, in the opinion of publishers, useful works for reprinting may have been approaching exhaustion or excessive expense.

The trebling of book production in the United States was amazing, but the upsurge in Europe was even greater. From 1970 to 1988 the annual rates of output of new titles in six Western European countries increased from 1.14 percent in the Netherlands to 3.93 percent in the United Kingdom; the average annual increase for the six countries was 3.17 percent. During the same period the average annual increase for the United States was 2.07 percent. Over the nineteen years the six Western European countries produced one-fifth more titles than the United States.[14]

The annual percentage increases and decreases in numbers of new titles in thirteen subject fields published in the United States from 1970 to 1988 are recorded for every other year in a table in *University Libraries and Scholarly Communication*. The table contains two major categories: Arts and Sciences, with seven fields, and Professional/Applied, with six. The annual decrease in the new Arts and Sciences titles went from an average of 77.2 percent for the first three biennial years to an average of 70.4 percent for the last three biennial years. The field in the first category that declined the most was Literature/Poetry/Drama, in which new titles ranked from 15.0 to 9.1 percent. The annual increase in the Professional/Applied category went from an average of 22.8 percent for the first three biennial years to an average of 29.6 percent for the last three biennial years. The field in the second category that gained the most was Medicine, with an annual increase in new titles rising from 6.6 percent to 9.8 percent. In Technology, in the second category, the annual increase also grew, from 4.9 percent to 7.2 percent, but in Science, in the first category, it remained nearly stable, with only a slight drop from 9.5 percent to 9.3 percent.[15]

Although I first heard the term "STM"—in reference to a group of publishers specializing in science, technology, and medicine—in Europe in the early 1980s, there had been specialty publishers in these fields long before the Second World War. As an example, three well-known medical-book publishers in the United States, C. V. Mosby Co., W. B. Saunders, and Williams and Wilkins, published their first books before the First World War. As the end of the twentieth century approaches, there are more than two hundred medical publishing houses in the United States alone. As pointed out above, medicine and technology titles increased by nearly half in the 1970s and 1980s, whereas the number of science titles did not. As early as 1965 Curtis Benjamin, then president and chairman of the management board of the McGraw-Hill Book Company, foresaw the stabilization and the probable decline in the publishing of scientific books, which he likened to the "twigs" on a tree in which "the trunk" is "represented in technical literature by basic textbooks and handbooks" and "main limbs and secondary boughs [are] represented by intermediate textbooks and general treatises. . . ."[16] While the number of "twig" books increases as science grows the unit cost of production rises, and scientific monographs encounter increasing market resistance.

University presses, another kind of specialty publishing, came into being largely in the twentieth century as far as the United States is concerned, although they had long existed in Europe. Both the Cambridge and Oxford University

Presses began operations in the sixteenth century; the Johns Hopkins University Press, the oldest university press in the United States, wasn't established until two centuries later, in 1878. When the Association of American University Presses (AAUP) was founded in 1937 it had a score of founding members, and its membership has been increasing since 1960; in 1995 it claimed 114 members, who published some four thousand titles. American university presses are not-for-profit entities that publish scholarly monographs, which are not unlike Curtis Benjamin's "twig" monographs in that they have small markets and are costly to print. However, their not-for-profit status enables university presses to price their products lower than a commercial publisher could afford to do. In Benjamin's analogy, they are "twig" specialists.

In contrast, other specialty publishers, and existing publishers who have developed specialties in specific types of book for specified readers, have enjoyed financial success. Avon Books, a leader in publishing romance novels for women readers, began its success story with the publication of *The Flame and the Flower* in 1972. As Janice Radway tells the story of its publication, the executive editor at Avon, looking for something to get her through a long weekend, "picked up an unsolicited manuscript and couldn't put it down." It was published as an Avon Spectacular, as indeed it became; five years later it had sold more than two and a half million copies. In 1974 Avon published two more successful romances, and publishers began to realize that a new genre had been created.[17]

Following the advent of desktop publishing in the early 1980s, small presses that publish perhaps as few as two books each year rapidly swelled the ranks of publishers. In 1990, four thousand new publishers registered for International Standard Book Numbers (ISBNs); in 1995 more than ten thousand new publishers registered. The desktop publishing systems can format text and graphics into pages that can be stored in the desktop computer for later transmission to an electronic printer, a computer-driven photocompositor, or, following 1990, the Kodak LionHeart system or a Xerox DocuTech printer. These new technologies have opened to many authors a new field of publishing previously available only to those who could afford expensive so-called vanity publishing. A few of the books from small presses have even been bought up by conglomerates.

The small presses have faced the same distribution and selling problem that Gutenberg had not been able to resolve. Only a very few of the small presses have resolved the problem on their own, but a dozen or more distribution and wholesale houses have come to the rescue. Other assistance has come from mostly not-for-profit trade associations. These organizations inform their members, which number in the thousands, by newsletters, seminars, and, most recently, by such channels as Internet bulletin boards and home pages.

The establishment of new newspapers began to decline in the 1890s after having been 14,070 new titles in the decade of the 1880s. They continued to decline until the 1950s when there were only 3,728 new titles. The numbers of new titles rose in the next two decades, only to sink again in the 1980s. Why the rate of inception of new newspapers should have dropped by 15 percent from the previous decade in the 1980s is neither obvious nor intelligible, particularly in light of extraordinary increases in U.S. book titles.

A phenomenon of the twentieth century occurring after the Second World War and almost entirely in the United States was the conglomerate merger, which had as its principal characteristic the acquisition of businesses whose activities were not related to those of the acquirer. Three of the largest conglomerates—Gulf and Western Industries, International Telephone and Telegraph Corporation (ITT), and Litton Industries—acquired publishing houses. In 1966 ITT purchased Howard W. Sams & Co., a textbook and technical-book publisher, which had itself bought the century-old Bobbs-Merrill trade-book publisher in 1959. Gulf and Western acquired Simon and Schuster along with its subsidiary, Pocket Books, in 1975. Litton Educational Publishing was organized in 1977 by Litton Industries from its acquisitions of the American Book Company, an educational house; Delmar Publishers, which published vocational books; and the Van Nostrand Reinhold Company, a publisher of scientific books. Four years later, in 1981, Litton Educational Publishing was sold to Thomson Organization in Canada. RCA Corporation purchased Random House in 1965 and in 1980 sold it to Newhouse, a newspaper company. In 1981 the Hearst Corporation purchased William Morrow and Company together with its subsidiaries, whose names, as John Tebbel put it, "read in part like a roll call of vanished independents."[18] Near the end of the century, however, there are still many independent traditional publishers as well as more than fifty independent electronic-book publishers.

Bookstore Chains, Book Clubs, and Libraries

The advent in the 1980s of chains of so-called superstores was the most spectacular occurrence in the bookstore industry in the last two centuries. In the United Kingdom, by 1991 the chains had attained a portion of the book market that enabled them to obtain increasingly beneficial relationships from publishers; by 1995 they provided the major increase in bookselling in that country. In the United States, for the four fiscal years ending January 31, 1993–January 31, 1996 the proportion of retail bookstore sales that occurred in superstores had risen from 30 to 44 percent, and in the next couple of years superstores would capture more than half of bookstore sales. The average annual sales increase for superstores was 4.67 percent, as compared with an overall book sales increase of only 2.0 percent. It is obvious that the ratio of sales of superstore chains to sales of independents has not stabilized, but presumably it will sometime in the foreseeable future.

The principal characteristic that sets a superstore apart from an independent bookstore is the size of its book collection. A superstore that I visited in the early 1990s had a huge collection ranging from the Loeb Classics to the most newly published books. It also had easy chairs in which people were reading, tables where students and others were writing, and the extra attraction of a cafe purveying coffee, tea, and sweets, somewhat like an inverted coffee shop of eighteenth-century London, which provided newspapers for patrons to read while sipping.

By the mid 1990s, Bertelsmann, the German book-club giant, had thirty-five million members worldwide, and Britain's Book Club Associates had two million members. Of the 150 book clubs for adult readers in the United States, the Book-of-the-Month Club, with a membership of one million, was perhaps the largest. Book clubs suffered a decline in sales of about 20 percent during most of the 1980s and early 1990s. As an example, United Kingdom book-club sales in 1991 dropped one-third below sales in the mid-1980s. Beginning in 1992, however, book-club sales began to rise, with some clubs enjoying an annual increase of 10 percent or more.

Libraries are a third significant market for publications, but with rising prices of books and journals university libraries were forced to nearly double their expenditures from 1972 to 1990 in order to add to their collections slightly declining gross numbers of volumes. An Andrew W. Mellon Foundation publication presents findings that depict this divergence.[19] The rate of increase of expenditures for books and journals began to soar above the rate of acquisition beginning in the late 1960s. Indeed, from 1972 to 1991, the number of volumes acquired yearly by university libraries remained flat and may even have declined slightly, whereas expenditures in constant dollars increased by nearly 75 percent. A somewhat similar relationship exists in a sample of the nearly fourteen hundred U.S. public libraries serving populations in excess of twenty-five thousand. With 1990 figures for adult circulation and material expenditures normalized at 100, circulation rose 20.7 percent from 1986 to 1995, while material expenditures rose 65 percent.[20] Whatever the causes of the disparity between the rates of expenditure and acquisition, it is clear that the library market for publications may not increase much in the immediate future in terms of numbers of volumes acquired, but will certainly increase in terms of expenditure.

Summary

The last quarter of the twentieth century witnessed the start of the sixth punctuation of equilibria in book production. Except for the Gutenberg decade never was there so much effective innovation in so brief a time. Flexography, which had come into being earlier in the century, flourished as a printing system; and litho-offset, after the development of successful photocompositors, became the preferred book production system. The Kodak LionHeart System and the Xerox DocuTech machine were two electrostatic printing innovations of the last quarter of the century. A third innovation was the electronic book, the subject of the next and final chapter.

12 | *The Electronic Book*

THE ELECTRONIC BOOK production system, although it also came into being in the last quarter of the twentieth century, has nothing in common with the three late-century printing systems, offset printing, flexography, and electrostatic printing, discussed in the previous chapter. It uses neither ink, paper, nor press, and it does not permanently print on anything; the format of the electronic book in no way resembles that of the convenient codex that has been traditional for nearly the last two thousand years, and it has met with unenthusiastic reception, chiefly because it presents a radical physical change for the user: from the familiar bound book in the hand to the monitor screen of a desktop computer or the flat-panel display of a laptop machine. The present situation with respect to electronic books is analogous to that of most late-nineteenth-century automobiles, which for nearly a decade after Karl Benz's successful 1885 motorized tricycle were "horseless carriages," until the French firm of Panhard and Lavassor built a machine having a design that has lasted more than a century: an engine in front under a hood instead of over the rear axle, a slanted post with steering wheel in place of a vertical post with tiller, and floor pedals rather than hand levers. The electronic book of the latter 1990s might be described as still being in the "horseless-carriage" stage.

Like the clay tablet and the papyrus-roll book, the electronic book employs a technology that was brought into being primarily to resolve problems of record keeping by administration and commerce. The first computer (1945) was built for the U.S. Army and the second (1949) by Cambridge University. Sales of early computers were a BINAC to the Northrup Aircraft Company and an ERA 1101 to the Georgia Institute of Technology, both in 1950; a Ferranti Mark I to Manchester

University and a UNIVAC I to the U.S. Bureau of the Census in 1951; and three ERA 1102s to the U.S. Air Force in 1952. In April 1953, IBM announced its 701 Calculator, and later that year J. Lyons and Company, a British catering firm, announced full business data processing services, such as accountancy and inventory control, by its LEO computer. Once again, the needs of business and government fostered a basic technology for book production.

Although books in electronic form have been with us for a quarter century, one can hardly say that there is yet an electronic-book industry. The reason is clear. In their present form electronic books have no appeal whatsoever for the vast majority of book users and readers, and they will not be widely accepted until at least two major innovations have appeared: first, an electronic reading device that must be even easier to use than the printed book; and second, an easy-to-use system, containing large and continuously updated databases, both remote and local, that will supply information whenever and wherever users may need it and from which they may withdraw items either for retention or onetime use. The databases must include digitized books, journals, reports, brochures, dramatic presentations, musical scores, concerts, audio and video material, and other forms of information not yet thought of. The overall system should also be hospitable to future functions.

The unacceptability of the present electronic book is often expressed in what has come to be known as the "can't curl up in bed with it" syndrome, closely followed by the "can't read it at the beach" complaint. Both protests are valid, but it may be supposed that advances in technology and design will soon overcome these insufficiencies as they have overcome others in the history of the book. After all, second- and third-century codices, many a foot or more tall, hardly constituted bedfellows, any more than did the seventeen-inch-tall 42-line Gutenberg Bible, or the taller-than-a-foot folios that followed in 1457, 1459, 1460, and 1462.

Electronic Book System

To be acceptable, the future electronic-book device should possess at least six specifications: (1) its legibility should be better than that of the most legible books; (2) its display should accommodate at minimum the five hundred words printed on an average six-by-nine-inch book page; (3) its size and weight should both be less than those of an average novel; (4) it should be possible to hold, manipulate, and read with one hand; (5) its one-time cost should be less than the average price of a novel; and (6) it should be able to access text in any one of millions of databases anywhere and at any time. Wireless telephony in the form of personal communications networks might make the last specification possible, but there will also need to be further technological changes in the entire system for producing, disseminating, and storing electronic information. All of the foregoing specifications must be met before the electronic book will become widely acceptable.

At the time of this writing, in the last decade of the twentieth century, there are a significant number of electronic-book publishers in existence. Although they are not threats to the current publishing community, they cause unease among traditional publishers. Electronic books will not be serious competitors of printed books, however, until a new publishing and distribution system has been established and electronic books have become far more attractive to the general community of book readers and users, which is not thirsting for a book that at present is decidedly less easy to read than a printed one.

The word "system" has acquired so many meanings (there are binary, mountain, railway, and solar systems, for example) that it has become a coat to fit any wearer. As used in this discussion "system" describes an ongoing process that produces some wanted operation and is thought of as a whole rather than as an assemblage of pieces and procedures. An electronic-book system might have as its purpose to promote the availability of information and knowledge to individuals, and one of the several goals to attain that purpose might be to make it possible for anyone to have access to a personalized database unit in the system.

A simplified electronic-book system, if it were to mimic the present flow of books from authors to users, would operate somewhat as follows: authors would submit manuscripts in electronic form to publishers, who would edit and "print" them, and then sell the electronic "books" to book clubs, bookstores, and libraries, which would distribute, sell, or lend, copies to individual users. All routes would end with the user, without whom there would be no justification for any of the system; hence, a system designer or analyst must start with the user, which should not be news to anyone engaged in the selling or lending of books. The primary goal of an electronic-book system should be to enable users to assemble personal libraries for their own purposes from material stored in remote databases, or on their own reading devices, or from compact discs.

Development of the Electronic Book

The advent of the computerized electronic book began in laboratories in the 1960s, with images on CRT screens replacing printed images on paper bound into codex form and computer power making it possible to enhance text with active images and audio projection in a manner hitherto impossible. Computerization also enabled the birth of hypertext, an intellectually revolutionary type of nonsequential literature, to be described in a following section.

In 1971 Project Gutenberg began converting to electronic form classic texts that had passed out of copyright; these were the earliest electronic books generally available. A quarter century later some 250 titles had been transcribed, entirely by volunteers, and made available on the Internet. A few examples of Project Gutenberg titles are *The Oedipus Trilogy*, the *Rubaiyat of Omar Khayyam*, *The Complete Works of William Shakespeare*, *The Federalist Papers*, *Treasure Island*, and *Tess of the d'Urbervilles*. A similar conversion activity is being conducted by Project Bartleby at Columbia University, which describes itself as "the public library of the Internet." Some traditional publishers have formed partnerships with software houses to convert their already printed books to digital form.

Portability of electronic books was becoming a feature in the mid-1980s with the appearance of display screens on handheld devices containing computerized spelling checkers, dictionaries, and thesauruses; by the early 1990s some of these little machines also contained encyclopedias. Their major disadvantage was that they lacked the capacity to display multiple works. However, in 1991 Sony introduced in the United States the Electronic Book Player, a palm-held device, measuring $4\frac{1}{2}$ by $\frac{11}{16}$ by $6\frac{3}{8}$ inches and weighing less than two pounds, that displays the contents of an 8-centimeter (approximately $3\frac{3}{8}$-inch) CD-ROM disc having a capacity of "100,000 pages of printed text." At the time of its introduction there were a dozen or so discs available, among them a disc containing the twenty-six-volume *Compton's Concise Encyclopedia* and another containing *The American Heritage Electronic Dictionary* together with *Roget's Electronic Thesaurus*. Reference works like these were the first popular electronic books. The Sony device, the first of its kind, is a true incunable and, like the incunables of the mid–fifteenth century not easy to use, but with it one can search for information in several ways: for a topic by word, for broad topics listed in a menu, for an article by the keywords in a title, or by using hypertext links, which are "see" references.

In 1991 the Apple Computer Company introduced a personal computer entitled PowerBook, which had a larger and more readable screen than that of Sony's Electronic Book Player; it was free of flicker and had a contrast ratio (the range between the blacks and whites in an image) of 95:1 approaching that for print on white paper. Early the next year the Voyager Company began publishing a series of multimedia works on CD-ROMs (Compact Disc-Read Only Memory) to display on the PowerBook, which the company referred to as "expanded books," because they provided sound and motion. As the *Economist* put it: "In Michael Crichton's 'Jurassic Park,' for instance, you can gawk at the picture of a cuddly tyrannosaurus while it briefly roars at you from the screen."[1]

The best known of compact discs is the CD-ROM, an enhancement of the original CDs introduced in 1982 by co-inventors Sony Corporation and Philips Electronics. Since that date 6 billion 12 cm CD-ROM discs have been sold, and more than 400 million CD-ROM players. Beginning in the early 1990s, the number of players installed in the United States each year was more than 100 percent higher than the number installed the previous year; for example, the 6.5 million installed in 1993 was nearly 170 percent more than the 2.4 million installed in 1992.

Research and development has led to new disc products named DVD-ROMs (Digital Versatile Disc-Read Only Memory), that were expected in mid-1996 to be first introduced in 1997, whose capacity is fourteen times that of CD-ROMs. DVD players can also read existing CD-ROMs. Continuing research will produce within a few years DVD-RAMs (Random Access Memory) whose memories will greatly facilitate retrieval of books and journal articles. Anticipated further research may lead to DVD derivatives that might have the capacity to house "a small library on a single disc."[2]

In the production of CD-ROMs the analog of the press in paper printing is a disc duplicator, a computer-driven device. The copying process is essentially the same as in a personal computer, but the large commercial disc duplicators have quality control capabilities smaller machines lack. In the mid 1990s there were nearly two dozen major commercial firms duplicating discs not just for publishers but also for various types of organizations selling or providing online and other computer services. By 1993, there were so many publishers of electronic works that the Frankfurt Book Fair devoted one of its large halls to some 170 publishers of electronic books, journals, and multimedia. The *Economist* reported, "With its display of colourful technical gadgetry that moved, spoke and sang, the electronic publishing hall looked more like a slot-machine arcade than a show-case for what some see as the greatest revolution in publishing since Gutenberg."[3] In June of the following year, the American Booksellers Association for the first time devoted a section of its exhibit hall to electronic publishing.

Ulrich's International Periodicals Directory began to list electronic journals in its 1986–1987 edition, with 1,200 titles being recorded. Nine years later there were 5,517 listed, a 360 percent increase; however, that figure was a mere 3.3 percent of the nearly 165,000 serials listed in *Ulrich's*. A significant portion of electronic journals have been produced in the so-called bit-mapped form rather than in ASCII, the American Standard Code for Information Interchange, apparently because some journal publishers were hoping to thwart piracy. Unfortunately, bit mapping also thwarts computer searching of text to obtain content information. As one of the major expectations for the near future is the development of retrieval of content information from both books and journals, texts for the latter will also have to be in ASCII.

Table 12.1 succinctly summarizes the three sets of technologies employed for the mechanical reproduction of copies of books in the last five and one-half centuries. Interestingly, the table reveals that of the six related processes of Gutenberg and offset technologies only one, binding, is the same in both, whereas of the five related major processes of offset and electronic book technologies four are the same, with only one pair, "presses," having unlike components, in that one produces printed and bound codices and the other CD-ROMs. To anyone aware that computer technology is the fundamental component of both offset and electronic book technology, the similarity of their related components is not surprising.

Hypertext

The most remarkable species of book to punctuate the equilibrium of the twentieth century was the entirely new literary form of hypertext. Vannevar Bush, director of the United States Office of Scientific Research and Development during

Table 12.1. Multi-copy printing technologies and products, 1450–2000

Gutenberg	Offset	Electronic Book
character matrices	digitized characters	digitized characters
type casting	keyboarding	keyboarding
type case	computer memory	computer memory
typesetting	keyboarding	keyboarding
hand press	offset press	disc duplicator
binding	binding	
bound codex	bound codex	CD-ROM

the Second World War and former professor at the Massachusetts Institute of Technology, is generally credited with heralding hypertext. In his much-cited article "As We May Think," which appeared in July 1945 in *The Atlantic Monthly*, Bush proposed a machine, which he called Memex, that has been described as "An aid to memory. Like the brain, Memex would file material by association. Press a key and it would run through a 'trail' of facts," to which one could add one's own observations. Bush described the operation of Memex: "when numerous items have thus been joined together to form a trail, they can be reviewed in turn, rapidly or slowly, by deflecting a lever like that used for turning the pages of a book. It is exactly as though the physical items had been gathered together from widely separated sources and bound together to form a book." Statements like this one suggested a new kind of literature.[4]

One person motivated by Bush's article was Douglas C. Engelbart at Stanford University, who wrote to Bush on May 24, 1962, requesting permission to quote lengthy passages. Engelbart told Bush that "this article of yours has probably influenced me quite basically. I remember finding it and avidly reading it in a Red Cross library on the edge of the jungle on Leyte . . . in the Fall of 1945." Engelbart also wrote that he was working toward "launching a serious research program on 'human intellectual effectiveness,'" and in 1991 he could report that "the possibilities we are pursuing involve an integrated man-machine working relationship, where close, continuous interaction with a computer avails the human of radically changed information-handling and portrayal skills, and where clever utilization of these skills provides radical changes in the way the human attacks problems."[5]

One of the "radical changes" to come from the work of Bush and Engelbart was apparent in the early 1960s: nonsequential, linked writing produced and read only on a computer, for which Theodore H. Nelson coined the term "hypertext" in 1965. Hypertext comprises blocks of text interconnected by electronic links that give the reader freedom to construct his own pathway through the assemblage of blocks. It "blurs the boundaries between reader and writer,"[6] the reader becoming a reader-producer in contradistinction to being only a passive consumer of the product of print technology.

Brown University has been home for a group doing research and development on hypertext writing and reading, and their use in university instruction. In 1985 three members of the group described approximately two decades of activity and accomplishment in a journal article on Brown's File Retrieval and Editing System (FRESS), a text-only hypertext document system developed in the late 1960s that had both one-directional and bidirectional links. FRESS attracted considerable interest and was in operation for more than a decade, but beginning in 1982 it began to be superseded by Brown's Electronic Document System, a hypermedia system of communication that incorporated text, animation, and high-resolution color.[7]

Commercial publishers of hypertext books did not start operation until the latter half of the 1980s. For example, Eastgate Systems, which boasts of having "the largest catalog of top-notch hypertexts available anywhere," marketed its first title in 1988. Five years later creative writers had produced enough hypertext fiction, readable only on a computer, for the *New York Times Book Review* (August 29, 1993) to devote a half-dozen pages to description and reviews by Robert Coover. The description on page 8 reads, "Hypertext, in effect, introduces 'purpose' or 'design' into the scatter of electronic writing, and its principal tool for doing this is its linking mechanism: in place of print's linear, page-turning route, it offers a network of alternate paths through a set of text spaces by way of designated links." As Coover subsequently put it, "Reading through a hypertext, one senses that just under the surface of the text on the screen is a vast reservoir of story waiting to be found." Coover listed seven publishers of hypertext fiction, perhaps all of which were publishing hypertext nonfiction as well. At this writing anyone wanting to read hypertext books on a screen must buy them in the form of 8-centimeter discs or have access to one of the several universities establishing collections of them.

Multimedia and Hypermedia

Multimedia technology combines and displays several media at once, such as text, synthesized voice, sound, music, video, animation, and graphics. Hypermedia, like hypertext, has bidirectional links, but the links are for full-motion video, images, graphics, and sounds in addition to text. In the mid-1980s a third Brown University system, the Intermedia Project, explored and developed linkage among text, two-dimensional graphics (such as photographs and paintings), and three-dimensional models. Students watching a musical score on a screen while the music is being rendered by an orchestra, is one example of hypermedia use in education. Another type of example of a teaching tool is the Perseus Project at Harvard University, that provides digitized Greek texts, translations, topographical drawings, and photographic images of archaeological objects. A user finding in a text mention of a theater in which he is interested can click on the name of the theater to obtain a floor plan; placing the arrow control so that it points to the stage and clicking again will yield a photographic display of it. Links within Perseus are bidirectional, so that the user can readily return to the text.

Like printed books, some multimedia presentations are designed for different levels of viewers and listeners, including both young learners and advanced students. A viewer wishing to hear words displayed on a screen can click on the icon preceding the first word to bring forth a voice reading the sentence. If the viewer then wishes to go to the next two pages, clicking on the turned-up, lower right-hand corner will display them. An example of secondary instruction is "A hyper-media biology package [that] will let a student or teacher select by kingdom, class, phylum, species, or common name from over 50,000 slides stored on a videodisc. The user can save a list of slides selected in a computer file, then use the file to re-call and project the images to accompany a lesson or a report at a later date."[8]

Publication of multimedia titles appears to involve many or all of the following three enterprises: (1) publishing houses of all types; (2) software houses; and (3) television and movie studios. There are already some contractual arrangements between publishing and software houses. Sales channels vary according to whether the publisher's customary product is books, videos, music, or software; interestingly, software stores appear to have been the first to stock multimedia, preceding the book and video stores. In a 1994 special supplement, *Publishers Weekly* listed eighty publishers and producers of multimedia, of which a quarter were software houses and twenty-one were wholesalers and distributors; altogether they published and distributed nearly four thousand titles. These firms are in the process of building a new industry.

Anticipation

Untold millennia of unrecorded oral presentations preceded the appearance, about 2500 B.C., of the clay literary works described in chapter 2, the first punctuation of equilibria in the history of the book. Five hundred years later the advent of the papyrus-roll book produced the second punctuation. Clay tablets and papyrus-roll books co-existed for two thousand years, much as two biological species may live together in the same environment. The codex book, however, coming into being in the second century A.D. as the third punctuation, rapidly became the dominant form of the book, the status that it still enjoys today. Moreover, the codex proved hospitable to the three further punctuations in the equilibria of book production: (1) the Gutenberg mechanization of copying books in the fifteenth century; (2) the introduction of nonhuman sources of power to cast type, drive presses, and manufacture paper in the early nineteenth century; and (3) the replacement of printing from cast type with computer-driven composition and offset printing early in the last third of the twentieth century. The seventh and most recent punctuation, in the form of the electronic book, also began in the last third of the twentieth century, and it may be presumed that books on paper and books on electronic screens, will, like clay tablets and papyrus books, coexist for some time, but for decades rather than centuries.

Meanwhile, the printed book continues to flourish. Preliminary figures for new book titles produced in 1995 suggest not only that there will be an increase over the 1994 total, but also that it may be in the vicinity of the 9.1 percent average annual increase experienced from 1960 to 1987. The rate of rise from 1993 to 1994 was very similar to that from 1985 to 1987, apparently because publishing recovered from the 1988–1992 recession. If recessions were the only factor causing decline, one might look forward to an average annual rate of 9 percent until the next decline in the economy. However, there are a variety of other factors to consider, one of which is the size of the population segment per title. From 1960 to 1987 U.S. population per new title declined from 1,195 to 468; in 1994 the figure was 505, which is dramatically lower than that for 1900—11,989 per new title.

As this book winds down, we are in the punctuation of a century and a half of power-press, cast-type equilibrium, in which the so-called traditional printing of the last twenty years will continue to evolve in the direction of digital books. It should be pointed out that the great majority of printed books are already digitized, in that photocompositors require digital format to produce offset plates for printing. Kodak's LionHeart and Xerox's DocuTech, discussed in the previous chapter, have already undergone improvement and enhancement and will continue to benefit publishers by making short-run printings increasingly economical, particularly of the journals whose subscribers are mostly institutions. The probable advent of direct-digital printing by high-speed photocompositors will also significantly reduce printing costs to publishers.

The new technologies of the last quarter century were initiated largely by the introduction in 1971 of the powerful microprocessors that do all the computing in modern computers and are the sources of most of the advances in computer capabilities. Interestingly enough, it is the print lithography process of the last century and a half that produces the tiny integrated circuits of microprocessor chips. Other technologies that will almost certainly play a new role in the production of various types of books are direct-digital printing, increased diversity in microchips, intelligent software, blue laser CD-ROM technology, electronic book readers, and the wireless networks that already service cellular telephones. In 1995, market analysts were projecting that three-quarters of the households in the United States will be subscribers to wireless service by 2001; the worldwide projection was that nearly half a billion people would be subscribers. Wireless networks will make it possible for electronic book readers to access databases of electronic books, as well as other types of information databases, from almost anywhere in the United States at almost any time. The new blue-laser CD-ROM technology is still in development; it will greatly increase the amount of information provided. Miniaturization of DVD pits and of track separation, the shorter wavelength of the DVD blue laser as compared with the red laser of CDs, together with innovative disc structure, has yielded a DVD capacity fourteen times greater than that of CDs.

Several software development projects are proceeding in the direction of enabling an individual to assemble virtual libraries for specific purposes. As an example, a scholarly user might consult a specific library for a university research project, and also consult a personalized database to retrieve information that would help him decide whether to accept a position in a for-profit corporation with which he is unfamiliar, located in an area of the country with which he is equally unacquainted. Three software projects, while not specifically related to retrieval of content information from electronic publications, will play a significant role in the easy assembly of such personalized, temporary, virtual libraries in only a few hours that formerly would require weeks to bring together. The three software projects are artificial intelligence, which apparently is becoming productive after forty years of development; genetic programming, whose disciples held their first conference in 1996; and intelligent software, also a recent field of investigation.

It is not possible to anticipate the demise of the printed book in terms of dates, but one can anticipate that the acceptance of the yet to be introduced successful electronic book will bring it to an end. We are not able to trace the events that marked the change from papyrus roll book to codex, but we do know that the former survived for four centuries after the advent of the latter. It may take less than four decades for electronic publications to share equal popularity with printed books.

Notes

Chapter 1: Dynamics of the Book

1. Niles Eldredge and Stephen Jay Gould, "Punctuated Equilibria: An Alternative to Phyletic Gradualism," in *Models in Paleobotany*, ed. T. J. M. Schopf (San Francisco: Freeman Cooper,1972), 82–115. Reprinted in Niles Eldredge, *Time Frames* (New York: Simon and Schuster, 1985), 193–223.

2. Ibid., 106.

3. Kurt Weitzman, *Illustrations in Roll and Codex* (Princeton, N.J.: Princeton University Press, 1970), 69.

4. Fritz Machlup, *The Production and Distribution of Knowledge in the United States* (Princeton, N.J.: Princeton University Press, 1962).

Chapter 2: Incunables on Clay

1. James H. Breasted, *Ancient Times: A History of the Ancient World* (Boston: Ginn, 1916), 102–3.

2. Denise Schmandt-Besserat, *Before Writing* (Austin: University of Texas Press, 1992).

3. Ibid., 10.

4. Ibid., 108.

5. Niles Eldredge and Stephen Jay Gould, "Punctuated Equilibria: An Alternative to Phyletic Gradualism," in *Models in Paleobotany*, ed. T. J. M. Schopf (San Francisco: Freeman Cooper, 1972). Reprinted in Niles Eldredge, *Time Frames* (New York: Simon and Schuster, 1985), 193.

6. Jean Bottéro, *Mesopotamia* (Chicago: University of Chicago Press, 1992), 70.

7. Samual Noah Kramer, *History Begins at Sumer* (Philadelphia: University of Pennsylvania Press, 1981), 5.

8. Seton H. F. Lloyd, "History: The Origin of Mesopotamian History," in *Encyclopaedia Britannica* (Chicago: Encyclopaedia Britannica, 1987), 21:907.

9. Giovanni Pettinato, *Ebla: A New Look at History* (Baltimore: Johns Hopkins University Press, 1991), 54.

10. Samuel Noah Kramer, "Three Old Babylonian balag-Catalogues from the British Museum," in *Societies and Languages of the Near East: Studies in Honor of I. M. Diakonoff* (Warminster: Aris and Phillips, 1982), 206.

11. Kramer, *History Begins*, 3–9.

12. George Sarton, *A History of Science: Ancient Science through the Golden Ages of Greece* (Cambridge: Harvard University Press, 1952), 71.

13. Kramer, *History Begins*, 45–50.

14. Ibid., 36–44.

15. Ibid., 54.

16. *Glass and Glassmaking in Ancient Mesopotamia* (Corning, N.Y.: Corning Museum of Glass, 1970).

17. Niles Eldredge, *Time Frames* (New York: Simon and Schuster, 1985), 168.

Chapter 3: Papyrus Rolls

1. Alan H. Gardiner, "Ramesside Texts Relating to the Taxation and Transport of Corn," *Journal of Egyptian Archaeology* 2 (1941): 19–20.

2. Alan H. Gardiner, *Egypt of the Pharaohs* (London: Oxford University Press, 1964), 297.

3. Ibid., 393.

4. Ibid., 404.

5. Georges Posner, "Sur l'emploi de l'encre rouge, dan les manuscrits Égyptians," *Journal of Egyptian Archaeology* 37 (1951): 75–78.

6. *The Edwin Smith Surgical Papyrus*, trans. James Henry Breasted (Chicago: University of Chicago Press, 1930).

7. Frederick G. Kilgour, "Locating Information in an Egyptian Text of the Seventeenth Century B.C.," *Journal of the American Society for Information Science* 44 (1993): 292–97.

8. *The Ancient Egyptian Book of the Dead*, trans. Raymond O. Faulkner, ed. Carol Andrews (London: British Museum Publications, 1985).

9. Gay Robins and Charles Shute, *The Rhind Mathematical Papyrus: An Ancient Egyptian Text* (London: British Museum Publications, 1987), 10.

10. Ibid., 10–11.

11. Kurt Weitzmann, *Illustrations in Roll and Codex* (Princeton, N.J.: Princeton University Press, 1970), 68.

12. Alfred Lucas, *Ancient Egyptian Materials and Industries* (London: Edward Arnold, 1962), 15.

13. Walter B. Emery, *Archaic Egypt* (Baltimore: Penguin Books, 1971), 235.

14. Tsien Tsuen-Hsuin, *Paper and Printing* (Cambridge: Cambridge University Press, 1985), 2.

15. *Ancient Egyptian Book of the Dead*, 11.

16. Francis Llewellyn Griffith, *The Petrie Papyri* (London: B. Quaritch, 1898).

17. Gardiner, *Egypt*, 130.

18. *Ancient Egyptian Book of the Dead.*

19. Henry E. Sigerist, *A History of Medicine* (New York: Oxford University Press, 1951), 1:301.

Chapter 4: The Greco-Roman World

1. John Boardman, Jasper Griffin, and Oswyn Murray, eds., *The Roman World* (Oxford: Oxford University Press, 1991).

2. George Sarton, *Introduction to the History of Science* (Baltimore: Williams and Wilkins, 1927), 1:172.

3. Joseph Naveh, *Early History of the Alphabet*, 2d. ed. (Jerusalem: Magnes Press, Hebrew University, 1987), 42.

4. Ibid., 53–54, 175–86.

5. Ibid., 181–82.

6. I. J. Gelb, *A Study of Writing*, 2d ed., rev. (Chicago: University of Chicago Press, 1963), 173.

7. Ibid., 179.

8. Naveh, *Early History*, 185.

9. John Noble Wilford, "Scholars Track the Alphabet with New Precision," *New York Times*, November 8, 1988, C1, C2.

10. Frederic G. Kenyon, *Books and Readers in Ancient Greece and Rome* (Oxford: Clarendon Press, 1951), 66–67.

11. Eric G. Turner, *Greek Papyri* (Oxford: Clarendon Press, 1980), 79.

12. Cicero, *Letters to Atticus*, vol. 1, 4, 4a, 283.

13. W. John Hackwell, *Signs, Letters, Words: Archaeology Discovers Writing* (New York: Scribner's, 1987), 52.

14. Eric G. Turner, *Greek Manuscripts of the Ancient World*, 2d ed. (London: University of London Institute of Classical Studies, 1987), 2.

15. Ibid.

16. R. Reed, *Ancient Skins, Parchments, and Leathers* (London: Seminar Press, 1972), 90.

17. Ibid., 119.

18. Reed, *Ancient Skins*, 88.

19. Herodotus, *The Histories of Herodotus* (New York: Heritage Press, 1958), 323.

20. Paul-Marie Duval, "Antiquité Mediterranéenne," in *Les origines de la civilisation technique*, ed. Henri Dauman, vol. 1 (Paris: Press Universitaires de France, 1964), 249.

21. K. D. White, *Greek and Roman Technology* (Ithaca, N.Y.: Cornell University Press, 1984), 192.

22. Hero of Alexandria, *Les Mécaniques* (Paris: Les Belles Lettres, 1988), 199–214. (This work had been translated from Arabic because no Greek version existed.)

23. White, *Greek and Roman Technology*, 34–35.

24. Pliny, *Natural History*, vol. 9 (Cambridge: Harvard University Press, 1989), 114.

25. Paul Saenger, "Silent Reading: Its Impact on Late Medieval Script," *Viator* 13 (1982): 367–414, 371.

26. William V. Harris, *Ancient Literacy* (Cambridge: Harvard University Press, 1989), 114.

27. William Harlan Hale, *Ancient Greece* (New York: American Heritage Press, 1970), 121.

28. Plato, *Phaedrus*, (Cambridge: Harvard University Press, 1977), 565, 567.

29. Harris, *Ancient Literacy*, 236.

30. Ibid., 259, 267.

31. Colin H. Roberts and T. C. Skeat, *The Birth of the Codex* (London: Oxford University Press, 1983), 37.

32. Kenyon, *Books and Readers*, 24.

33. Ibid., 23–24.

34. Turner, *Greek Papyri*, 87.

35. Luciano Canfora, *The Vanished Library* (Berkeley: University of California Press, 1987), 63.

36. Ibid., 141.

37. For examples see David Diringer, *The Book before Printing* (New York: Dover Publications, 1982), 270; Karl Dziatzko, "Bibliotheken," in *Paulys Real-Enclopaedie der Classischen Altertums-wissenschaft* (Stuttgart: J. B. Metzlerscher, 1899), vol. 3, col. 410; Edward Edwards, *Libraries and Founders of Libraries* (London: Trubner, 1864), 7; Elmer D. Johnson and Michael H. Harris, *History of Libraries in the Western World*, 3d ed., rev. (Metuchen, N.J.: Scarecrow Press, 1976), 49; Edward Alexander Parsons, *The Alexandrine Library* (London: Cleaver-Hume Press, 1952), 172.

38. Christian Callmer, "Antike Bibliotheke," *Opuscula Archaeologica* 3 (1944): 152–53.

39. Alan Rowe, *Discovery of the Famous Temple and Enclosure of Serapis at Alexandria* (Le Caire: Institute Francais d'Archéologie Orientale, 1946), 25.

40. Peter Marshall Fraser, *Ptolemaic Alexandria*, 3 vols. (Oxford: Clarendon Press, 1972), 1:323.

41. Canfora, *Vanished Library*, 63.

42. The last four paragraphs are based on Clarence Eugene Boyd's *Public Libraries and Literary Culture in Ancient Rome* (Chicago: University of Chicago Press, 1913).

43. Lawrence Richardson, *Pompeii: An Architectural History* (Baltimore: Johns Hopkins University Press, 1988) 273–75; and "The Libraries of Pompeii," *Archaeology* 30: 400–402.

44. Canfora, *Vanished Library*, 196.

45. Carl Wendel, "Die Erst Kaiserliche Bibliothek in Constantinople," *Zentralblatt fur Bibliothekwesen* 59 (1942): 193–209.

46. Jean Irigoin, "Centres de copie et bibliotheques," in *Byzantine Books and Bookmen* (Washington, D.C.: Dumbarton Oaks, 1975), 19.

47. Cyril Mango, "The Availability of Books in the Byzantine Empire, A.D. 750–850," in *Byzantine Books and Bookmen* (Washington, D.C.: Dumbarton Oaks, 1975), 39, 43.

48. Nigel Guy Wilson, *Scholars of Byzantium* (Baltimore: Johns Hopkins University Press, 1983), 120–29.

49. Sarton, *Introduction*, vol. 2, pt. 1, 403.

50. *Announcing New Editions in The Loeb Classical Library 1992* (Cambridge: Harvard University Press, 1992), 2.

Chapter 5: The Codex, 100–700 A.D.

1. Terturian, *Apology*, 40, 1–2, quoted in Robert M. Grant, *Apologists of the Second Century* (Philadelphia: Westminster Press, 1988), 10.

2. Grant, *Apologists of the Second Century*, 30.

3. Alan K. Bowman, *The Roman Writing Tablets from Vindolanda* (London: British Museum, 1938).

4. Homer, *The Iliad of Homer* (New York: Macmillan, 1945), 129.

5. Courtesy of the Ohio State University Library.

6. Edward Maunde Thompson, *An Introduction to Greek and Latin Paleology* (Oxford: Clarendon Press, 1912), 13, 14.

7. George F. Bass, "Oldest Known Shipwreck Reveals Splendors of the Bronze Age," *National Geographic Magazine* 172 (1987): 730–31.

8. Thompson, *Introduction*, 15.

9. Herodotus, (Oxford: Clarendon Press, 1949), v. 2, book 7, chapter 239, 569.

10. Giovanni Pugliese Carratelli, "L'Instrumentum Scriptorium Monumenti Pompeiana ed Ercolanesi," *Pompeiana* (Naples: Gaetano Macchiaroli, 1950), 270–73.

11. Berthe van Regemorter, "La Reliure des Manuscrits Grecs," *Scriptorium* 8 (1954): 17.

12. Eric G. Turner, *The Typology of the Early Codex* (Philadelphia: University of Pennsylvania Press, 1977), 1.

13. Eric G. Turner, *Greek Papyri* (Oxford: Clarendon Press, 1980), 2.

14. Berthe van Regemorter, "Le codex relié depuis son origine jusqu'au Haut Moyen-Age," *Le Moyen Age* 61 (1995): 15.

15. Turner, *Greek Papyri*, 87–88.

16. Colin H. Roberts and T. C. Skeat, *The Birth of the Codex* (London: Published for the British Academy by the Oxford University Press, 1983), 38.

17. Turner, *Typology*, 37.

18. Seneca, "On the tranquillity of mind," in *Moral Essays* (Cambridge, Mass.: Harvard University Press, 1965), vol. 2, 247–49.

19. Turner, *Typology*, 50, 51.

Chapter 6: Islam, 622–1300

1. George Sarton, *Introduction to the History of Science* (Baltimore: Williams and Wilkins, 1927), 1:7.

2. Tsien Tsuen-Hsuin, *Paper and Printing* (Cambridge: Cambridge University Press, 1987), 297–99.

3. Dard Hunter, *Papermaking through Eighteen Centuries* (New York: William Edwin Rudge, 1930), 186–90.

4. Ibid., 159.

5. Ibn Badis, Al-Mu'izz, "Staff of the scribes and implements of the discerning, with a description of the line, the pens, soot inks, *LIQ*, gall inks, dyeing, and details of bookbinding," in *Mediaeval arabic bookmaking and its relation to early chemistry and pharmacology*, by Martin Levey. *Transactions of the American Philosophical Society* 52 (1962): 3–79, 13.

6. Ibid., 14.

7. Sarton, *Introduction*, vol. 1, 666.

8. Cited in Gulnar Bosch, John Carswell, and Guy Pethridge, *Islamic Bindings and Bookmaking* (Chicago: Oriental Institute, University of Chicago, 1981), 6.

9. George Makdisi, *The Rise of Humanism in Classical Islam and the Christian West* (Edinburgh: Edinburgh University Press, 1990), 72, 74.

10. Ibid., 72.

11. Ibid., 74.

12. Ibid.

13. Ibid., 79.

14. Johannes Pedersen, *The Arabic Book* (Princeton, N.J.: Princeton University Press, 1984), 27.

15. Makdisi, *Rise of Humanism*, 246.

16. Ibid., 245.

17. C. E. Bosworth, "Administrative Literature," in *Religion, Learning, and Science in the ʿAbbāsid Period* (Cambridge: Cambridge University Press, 1990), 159.

18. Pederson, *Arabic Book*, 101–2.

19. Martin Levey, *Mediaeval Arabic Bookmaking and its Relation to Early Chemistry and Pharmacology* (Philadelphia: American Philosophical Society, 1962), 13.

20. Ibn Badis, "Staff," 13–50.

21. Al-Sufyānī, Abul-Abbas Ahmed ibn Muḥammed, "Art of bookbinding and of gilding." From the Arabic text published by P. Richard, 1925, in "Mediaeval arabic bookmaking and its relation to early chemistry and pharmacology, by Martin Levey, *Transactions of the American Philosophical Society* 52 (1962):3–17, 51–55.

22. Ibn Badis, "Staff," 42.

23. Al Sufyānī, "Art of Bookbinding," 52.

24. Pedersen, *Arabic Book*, 50.

25. Ross E. Dunn, *The Adventures of Ibn Battuta* (Berkeley: University of California Press, 1986), 37.

26. Pederson, *Arabic Book*, 52, 50.

27. L. E. Goodman, "The translation of Greek materials into Arabic" in *Religion, Learning, and Science*, 495.

28. Pedersen, *Arabic Book*, 120.

29. Bayard Dodge, *Muslim Education in Medieval Times* (Washington, D.C.: Middle East Institute, 1962), 23.

30. Pedersen, *Arabic Book*, 121–24.

31. Adam Gacek, "Some Remarks on the Cataloguing of Arabic Manuscripts," *Bulletin of the British Society for Middle Eastern Studies* 10 (1983): 173, 179 n. 9.

Chapter 7: Western Christendom, 600–1400

1. Helmut Georg Koenigsberger, *Medieval Europe 400–1500* (Harlow, U.K.: Longman, 1987), 42.

2. Henri-Jean Martin, *The History and Power of Writing* (Chicago: University of Chicago Press, 1994), 121.

3. Mark Alfred Schroll, *Benedictine Monasticism As Reflected in the Warnefrid-Hildemar Commentaries on the Rule* (New York: Columbia University Press, 1941), 122.

4. Rosamond McKitterick, *The Carolingians and the Written Word* (Cambridge: Cambridge University Press, 1989), 166, 169, 170, 173, 179, 183.

5. Saint Benedict, *The Rule of St. Benedict in Latin and English with Notes* (Collegeville, Minn.: Liturgical Press, 1981), 48, 15, 16.

6. Schroll, *Benedictine Monasticism*, 54, 206.

7. Cassiodorus, *An Introduction to Divine and Human Readings* (New York: Octagon Press, 1966), 133–35.

8. Florence Edler De Roover, "The Scriptorium," in *The Medieval Library*, ed. James Westfall Thompson (New York: Hafner Publishing, 1965), 595.

9. *Registrum Anglie de Libris Doctorum et Auctorum Veterum* (London: British Library, 1981), xiii.

10. Richard H. Rouse, "Bostonus Buriensis and the Author of the *Catalogus Scriptorium Ecclesiae*," *Speculum* 66 (1966): 493.

11. Roover, "Scriptorium," 610–11.

12. Ibid., 607–8.

13. Leila Avrin, *Scribes, Script, and Books* (Oxford: Phaedon Press, 1991), 224.

14. Roover, "Scriptorium," 601.

15. Falconer Madan, *Books in Manuscript* (New York: Haskell House, 1968), 42.

16. Paul Saenger, "Silent Reading: Its Impact on Medieval Script and Society," *Viator* 13 (1982): 377.

17. Janet Backhouse, *The Illuminated Manuscript* (Oxford: Phaedon Press, 1979), 7.

18. David Diringer, *The Book before Printing* (New York: Dover Publications, 1982), 501.

19. Jean Vezin, "La reliure occidentale au moyen age," in *La reliure médiévale* (Paris: Presses de l'École Normale Supérieure, 1978), 38.

20. Koenigsberger, *Medieval Europe*, 215.

21. Marcel Thomas, "Manuscripts," in Lucien Febvre and Henri-Jean Martin, *The Coming of the Book* (London: Verso, 1984), 22.

22. David C. Lindberg, *The Beginnings of Western Science* (Chicago: University of Chicago Press, 1992), 203.

23. Saenger, "Silent Reading," 387.

24. Richard H. Rouse and Mary A. Rouse, *Preachers, Florilegia, and Sermons* (Toronto: Pontifical Institute of Medieval Studies, 1979), 7, 8.

25. Ibid., 8.

26. Ibid., 9.

27. Ibid., 23.

28. Edward Rosen, "The Invention of Eyeglasses," *Journal of the History of Medicine and Allied Sciences* 2 (1956): 29, 217, 214, 204, 203.

29. Michael Rhodes, "A Pair of Fifteenth-Century Spectacle Frames from the City of London," *Antiquaries Journal* 62 (1982): 57–73, 66, 73, n. 71.

30. Horst Appuhn, "A Memorable Find," *Zeiss Werkzeitschrift* 27 (1958): 4, 5.

31. Rhodes, "Fifteenth-Century Spectacle Frames," 57.

32. Richard de Bury, *Philobiblon* (Oxford: Shakespeare Head Press, 1960), 161.

33. Oriel Valls i. Subirà, *La Historia del papel en España* (Madrid: Empresa Nacional de Celulosa, 1978), 3:129–33.

34. Marius A. Péraudeau and Ernst Maget, *Le moulin à papier Richard-de-Bas* (Paris: Pierre Gaudin, 1985), 10.

Chapter 8: Printing, 1400–1800

1. Richard H. Rouse, "Backgrounds to Print: Aspects of the Manuscript Book in Northern Europe of the Fifteenth Century," *Proceedings of the PMR Conference* 6 (1981): 38.

2. Ibid., 40.

3. John M. Lenhart, *Pre-Reformation Printed Books: A Study in Statistical and Applied Bibliography* (New York: Joseph P. Wagner, Inc., 1935), 26, 28.

4. Lucien Febvre and Henri-Jean Martin, *The Coming of the Book* (London: Verso, 1984), 248.

5. Warren Chappell, *A Short History of the Printed Word* (New York: Dorset Press, 1970), 84.

6. Rouse, "Backgrounds," 48.

7. Theodore L. DeVinne, *The Invention of Printing* (New York: Francis Hart, 1876; reprint, Detroit: Gale Research, 1969), 204–5.

8. Ibid., 203.

9. Heinrich T. Musper, "Xylographic Books," in *The Book through Five Thousand Years*, ed. H. D. L. Vervliet (London: Phaidon, 1972), 346.

10. Allen Stevenson, "The Quincentennial of the Netherlandish Blockbook," *British Museum Quarterly* 21 (1966–67): 84.

11. Musper, "Xylographic Books," 341, 345.

12. Rouse, "Backgrounds," 48.

13. Karl C. Bochenheimer, *Johann Brito aus Brügge* (Mainz: Verlangsaustalt und Druckerei, 1898).

14. Pierre Henri Requin, *L'Imprimerie à Avignon en 1444* (Paris: Alphonse Picard, 1890).

15. Antonio Valsecchi, *Intorno a Panfilo Castaldi da Feltre e alla Invenzione dei Caratteri Mobile per la Stampa* (Milan: Pietro Aquelli, 1866).

16. Jacobus Scheltema, *Levens-schets van Laurens Janozorn-Koster* Utrecht: J. G. van Terveen en zoon, 1834).

17. Curt F. Bühler, *The Fifteenth-Century Book* (Philadelphia: University of Pennsylvania Press, 1960), 51, 52.

18. Vannoccio Biringuccio, *The Pirotechnia* (New York: Basic Books, 1959), 388.

19. DeVinne, *Invention of Printing*, 380.

20. Maurice Audin, "Types du XVe Siècle," *Gutenberg Jahrbuch* 18 (1954): 92.

21. Biringuccio, *Pirotechnia*, 374.

22. Joseph Moxon, *Mechanik Exercises on the Whole Art of Printing* (New York: Dover Publications, 1978), 165, 167.

23. Bruce Gonser and J. Homer Winkler, "Type Metals," in *Metals Handbook*, ed. Lyman Taylor (Cleveland: American Society for Metals, 1948), 958. I am grateful to Professor H. H. Stademaier for bringing this work to my attention.

24. DeVinne, *Invention of Printing*, 66–67.

25. Ibid., 60.

26. Moxon, *Mechanik Exercises*, 254.

27. Douglas C. McMurtrie, *The Gutenberg Documents* (New York: Oxford University Press, 1941), 105.

28. Ibid., 116, 117.

29. Aloys Ruppel, *Johannes Gutenberg*, 3d ed. (Nieuwkoop: B. de Graaf, 1967), 116–22.

30. Ibid., 137.

31. DeVinne, *Invention of Printing*, 422.

32. Ruppel, *Gutenberg*, 132.

33. Albert Kapr, *Johannes Gutenberg* (Munich: Verlag C. H. Beck, 1987), 220–24.

34. Febvre and Martin, *Coming of the Book*, 182–86.

35. Douglas C. McMurtrie, *The Book* (New York: Dorset, 1943/1989), 568.

36. Margaret M. Smith, "Printed Foliation: Forerunner to Printed Page Numbers?" *Gutenberg Jahrbuch* 63 (1988): 54–70.

37. Ulrich Boner, *Der Edelstein* (Bamberg: Albrecht Pfister, 1461).

38. William M. Ivins, *Prints and Visual Communication* (Cambridge: Harvard University Press, 1953), 43–44.

39. Andreas Vesalius, *The Illustrations from the Works of Andreas Vesalius,* with annotations and . . . a discussion . . . by J. B. de C. M. Saunders and Charles D. O'Malley (Cleveland: World Publishing, 1950), 20–21.

40. Ivins, *Prints,* 166.

41. Adolf Dresler, *Die Älteste Periodische Zeitung und Zeitschrift: Die Rorschacher Monatsschrift* (Munich: Pohl, 1963).

42. David A. Kronick, *A History of Scientific and Technical Periodicals* (Metuchen, N.J.: Scarecrow Press, 1976), 90–91.

43. Ibid., 171.

Chapter 9: Power Revolution, 1800–1840

1. Robert Luther Thomson, *Wiring a Continent* (Princeton, N.J.: Princeton University Press, 1949), 91, 74.

2. William Turner Berry, "Printing and Related Trades," in *A History of Technology,* vol. 5 (Oxford: Clarendon Press, 1958), 702.

3. Harvey J. Graff, *The Legacies of Literacy* (Bloomington: Indiana University Press, 1987), 353.

4. Harvey B. Weiss, "A Graphic Summary of the Growth of Newspapers in New York and Other States, 1704–1820," *Bulletin of the New York Public Library* 52: 184.

5. Raymond Irwin, *The English Library* (London: George Allen and Unwin, 1966), 282.

6. Jesse H. Shera, *Foundations of the Public Library* (Hamden, Conn.: Shoe String Press, 1949), 231, 232.

7. Frederick G. Kilgour, "Modern Medicine in Historical Perspective," *Bulletin of the Medical Library Association* 50: 42–56. Reprinted in *Collected Papers of Frederick G. Kilgour,* vol. 1 (Dublin, Ohio: Online Computer Library Center, 1984), 161–69.

8. Graff, *Legacies of Literacy,* 303–14.

9. Leslie Howsam, *Cheap Bibles* (New York: Cambridge University Press, 1991), 79.

10. Ibid., 117–18.

11. James Moran, *Printing Presses* (Berkeley: University of California Press, 1973), 39.

12. Michael Turner, "Reading for the Masses: Aspects of the Syndication of Fiction in Great Britain," in *Book Selling and Book Buying: Aspects of the Nineteenth-Century British and North American Book Trade,* ed. Richard D. Landon (Chicago: American Library Association, 1978), 33.

13. This paragraph and the following five paragraphs are based on Moran, *Printing Presses,* 50–97.

14. *Printing The Times* (1953), 30, 31.

15. *The History of The Times,* (New York: Macmillan, 1935), 1:112.

16. Moran, *Printing Presses,* 106.

17. Ibid., 116, 117.

18. Lucien Alphonse Legros and John Cameron Grant, *Typographical Printing-Surfaces* (New York: Garland Publishing, 1916; reprint, 1980), 471–72.

19. Ibid., 581.

20. John Carter, "William Ged and the Invention of Stereotype," *Library* 15: 163.

21. Howsam, *Cheap Bibles*, 3.

22. David Paul Nord, *The Evangelical Origins of Mass Media in America 1815–1838* (Columbia, S.C.: Association for Education in Journalism and Mass Communications, 1984), 8, 19.

23. Ibid., 12.

24. Legros and Grant, *Typographical Printing*, 302.

25. Aloys Senefelder, *A Complete Course of Lithography* (London: R. Ackermann, 1819), v.

26. Ibid., 7–8, 9.

27. Douglas C. McMurtrie, *The Book* (New York: Dorset, 1943/1989), 551.

28. Senefelder, *Complete Course*, 9–11, 38.

29. Terry Belanger, "From Bookseller to Publisher: Changes in the London Book Trade, 1750–1850," in *Bookselling and Book Buying: Aspects of the Nineteenth-Century British and North American Book Trade*, ed. Richard G. Landon (Chicago: American Library Association, 1978).

30. Henri-Jean Martin, *The History and Power of Writing* (Chicago: University of Chicago Press, 1994), 259–60.

31. James Lackington, *Memoirs of the First Forty-Five Years of James Lackington, 1794* (New York: Garland Publishing, 1974), 335–36.

32. Martin, *History and Power*, 438.

Chapter 10: *Climax of Books Printed from Cast Type, 1840–1940*

1. Lucien Alphonse Legros and John Cameron Grant, *Typographical Printing-Surfaces* (London: Longmans, Green, 1916), 577–78.

2. Henry Bessemer, *Sir Henry Bessemer, F.R.S., An Autobiography* (London: Offices of "Engineering," 1905; reprint, 1989), 47.

3. Ibid.

4. James Moran, *Printing Presses* (Berkeley: University of California Press, 1973), 176–77.

5. Theodore L. DeVinne, "Perfecting the Press," *Scientific American Supplement* 1380 (June 14, 1902): 22,122.

6. Moran, *Printing Presses*, 190.

7. James Moran, "Printing," in *A History of Technology, vol. 7* (Oxford: Clarendon Press, 1978), pt. 2, 1,268.

8. Victor Fouque, *The Truth Concerning the Invention of Photography* (New York: Tennant and Ward, 1935), 37.

9. Frank E. Comparato, *Books for the Millions* (Harrisburg, Pa: Stackpole, 1971), 184.

10. William Turner Berry, "Printing and Related Trades," in *A History of Technology*, vol. 5 (Oxford: Clarendon Press, 1958), 714.

11. Henri-Jean Martin, *The History and Power of Writing* (Chicago: University of Chicago, Press, 1994), 414.

12. John Feather, *A Dictionary of Book History* (New York: Oxford University Press, 1986), 186.

13. Ibid., 187.

14. Berry, "Printing and Related Trades," 686.

15. Legros and Grant, *Typographical Printing-Surfaces*, 480.

16. Matthew Schneirov, *The Dream of a New Social Order: Popular Magazines in America 1893–1914* (New York: Columbia University Press, 1994), 92.

17. Theodore Peterson, *Magazines in the Twentieth Century* (Urbana: University of Illinois Press, 1956), 58.

18. William J. Thorn and Mary Pat Pfell, *Newspaper Circulation* (New York: Longman, 1987), 48.

19. Peterson, *Magazines*, 90–91.

20. Wilfred A. Beeching, *Century of the Typewriter* (London: Heinemann, 1974), 36.

21. Mark Twain, *Mark Twain-Howells Letters* (Cambridge: Harvard University Press, 1960), 133.

22. Donald Hoke, *Ingenious Yankees* (New York: Columbia University Press, 1990), 133.

23. Paul Kaufman, *Libraries and Their Users* (London: Library Association, 1969), 143.

24. Sir Allen Lane, "Penguins and Pelicans," *The Penrose Annual*, 1938. Reprinted in *Printing in the Twentieth Century*, ed. James Moran (London: Northwood Publications, 1974), 160.

25. Ibid.

26. John Tebbel, *A History of Book Publishing in the United States* (New York: R. R. Bowker, 1978), 3:510.

27. Jean Hassendorfer, *Développement comparé des bibliothèques publiques en France en Grande-Bretagne et aux États-Unis dans la seconde moitié du XIXᵉ siècle (1850–1914)* (Paris: Cercle de la Librairie, 1967), 44–56.

28. Ibid., 46.

29. Arthur T. Hamlin, *The University Library in the United States* (Philadelphia: University of Pennsylvania Press, 1981), 230, 234.

Chapter 11: Computer-Driven Book Production

1. Henry Whetton, ed., *Practical Printing and Binding* (London: Oldham Press, [1946]; reprint, 1948), 230–42.

2. Stephen H. Horgan, "Twenty-five years of processwork," *The Inland Printer*, 63 (July 1919): 408.

3. James Moran, "Printing," in *A History of Technology*, vol. 7 (Oxford: Clarendon Press, 1978), pt. 2, 1,269.

4. Albro Tilton Gaul, *The Wonderful World of Insects* (New York: Rinehart, 1953), 291.

5. Moran, "Printing," 1,279.

6. William H. Taft, *American Magazines for the 1980s* (New York: Hastings House, 1982), 318.

7. Joseph Blumenthal, *Typographic Years* (New York: Frederic C. Beil, 1982), 126.

8. Lloyd P. DeJidas and Thomas M. Destree, *Sheetfed Offset Press Operating* (Pittsburgh: Graphic Arts Technical Foundations, 1995), 14–15, 214–15.

9. Ernest A. Hutchings, *A Survey of Printing Processes*, 2d ed. (London: Heinemann, 1978), 169.

10. Jill Roth, "Book Marks," *American Printer*, January 1991, 44–45.

11. Xerox Corporation, *Xerox Launches DocuPrint 6135* (Chicago: Xerox Production Systems, 1995).

12. *University Libraries and Scholarly Communication* (Washington, D.C.: Published by the Association of Research Libraries for the Andrew W. Mellon Foundation, 1992), 200.

13. Frank L. Schick, *The Paperbound Book in America* (New York: R. R. Bowker, 1958), 104.

14. *University Libraries*, 75.

15. Ibid., 67.

16. Curtis G. Benjamin, "The High Price of Technical Books," *ALA Bulletin*, 1965, 62–63.

17. Janice A. Radway, *Reading the Romance* (Chapel Hill: University of North Carolina Press, 1991), 33–34.

18. John Tebbel, *Between Covers* (New York: Oxford University Press, 1987), 448.

19. *University Libraries*, 4, 5.

20. Lisa A. Wright, "Public Library Circulation Rises along with Spending," *American Libraries* 27 (Oct. 1996): 57–58.

Chapter 12: The Electronic Book

1. "Roll Over Gutenberg," *Economist*, Oct. 18, 1993, 105.

2. Alan E. Bell, "Next Generation Compact Discs," *Scientific American* 275 (July 1996): 42, 44, 46.

3. "Roll Over Gutenberg," 105.

4. Vannevar Bush, "As We May Think," *Atlantic Monthly* (July 1945): 641–49. Reprinted in *From Memex to Hypertext*, ed. J. M. Nyce and P. Kahn (Boston: Harcourt Brace Jovanovich, 1991), 87, 104.

5. Douglas C. Engelbart, "Letter to Vannevar Bush and Program on Human Effectiveness," in *From Memex to Hypertext*, ed. J. M. Nyce and P. Kahn (Boston: Harcourt Brace Jovanovich, 1991), 235, 236, 237.

6. George P. Landow, *Hypertext: The Convergence of Contemporary Critical Theory and Technology* (Baltimore: Johns Hopkins University Press, 1992), 5.

7. Nicole Yankelovich, Norman Meyrowitz, and Andries van Dam, "Reading and Writing the Electronic Book," *Computer*, Oct. 1985, 15–30.

8. Donna Baumbach, "Hypermedia," *Macmillan Encyclopedia of Computers* (New York: Macmillan, 1992), 508.

Index